APPLICATIVE JUSTICE

APPLICATIVE JUSTICE

A Pragmatic Empirical Approach to Racial Injustice

Naomi Zack

ROWMAN & LITTLEFIELD
Lanham • Boulder • New York • London

Published by Rowman & Littlefield
A wholly owned subsidiary of The Rowman & Littlefield Publishing Group, Inc.
4501 Forbes Boulevard, Suite 200, Lanham, Maryland 20706
www.rowman.com

Unit A, Whitacre Mews, 26-34 Stannary Street, London SE11 4AB

British Library Cataloguing in Publication Information Available

Library of Congress Cataloging-in-Publication Data

Names: Zack, Naomi, 1944-
Title: Applicative justice : A pragmatic empirical approach to racial injustice / Naomi Zack.
Description: Lanham & Rowman Littlefield, 2016 | Includes bibliographical references and index.
Identifiers: LCCN 2015039250| ISBN 9781442260009 (cloth : alkaline paper) | ISBN 9781442260023 (electronic)
Subjects: LCSH: Justice (Philosophy) | Equality--Philosophy. | Equality before the law.
Classification: LCC Classification: LCC B105.J87 Z34 2016 | DDC 320.01/1--dc23 LC record available at http://lccn.loc.gov/2015039250

∞ ™ The paper used in this publication meets the minimum requirements of American National Standard for Information Sciences Permanence of Paper for Printed Library Materials, ANSI/NISO Z39.48-1992.

Printed in the United States of America

To Alex, Bradford, Jessica, Coco, and Winnie

Why then do most philosophers refuse
to think about injustice as deeply and subtly as they
think about justice?

—Judith Shklar, *The Faces of Injustice*

CONTENTS

Preface xi

Introduction: Key Ideas and Chapter Scopes 1

1 Ideal Theory, Nonideal Theory, and Empirical Political Theory 9

2 Limits of Law and Government 35

3 Ideal Equality and Real Inequality 65

4 The Distribution of Procedural Justice 89

5 Discourse, Prophecy, and Atmosphere 117

6 The Discourse of Political Activism 145

7 Postscript: An Invitation to the Reader 175

Notes 183

Select Bibliography 217

Index 227

About the Author 235

PREFACE

The story of how President Lyndon B. Johnson came to sign into US law the Civil Rights Act of 1964 has many anecdotal sidebars and conflicting accounts, which can be distilled into these three facts: He was a Southerner, from a culture that would be considered unjustly racist today. He was a master politician who orchestrated many complex political gyrations in getting the act passed. The act was passed. That entire struggle toward written justice, the importance of the law itself, and the disappointment of subsequent events that have not lived up to either its letter or spirit is a symbol of what motivates this book, which is its real subtitle: *How we can make sense of the combination of good intentions, bad intentions, self-serving grasps at power, good laws, and bad practices, as all part of the same political life, in our time and earlier, both in general and down to small detail?* Of course, I have chosen to avoid a subtitle more suitable to the seventeenth century,[1] and described the project of this book as *A Pragmatic Empirical Approach to Racial Injustice*. My approach is pragmatic by focusing on the silent cry for help from many quarters that has not so far been answered, and it is pragmatic in drawing on the philosophical tradition of pragmatism.

For several years, a copy of Bentley's 1908 *The Process of Government* reposed unread on one of my office bookshelves. When I finally began reading it during the winter of 2009–2010, a slow process began of understanding its relevance to contemporary political struggles. I realized that Bentley's noncynical political realism offered a way to think about injustice as part of the same reality of political life that promulgates just laws and principles. There is no contradiction between formal equality in law and real life inequality in reality because law is verbal and reality is a matter of action. The task is therefore to figure out what to do when stated rules and principles are violated in practice. I feel this to be a very urgent task, although I could not do more in this book than gesture at its challenges in the changing political world of our time.

I began writing this book before I realized it, in a short piece published in the 2013 Fall APA *Newsletter on Philosophy and the Black Experience*, "Racial Inequality and a Theory of Applicative Justice."[2] This was followed by longer examination of the futility of absolute ideas of human equality in "Philosophical Theories of Justice, Inequality, and Racial Inequality," appearing in a special issue of the New School *Graduate Faculty Philosophy Journal*,[3] which became the basis for chapter 3, here. My proper work on the book began during the summer of 2014 but I interrupted it during the winter of 2014–2015 to write about very specific contemporary pressing issues in *White Privilege and Black Rights: The Injustice US Police Racial Profiling and Homicide.*[4] The content of that interruption was valuable for its sobering acquaintance with contemporary injustice and the legal support of it, when I took up this book again, finished it, and then revised it.

The final revisions benefited from excellent criticism. I am grateful to the Philosophy Department at Georgia State University for their reactions to a colloquium paper I gave, "How Police Racial Profiling and Homicide Are Now Legal but Unjust," in March 2015. That paper was an expansion of ideas I presented at a University of Oregon panel presentation for the Multicultural Center and Ethnic Studies event, "Black Lives Matter," in January 2015. In those presentations, my criticism of ideal theory and description of the legal structure that supports contemporary police racial profiling and homicide with impunity, both drew from the main ideas in *White Privilege and Black Rights* and extended them to the concerns of the present book.

I have had truly wonderful critics of the penultimate manuscript, who are concerned about the same kinds of injustice that concern me! Janine Jones was a conscientious reader of parts of chapters 5 and 6, with a number of insightful criticisms, although I did not follow all of them. I am also grateful to the two anonymous external reviewers for Rowman and Littlefield. One insisted that I had completely misunderstood John Rawls's thought experiment of deliberation behind the veil of ignorance in his *A Theory of Justice* and the second wanted me to say more about work in legal pragmatism. Closer to home, Alan Reynolds, a recent University of Oregon Philosophy Department PhD graduate said the same thing about my reading of Rawls. And so did Cheyney Ryan, my ongoing colleague, and to some extent Colin Koopman, my present colleague in the University of Oregon Philosophy Department. I have not taken up legal pragmatism in the final version of the manuscript, because I realized that my concerns are with methodological pragmatism, instead. As for Rawls, I saw that I had indeed misunderstood him, but I believe that my better understanding has resulted in a stronger criticism of ideal theory. I also learned from Sarah Hamid, a University of Oregon graduate student in journalism and communications, who pointed the way toward research in contemporary digital culture, which I had much neglected. Jon La Rochelle, a University of Oregon PhD student in philosophy, motivated me to think about locally focused political activism in terms of the second half of the book. Of course, I have not done all of this criticism full justice! Not only would it take several more books to accomplish that, but I confess to the usual kinds of inertia and stubbornness, as well. Still, this version now going to press is much improved as a result of all that response and feedback. The remaining flaws are not only all mine, but no one can say I did not have a chance to do a better job of correcting them.

I could not have completed the book when I did without sabbatical leave for spring term 2015, for which I thank both the University of Oregon Department of Philosophy and College of Arts and Science. I am very grateful to Jon Sisk and his crew at Rowman and Littlefield, especially Natalie Mandziuk who as editor, saw the book through its contract and put this version into production and to Chris Utter who has been assisting Jon Sisk with final editorial processes. I am indebted to Crystal Clifton for copy editing, and thanks to Elaine McGarraugh for skilled, patient, and responsive production management.

Naomi Zack
Eugene, Oregon
July 2015

INTRODUCTION

Key Ideas and Chapter Scopes

I aim to philosophically reconcile ideas of justice with practices of injustice and end up with rational grounds for optimism and realistic foundations for action. Pragmatism is consulted because my method arrives at its goal, organically, and not teleologically. I use an empirical theoretical method to understand political life and envision real life action toward practical goals. I begin with considerations of injustice rather than constructions of justice within ideal theory. I maintain an ongoing critique of John Rawls, reclaim Arthur Bentley, and engage others, including: Amartya Sen, John Locke, Giogio Agamben, Hannah Arendt, Isiah Berlin, Cornel West, Michelle Alexander, Raymond Williams, and Judith Shklar.

The process of this book introduces new concepts and perspectives for considering social justice and injustice. Toward some initial clarity, I begin here with introductions of key ideas: the concern; progress versus revolution; the comparative approach; the theory of applicative justice; the history of applicative justice; the focus of the book. I then present the scope of the chapters.

KEY IDEAS

The Concern of the Book

Politicians use the language of ethics, ethicists speak of moral laws, and people in society strive as individuals and self-conscious members of groups to bring about social change, using both ethical and legal language, as rhetoric with varied faithfulness to its specialized meanings in ethics and law. Ethics may be the underlying motivation and justification for law, but ethics by itself does not have the authority and power of law. Justice or injustice in real life is ultimately a matter of the presence or absence of just law with the force of government backing it up. Where just law and government force is not applied, justice as a moral or ethical idea can motivate a political goal of just law backed up by government force. The problem is that just law and government force are not uniformly applied where it would be morally right, and making that application happen is very difficult.

Progress versus Revolution

Law broadly includes legal principles and practices, existing laws, the actions of police, the penal system, and decisions of juries and judges. In practical terms, law is attached to the rules and behavior of specific governments. Progressives and radicals who seek ways to bring about societal changes may focus on changing law by expanding it, extending it, revising it, or abolishing some aspect of it. Their goal is justice, not in an abstract or ideal sense, but as some change in law with force, which will correct what is experienced as unjust. Such change in law in aiming for justice as a correction of injustice would be futile if law were not already partly and often largely, just. If law, as attached to a specific government, was believed to be totally unjust, the goal would not be to change but to overthrow or destroy that government—revolution. I presume that enough of law in its broad sense is already just in the American democratic system for progress to be an effective goal.

The Comparative Approach

There is a substantial body of just law backed up by force in contemporary democratic society and large numbers of the populace benefit from that. But there is also a substantial amount of injustice and it is often believed that the corrective would be further application of just law and force to neglected cases. The challenge is to change law and force so that those who suffer from injustice experience their lives in ways that more closely resemble the lives of those who benefit from the support of just law and force.

The Theory of Applicative Justice

The practice of changing law and force to *apply* where injustice is experienced is not yet understood as a distinct kind of justice and practice. It lacks a name and self-conscious theory. The name and theory used here is *applicative justice*, which is a form of *injustice correction theory* or *injustice theory*. A theory of applicative justice explains past events and practices and generates thought about new practices for changing law and force. In its explanatory and predictive role, applicative justice theory is descriptive, but it also has a normative role. As normative, applicative justice identifies what is just in existing law so as to extend it or otherwise change and apply it to what is unjust (after what is unjust has been identified as unjust). The normativity of applicative justice theory relies on moral assessments in identifying justice and injustice, in order to persuade people to apply just law and force where there is injustice. This may make applicative justice sound like retributive justice, but it is distinct in not having a punitive intent. For instance, if slavery is legally abolished, slave owners may experience that as punishment, but the abolition of slavery is more properly viewed as applying the justice experienced by those who are not slaves to those who are slaves.

The so-called tension between the values of liberty and equality is too abstract to explain a correction of injustice which requires that some actions be curtailed, because those who invoke it assume that liberty and equality are equal in value. Liberty pertains to what the law does not prohibit. Ending slavery curtails the liberty of people to own slaves, but that liberty and the law protecting it is unjust and therefore not a value. Equality is always equality in some respect, in the case of slavery, an equal right to dignity and autonomy among would-be slave owners and slaves. Equality in this context is a higher value than the liberty to own slaves.

Normative applicative justice draws on broadly shared legal principles and moral doctrines such as human equality and procedural fairness, as well as the ideas in political philosophy, jurisprudence, and activism, from which they can be derived. The goal of normative applicative justice is to provide ways for correcting injustice that are compatible with existing justice, and feasible in a reasonable time span. Normative applicative justice is thereby not radical, but progressive, a matter of action that seeks progress in justice, as justice has already been partially applied. Applicative justice has mighty obstacles in contemporary reality: self-serving politics, ignorance, prejudice, ill will among many voters, media misrepresentations, business interests in a status quo, and lack of understanding of oppression and injustice by those who are treated unjustly.

The History of Applicative Justice

Law in reality is made up of specific laws, court decisions, the criminal justice system, rules and constraints over the workings of government, and a multiplicity of official and non-official norms and practices. The history of applicative justice is made up of corrections to discrete injustices that are part of law in reality, rather than deliberate undertakings toward more general liberatory social change. The history of progress in justice is an account of specific changes in law preceding more general change, as society adjusted to them, with individuals and groups adapting to new rules and practices, for example: the Emancipation Proclamation (1863), the Nineteenth Amendment to the US Constitution granting women the right to vote (1920), *Brown vs. Board of Education* (1954), the Civil Rights Act of 1964, the Voting Rights Act of 1965, the Immigration and Nationality Act of 1965, *Roe vs. Wade* (1973).

An alternative history of progress in justice might assume that wide social changes, resulting from political and economic events or changes in technology (e.g., war, depression and boom, the automobile) resulted in new *weltanschauungs*, *zeitgeists*, or lifestyle opportunities, of which the discrete events of applicative justice were but symbols, expressions, or even just symptoms, of something bigger and more general. Despite its emotional and aesthetic appeal, that kind of interpretation does not primarily inform my efforts here. In chapter 5, I will briefly explore the notion of "atmospheres" and "climates" of race (i.e., of racism), but I believe that these words refer to hypostatized metaphors that originate in shared, individual human imaginings. That is, I proceed from the perspective that even though people encounter strong systemic assumptions that seem to strike them in a top-down way (especially when they are the subjects of them), such "imaginaries" have been created by individual human beings, and not the other way around.

Focus of the Book

Any type of unjust human experience could be made more just compared to the experience of those who do not have that type of experience. Without mass voluntary changes, changes in written law or accepted policies or practices, backed up by official force, are required. The progress of this book is driven by such concerns of applicative justice for concrete, real life types of injustice, which include: police racial profiling, women victimized by domestic violence, vulnerable populations in disaster, the criminalization of homeless people, the criminalization of poor black people, cruel and exploitive treatment of undocumented immigrants, institutional violence against women, and substandard K–12 education in racially and ethnically segregated residential neighborhoods. However, it is impossible to write about all these types of injustice all at once, and a book such as this does require specific examples. I have therefore chosen to develop this book with a primary focus on African Americans and poverty. The main reasons are that many are interested in these problems in academic philosophy and I have written about race and race relations previously.

CHAPTER SCOPES

My work in this book is exploratory from chapter to chapter. The method does not rise to either ideal or nonideal theory, but stays close to the ground. Chapters 1 and 2 engage Arthur Bentley to show why, from a practical point of view, the idea of an ideal of justice is a mistake for liberatory scholarship. I begin with the premise that what people really care about in reality is not a perfect notion of justice, but real life injustice. I criticize Rawlsian ideal theory for the likely ignorance of injustice of those behind the veil, which also generates skepticism about their identities as non-knowers. Because ideal theory cannot be applied to nonideal reality and nonideal theory attends to injustice with ideal theory in view, it becomes necessary to develop empirical political theory. Amartya Sen develops nonideal theory with a comparative approach similar to the one developed here, but he fails to reconcile ideals with imperfect reality, merely noting the discrepancy.

Bentley's methodology in extending law to what people do in its name, that is, to political process, enables empirical description of the subject matter of applicative justice. The use of Bentley's descriptive method is compatible with an aim to make conditions of injustice better, instead of aiming for perfect justice. However, Bentley's analysis cannot be accepted uncritically. His reduction of written law and the apparatus of state to group activities and interests, taken as a description of society, is too extensive, with little room for normative evaluation as part of the analysis. Bentley presumes satisfactory democratic normality, in oblivion about those who were oppressed and disenfranchised in his time. It is not likely that Bentley could have imagined what critics today address as a "state of exception," when democratic rights and liberties are curtailed by government. Also, the nature of political processes have changed since Bentley's day. Large parts of the masses are now politically apathetic, but newly emergent waves of electronic journalism with opportunities for micro-opinion suggest that the masses are not altogether politically passive. Oppositional academic criticism could fulfill both Arendt's idea of the life of the mind and Agamben's longing for life outside of government.

Chapter 3 starts with the idea of human equality as an ideal, but an empirical analysis of equality fails to provide a plausible foundation for it and that in turn motivates a comparative approach to injustice. The rhetorical value of egalitarianism is duly recognized, nonetheless. In chapter 4, I consider the traditional distinction between procedural and distributional justice for a society where not all are treated with the same procedural justice. I conclude with the claim that procedural justice is a distributed good. Chapters 5 and 6 are devoted to the subject of political discourse, toward the goal of redistribution of procedural justice for American blacks and whites. In chapter 5, I survey the terrain of discourse, and consider the ideas of atmosphere and climate pertaining to racism, and the nature of symbols. Cornel West's construction of the Black Prophetic Tradition is engaged as a form of oppositional political discourse that relates academic speech to a liberatory historical trend and opens philosophy to the contemporary world. Chapter 6 focuses on important distinctions pertaining to discourse with the use of revisionist history of the US criminal justice system: the importance of the distinction between word and action and the importance of the distinction between big picture analysis for understanding and specific injustice attention for corrective action. The importance of historical perspective is also taken up, in reference to Raymond Williams's idea of "The Long Revolution" and the attitudes it supports and requires. Chapter 6 concludes with Judith Shklar's insight that oppositional discourse has its place in a democracy, the same democracy that the book has described as made up of both justice and comparative injustice in its political life. Chapter 7, the postscript, continues the discussion of the book by suggesting one thing that needs to be done in our time concerning racial justice, and inviting the reader to begin that project with me.

1

IDEAL THEORY, NONIDEAL THEORY, AND EMPIRICAL POLITICAL THEORY

> [The American President] has to take all sorts of abuse from liars and demagogues. . . . The people can never understand why the President does not use his supposedly great power to make 'em behave. Well, all the President is, is a glorified public relations man who spends his time flattering, kissing and kicking people to get them to do what they are supposed to do anyway.—Harry S. Truman[1]

I begin here with criticism of Rawlsian ideal and nonideal theory, from the perspective and starting point of a concern with injustice. That criticism discloses the necessity for a more empirical approach to justice. Arthur Bentley's pragmatic theory of government is introduced to help specify the subject described by empirical political theory.

JOHN RAWLS'S IDEAL THEORY OF JUSTICE

Any new philosophical theory of justice or injustice should begin with John Rawls, because his paradigm dominates political philosophy. There are a number of problems with how Rawls develops his conception of justice as fairness, which impede its ability to serve as a descriptive and normative theory of progress in justice. These include a problem with ignorance behind the veil, the context of origination of Rawlsian ideal theory, and the nonempirical ideality of Rawls's project. The first two problems arise from concern about experienced injustice and the third is a more general philosophical problem of how Rawlsian theory could be related to reality.

IGNORANCE BEHIND THE VEIL—A NAÏVE CRITICISM

Rawls's conception of justice as fairness is developed in a thought experiment requiring ignorance by the principal architects of major societal institutions about their own interest or social identities. They are presumed not to know whether they have traits that will position them for gain or loss in the institutions they design and select. It is also presumed that the society deliberated about is already "well organized," or law abiding, so that people will comply with the results of deliberation behind the veil. The deliberators share background legal and moral principles of justice, such as those affirmed in the founding documents of the United States.

The first problem with Rawls's setup seems to concern forms of ignorance of which he seemed to be unaware. Privileged people in societies where some are oppressed cannot be assumed able to achieve ignorance about their own identities without some kind of prior reeducation or training about the nature of their identities. Because they may not understand how they are elite or privileged, it would be necessary to develop a new form of awareness in those privileged, before they could design institutions that avoid bias in their favor.[2] For example, the prevalence of race-based disadvantage in contemporary "color blind" society is accompanied by widespread ignorance about that disadvantage. On a more general level, democratic masses have to be shown—and reshown—the suffering of members of oppressed groups in order to understand that those groups are or have been oppressed. Evidence of that is the importance of media images or graphic descriptions for creating important political turning points: the police dog lunging at a seventeen-year-old demonstrator in Birmingham, Alabama, in 1963; Phan Thi Kim Phuc fleeing burnt and naked from the 1972 napalm bombing of Trang Bang, her village in Vietnam; Senate testimony by disabled Americans who experienced discrimination based on their disabilities, which was needed to implement the 1990 Americans with Disabilities Act; the 2015 video of Walter Scott, an unarmed black man running away from the police officer who fatally shot him in the back.[3]

The necessity for dramatic imagery, poster-child individuals, direct testimony of suffering, or raw footage of unjust violence to motivate change in reality, suggests a default condition of public apathy toward injustice that noncognitive information disrupts. It also suggests prior ignorance of the injustice in question.

Rawls's deliberators might be ignorant not only about what their own identities were, but also in all likelihood, about the social meanings and effects of their identities and of other identities. This second degree of ignorance could be a major handicap in designing fair institutions and it might be difficult to correct if held in place by a psychological mechanism familiar in contemporary society, which is similar to denial.[4] Such denial might not constitute a full-blown clinical condition (because it is not blocking personal pain) but it is an attitude general enough to block the processing of information about real injustice in a society that is assumed to be just. The denial amounts to an apparent inability on the part of those not oppressed, who have the power to lift oppression, to imagine the perspectives of those who are oppressed or how their oppression is experienced by them.[5]

If the United States were the racially just color blind society that many white Americans believe it is, that would not entail that white Americans who correctly assumed the society was racially just, understood the disadvantages experienced by nonwhites. Even in a real racially just society, some groups might be more likely to be disadvantaged by certain institutions than other groups. If a white person behind a Rawlsian veil of ignorance doesn't know if she is white or nonwhite, it does not follow that she knows what her political perspective would be if she were black; or if able-bodied, what the consequences in institutional preferences would be if disabled; or if a hawkish patriot, what the effects of militarism are on those who would serve and their families. Given such ignorance about social identities that is deeper than the first ignorance behind the veil of simply not knowing which identities one has, decisions meant to be fair from behind the veil might be too arbitrary to amount to justice.

Ignorance behind the Veil—Who the Deliberators Really Are

I have correctly suggested with the foregoing interpretation of Rawlsian ignorance behind the veil that deliberators do not know their interests or identities in society, so that they are prevented from making self-interested choices. The problem seems deeper than that because they may be ignorant of how certain institutions affect members of groups different from their own. But this interpretation charges Rawls's deliberators with the ignorance that real people in society might have. According to Rawlsians, however, Rawls does not intend that, for instance, we imagine a white person behind the veil who puts aside her racial identity. The person behind the veil is not a real person, but a fictional partial-person who, as a character in the thought experiment, has no racial or any other social identity.[6] The imagined Rawlsian deliberator really is ignorant, through and through. There is something odd about this posit. To be ignorant in the usual sense requires that knowledge be available or at least possible. We do not say that a dog is ignorant about geography or history, because it is impossible for a dog to have knowledge of those fields. It would be more accurate to say that the dog was *unknowing* of geography or history.

Rawls's imagined deliberators do not have knowledge or attainable knowledge of their social identities, as information that they forget or block out. Rather, the thought experiment requires that as fictional, partial-people, they are unknowing, rather than ignorant of these things. But, if that was what Rawls really had in mind, other questions arise that are even more disturbing than the interpretation of the deliberators as real people who are ignorant in the usual sense. Why would the deliberations about just institutions undertaken by unknowing partial-persons be useful to those seeking justice? The answer might be that only such deliberators, uncontaminated by certain kinds of knowledge, could construct just institutions. We might also ask, how could the imagined fictional partial-person, who is unknowing about social identities that are advantaged and likely to receive just treatment, or disadvantaged and likely to receive unjust treatment, tell us anything about injustice? Of course, injustice is not her subject, justice is, and she would insist that to identify injustice and know how to avoid or correct it, it is first necessary to have a conception of justice. But could she conceive of justice without first conceiving of injustice, or at least, also conceiving of injustice? Consider Western medicine, which is often criticized for its focus on injury and disease instead of soundness and health. Still, a patient who is ill or injured needs that problem addressed by an experienced practitioner, who would have to approach the problem on its own terms, instead of beginning with optimal function or health.

Decades of work on institutional or inadvertent racism, as well as the personal and professional effects of implicit bias against women, people of color, lesbians and homosexuals, and those who are disabled have taught that members of oppressed groups require that their own voices, based on their own experiences of oppression, be heard. It is what those voices express about the lived experience of victims of injustice that educates listeners about what that experience feels like for another live human being. Justice as fairness—Rawls's conception of justice—would be fairness to real live people, because it is real live people who deserve to be treated fairly, because they are real live people. However, for the voices of the oppressed to engage in deliberation behind the veil of ignorance, those persons would have to be present behind the veil of ignorance, *with the knowledge of who they were*. And that would defeat the premise of the veil because there would be no veil.

The Distinction between Ideal and Nonideal Theory

A Rawlsian would continue to object to such criticism based on posited ignorance of oppression, by reminding us of the distinction between ideal and nonideal theory, such that societies with oppression are the subject of nonideal theory only. The thought experiment of what occurs behind the veil of ignorance belongs to the construction of ideal theory, the part of justice that pertains to a well-ordered society in which there is a shared background of ideas about justice and laws are followed. But this defense also invites skepticism.

Given that those who do not suffer from a type of injustice are likely to be ignorant of the experience of those who do suffer from it, how can they come to know what a just society that lacks injustice *is*? This skepticism about the nature of a just society is more than skepticism about whether such a society could exist. If we can't adequately describe a just society by imagining the deliberations of a partial-person who is unknowing about injustice, then why would anyone think that such deliberation would bring us closer to a conception of justice? Rawls's stipulation of compliance with law does not tell us much of substance unless we know that the law complied with is just. Simply positing shared background information about just laws and principles cannot in itself reassure us that there are just laws and principles in the background, in the absence of some positive description of what justice is. And such a positive description would have to be forthcoming from the partial-person deliberators who are unlikely to be able to provide it, given their unknowingness about injustice.

Such skepticism that justice can be described before injustice has been knowingly experienced may seem absurd given the academic success of Rawls's paradigm. So maybe it would be better advised to take a closer look at the separation between ideal and nonideal theory. John Simmons writes, quoting Rawls:

> In its barest outline, of course, the idea behind the distinction [between ideal and nonideal theory] is simple and appealing, no doubt accounting for the widespread acceptance of (or indifference toward) Rawls's version of it: "the intuitive idea is to split the theory of justice into two parts. The first or ideal part assumes strict compliance and works out the principles that characterize a well-ordered society under favorable circumstances." [*TJ*, p. 245] This "ideal part presents a conception of a just society that we are to achieve if we can. Existing institutions are to be judged in the light of this conception." [*TJ*, p. 246] "Nonideal theory asks how this long-term goal might be achieved, or worked toward, usually in gradual steps. It looks for courses of action that are morally permissible and politically possible as well as likely to be effective." LOP p. 89[7]

Simmons slightly rephrases Rawls on the gap between ideal and nonideal theory, so that "although 'the specific conditions of our world at any time' affect the appropriate conclusions of nonideal theory, they should not influence *ideal* theory."[8] On Simmons's interpretation of Rawls, ideal theory cannot provide remedies for oppression, because "the specific conditions of our world at any time" should not influence it. Oppression is part of the imperfect world addressed by nonideal theory and there is no indication that nonideal theory can influence ideal theory.

The normative aspects of applicative justice, in seeking to extend or revise existing law and force to correct injustice, could be called part of nonideal theory, but it is difficult to see how Rawlsian nonideal theory could contribute to the correction of injustice. The Rawlsian nonideal aim is to bring reality closer to the ideal as described by ideal theory.

Rawls did not suggest that he was providing a theory of justice that could be applied to create a just society. Rather, we would need to aim for that ideal with the theoretical resources provided by nonideal theory. However, nonideal theory is supposed to rely on the conclusions of ideal theory, as something to which reality needs to be brought closer. And, the ideals of ideal theory are not to be influenced or changed based on the work accomplished by nonideal theory.

Historically, those who have sought to correct oppression of one form or another are rarely so confident of their solutions to omit prohibitions of oppression in statements of their ideals. For example, the Bill of Rights as the first ten amendments to the US Constitution explicitly prohibits a number of government actions that were historically oppressive in ways known to founders. (The preamble to the Bill of Rights reads in part: "Conventions of a number of the States, having at the time of their adopting the Constitution, expressed a desire, in order to prevent misconstruction or abuse of its powers, that further declaratory and restrictive clauses should be added."[9]) This again raises the intriguing issue of the relevance of their own backgrounds to the deliberations of Rawls's ideal theorists behind the veil. Since such background information almost certainly contains references to corrections of fundamental injustices that would be part of nonideal theory, the sterile nature of ideal theory as uninfluenced by nonideal theory is likely to be contaminated in all times and places within human history.

THE CONTEXT OF ORIGINATION OF POLITICAL THEORY

The Tradition of Very Strong Property Rights

The actual historical backgrounds of those who construct an ideal is the context of origination of that ideal. The context of origination of any political theory, consisting of the social, political, and economic circumstances, interests, and motivations of theorists, may influence how the theory is subsequently applied, or if it cannot be applied, who its proponents are likely to be. Ideal theory is not something that we should think of as capable of application, but its context of origination can be viewed as influencing the thought and values of its proponents. A familiar historical example will help show how contexts of origination structure subsequent theoretical interest, as well as, in this case, its application.

When private property owners and their advocates have created theories of justice, this context of origination has structured the application of their theories. The importance of property rights in American ideals of justice can be tracked to John Locke's *Second Treatise of Government*. Locke was influential in justifying and perhaps even crafting the structure of English parliamentary government after the Glorious Revolution of 1688. That form of representative government was motivated by the need to protect the private property of the English aristocracy against the English crown and nobility, and against claims by the dispossessed who had lost access to their "commons" during the enclosure movement.[10] Locke's *Second Treatise* influenced Thomas Jefferson, a substantial owner of property that included slaves, the main author of the US Declaration of Independence, and an influential correspondent with those who drafted the Constitution. Jefferson served as secretary of state, vice president, and then president during a time when the United States doubled its size.[11]

The high value placed on private property ownership rights was used to justify protection of the rights of slave owners in *Dred Scott vs. Sanford* in 1857.[12] Long after slavery was abolished, strong property rights continue to be valorized. In 2003, President George W. Bush successfully used the slogan "the ownership society" to promote the buying and financing of US homes for first-time home buyers. One result was to increase the transformation of the home ownership of some, into a "derivative," intangible but monetarized form of property for a wealthier group, via highly leveraged and largely unregulated financial instruments based on mortgage debt.[13] Further attesting to property ownership and its attendant rights as an overriding American value is the tendency in some state courts to punish physical crimes against property as harshly as some violent crimes against persons.[14] But, less visible crimes against property, as committed by the derivative speculators who precipitated the real estate crash and Great Recession of 2008, go largely unpunished.[15] Thus, the more property someone owns, either in tangible goods, cash, or financial instruments, the stronger are their property rights, that is, the better their protection under law. More generally, Euro-American principles of justice that protect the rights of private property owners have enabled development and corporate globalization at the expense of natural environments and the well-being of low-paid workers throughout the world.

Progressives who criticize received themes of justice with their own theories of applicative justice (although not by that name) usually advocate for exploited workers and the poor, who do not benefit from the protection of private property ownership. The importance placed on private property ownership in the context of origination of the American legal system has powerfully influenced its contexts of application in ways that support injustice. Ongoing legal deference to private property rights has resulted in exploitation and disregard that violate principles of human dignity.[16] (As well, the lack of restraint on what can be owned—throughout global culture—indirectly enables practices of contemporary slavery.[17])

The problem with government design centered on very strong property rights can thus be directly related to the property-owning status of John Locke and his patrons (Lord Shaftesbury and friends).[18] I will return to the unjust results of Locke's equation of very strong property rights with liberty in chapter 4.

The Context of Origination of Ideal Theory

The Lockean historical example raises analogous concerns about the nature of the context of origination of Rawls's ideal theory. Rawls's context of origination for his conception of justice is, we already know, a thought experiment:

> The idea of the original position is to set up a fair procedure so that any principles agreed to will be just. The aim is to use the notion of pure procedural justice as a basis of theory. Somehow we must nullify the effects of specific contingencies which put men at odds and tempt them to exploit social and natural circumstances to their own advantage. Now in order to do this I assume that the parties are situated behind a veil of ignorance. They do not know how the various alternatives will affect their own particular case and they are obliged to evaluate principles solely on the basis of general considerations. . . . It is assumed, then, that the parties do not know certain kinds of particular facts. First of all, no one knows his place in society, his class position or social status; nor does he know his fortune in

> the distribution of natural assets and abilities, his intelligence and strength, and the like. Nor, again, does anyone know his conception of the good, the particulars of his rational plan of life, or even the special features of his psychology such as his aversion to risk or liability to optimism or pessimism. More than this, I assume that the parties do not know the particular circumstances of their own society. That is, they do not know its economic or political situation, or the level of civilization and culture it has been able to achieve. The persons in the original position have no information as to which generation they belong.[19]

What Rawls assumes about those who are behind a "veil of ignorance," and his assumption of a veil of ignorance itself, are both exercises in imagination. As noted, according to Rawls, the conception of justice as fairness is ideal theory, intended to be for well-ordered, law-abiding societies. Rawls thereby takes for granted an almost automatic implementation of the principles of justice:

> The principles of justice (in lexical order) belong to ideal theory (§39). The persons in the original position assume that the principles they acknowledge, whatever they are, will be strictly complied with and followed by everyone. Thus the principles of justice that result are those defining a perfectly just society, given favorable conditions. With the presumption of strict compliance, we arrive at a certain ideal conception.[20]

Altogether, Rawls's ideal theory is remote from real life. If there is perfect compliance with the principles of justice, then the struggles for justice that characterize progressive movements will not occur, because there will be no need for them. That ideal theory bypasses real injustice is bizarre, because in human history the practical concern with justice has been motivated by observed injustice(s). Furthermore, given the nonexistence of societies that are perfectly just, the context of origination of Rawlsian ideal theory is purely imaginative and speculative. Rawlsian ideal theory is thereby restricted to an "ideal" realm in a philosophical sense—that is, to the world of ideas that do not, and need not, refer to anything in the material world. This means that any context of application in real life would be imperfect, not unlike drawn geometrical figures in comparison to what those figures are as defined by the axioms of geometry. It also means, because some can always imagine and speculate, in any situation, that Rawlsian ideal theorizing can occur in situations with great ongoing injustice. Rawlsian ideal theorizing has nothing to offer for correcting real life injustice, and, while it can't be said to cause real life injustice, time spent pursuing it might be evaluated in terms of its "opportunity cost" of other kinds of theorizing. Also, Rawlsian theorizing itself requires a certain kind and amount of institutionally financed leisure, as well as personal insulation from human suffering. The social identities of political theorists are not irrelevant to the theories which attract them. Just as a certain type of property owner in this day would find Locke's version of social contract theory appealing, so might those whose life experience has made them more familiar with just than unjust treatment find Rawlsian ideal theory appealing.

We should also note that Rawls and Rawlsians assume that it is important to know what justice is before injustice can be identified and addressed. They often assert that an idea of justice is "analytically prior" to an idea of injustice. But there is little or no explanation or justification for that claim. For Rawls and Rawlsians, the conceptual priority of justice over injustice has every appearance of an article of faith.

Charles Mills and others have criticized Rawlsian justice-as-fairness for the failure of ideal theory to account for, or even consider, less than ideal societies. Mills argues that in the nonideal society of the United States, the effects of past injustice continue to diminish opportunities for people of color, even if they are treated fairly in the present.[21] This creates an intellectual divide between Rawlsians and those concerned with racial injustice. Mills writes:

> Rawls, the celebrated American philosopher of justice, had next to nothing to say in his work about what has arguably historically been the most blatant American variety of *injustice*, racial oppression. The postwar struggle for racial justice in practice and in theory and the Rawlsian corpus on justice are almost completely separate and non-intersecting universes.[22]

If those with comparatively less power and authority in society have found it necessary to conduct their theoretical work on justice, in isolation from paradigmatic theoretical discussion, that in itself seems unfair. If the intellectual concern is with justice, shouldn't those most in need of it be able to participate in the discussion? However, the problem with Rawlsian ideal theory in terms of racial oppression is even more general and drastic than a separation within political theory between those who ignore racial oppression and those who attend to it.[23] The fundamental separation is between those who are able to theorize justice without antecedent distress from injustice and those who demand of a theory of justice that it answer urgent, real life needs, wants, lacks—injustices that they have experienced or observed. The modern theory of private property was invented by those who wanted to protect and expand their existing ownership. *Rawlsian ideal theory is imagined to be the product of those who are not suffering from injustice!* In both cases, the context of origination of a theory biases its appeal to those whose goals and circumstances are similar to the originators. And, to add injury to insult, the nonreferentiality of Rawlsian ideal theory underscores how the theory is useless to those suffering from injustice.

Rawlsian ideal theory promises to provide a "realistic utopia" toward which progressives may aspire. It is difficult to dismiss the idea of an ultimate standard of justice, even if all we have is the name. But, again, what kind of a standard does Rawls describe? Rawlsian ideal theory is a perfect construct of justice, suspended *in* thought. Rawls does set up the original position against a backdrop of shared founding documents and egalitarian principles of justice. But this is not like some process of deriving the principles of jurisprudence from positive law. Rawls's ideal theory background is ultimately a psychological, moral, and intellectual imagining. A source like that may have a spiritual value, but such imaginings cannot do the work of a political background based on events that have occurred, or are occurring. In other words, Rawlsian ideal theory is not an *empirical* theory in any sense. The light shed by the perfection of a realistic utopia may reveal how things *could be* in the mind's eye(s), but it fails to illuminate how things *can be* in reality. But what about Rawlsian nonideal theory?

Amartya Sen and Nonideal Theory

For an example of nonideal theory, we might consider the thought of economist Amartya Sen, Rawls's student. Sen has been interested in developing a conception of justice that will express common sense ideals and expectations. Like Rawls, Sen assumes that the correct description of the right structure is important for progress toward justice.

However, unlike Rawls and instructive for concerns here, Sen describes his point of departure as starting with perceptions of injustice:

> The requirements of a theory of justice include bringing reason into play in the diagnosis of justice and injustice. Over hundreds of years, writers on justice in different parts of the world have attempted to provide the intellectual basis for moving from a general sense of injustice to particular reasoned diagnoses of injustice, and from there to the analyses of ways of advancing justice.[24]

Sen is concerned with "actualization" or peoples' real lives in a given society, more than he is with the justice or fairness of formal institutional structures, or what he calls "transcendental institutionalism."[25] His criticism of transcendental institutionalism is that there may not be a unique just institutional arrangement, so that for the guidance of social choices where options are less than perfect or ideal, knowledge of a fully just arrangement is neither necessary nor sufficient. His famous example is that in choosing between a Dali and a Picasso, whether or not the Mona Lisa is the most perfect picture in the world, is irrelevant.[26]

Sens's own starting point is that of "taking the comparative rather than the transcendental route" and "focusing on actual realizations in the societies involved, rather than only on institutions and rules."[27] Sen brings home the distinction between his approach and Rawls's, with the distinction between *niti* and *nyaya* from Sanskrit literature on ethics and jurisprudence: *Niti* refers to "organizational propriety and behavioural correctness"; *Nyaya* refers to "the world that actually emerges."[28] Sen writes, "A realization-focused perspective also makes it easier to understand the importance of the prevention of manifest injustice in the world, rather than seeking the perfectly just."[29]

The approach that I will now introduce and develop in subsequent chapters shares Sen's focus on injustice as a starting point. But my rejection of ideal theory goes beyond Sen's contrast between *niti* as ideal and *nyaya*, which is the world that actually emerges. I will attempt to go beyond noting that contrast into development of a political perspective that both practical standards and reality are part of the same political whole. This is a project in empirical political theory.

Requirements of Empirical Political Theory

The desirability and even necessity of political ideals is a good starting point for progressive ideas of justice. Such ideals inspire progressives in forming their goals. However, there are two senses of *ideal* at stake here. First, there is a Rawlsian sense of ideal as a product of thought, held in thought, which is a thoroughly *rationalist* ideal, suitable only for inspiring more perfection in thought. Second, in responding to the urgency of experiences of injustice, there is an ideal in the sense of a standard that can be realized in reality, as reality has been and continues to be experienced in political life. This would generate empirical ideal theory, a thoroughly *empiricist* project.

Is empiricist political theory the same thing as Rawlsian nonideal theory? Not exactly. The main activity of Rawlsian ideal theory is thought and discussion, whereas Rawlsian nonideal theory, in striving to approximate ideal theory, would seem to explicitly include action, legislation, and all of the struggles and plans that are taken for granted as part of political life, including practical applications of theoretical conclusions designed for their applicability. However, since Rawlsian nonideal theory does not influence Rawlsian ideal theory and Rawlsian ideal theory cannot be applied in a society that is not well ordered, it cannot be applied to reality. Rawlsian nonideal theory gets from Rawlsian ideal theory nothing more than something to think about and gaze upon as an ideal in the mind's eye. Rawlsian nonideal theory is no different from any other empirical political theory, and except for its unrequited mesmerization by Rawlsian ideal theory, it is on its own for all practical purposes that theorists know will not change the ideals of ideal theory.

What is empirical political theory? One part of empirical political theory has already been identified for applicative justice in its connection to existing positive law, principles, and practices. Another part of empirical ideal theory, which is of interest, now, is description of a state of affairs *better* than what is actually experienced, but conceivable and practical as a change in, addition to, or subtraction from, what is actually experienced. The process of getting from how reality is, to where it can be, is a practical process of changes in laws and practice to bring real conditions in accord with what would be better. Contra Rawlsian nonideal theory, that process would be backward looking toward what already has been and is, in order to attain an empirical goal that may be revised after attainment. If this sounds familiar, it is indeed a pragmatic approach.

An empirical goal or standard is posited to make things better for those who experience injustice, as compared to the circumstances of those who do not experience that same injustice or type of injustice. In growing out of what has been and is, the standard of what is "better" would be an attainable goal. This departure from Rawls is the difference between improving a condition in response to its shortcomings so that one can answer yes to the question, "Is it better?" versus improving a condition so that one can answer yes to the question, "Does it bring us closer to perfection?" (For example, after it was cleaned, "Is the room cleaner than it was or more like an already clean room?" and not "Is the room closer to perfect cleanliness?")

One job of political philosophy is to describe a better or more just form of existing reality. This job is starkly different from the job of Rawlsian nonideal theorists who seek to tell us how to reach a nonexistent, and not known to be attainable, ideal. The job getting to "better" as attainable in reality is the job of applicative justice theorists, but it need not apply to anything external to the situation addressed. If some people are allowed to vote and others are not allowed to vote, we don't have to strive for a fundamental ideal of representative government and free elections. All that is necessary is to remove the obstacles to voting that are preventing the group not allowed to vote from voting, as those who are allowed to vote are already voting.

The "better" to which philosophical and practical efforts aim is what is meant by an *empirical standard*. We need to be able to specify what kind of content any empirical standard would have. But before saying more about such descriptions of "better," we need a method for generating descriptions of how things are and how they could be, which is based on an accurate understanding of existing democratic political processes. For an empirical political theory or, more specifically, a theory of applicative justice, it is necessary to have accurate descriptions of the laws and practices that could be changed to result in progress in justice. It may also be nice to have a general theory of justice for rhetorical purposes and we will see, in chapter 2, that Rawls's conception of justice as fairness is rhetorically adequate for our purposes as well. However, this will be "fairness" without a veil of ignorance and as no more than a heuristic justification for getting from an existing state of affairs to something better—that is, fairness as a map instead of a blueprint or a receding mirage (Rawls was not aiming to provide a blueprint). But, for now, how can our understanding of political processes generate descriptions of empirical ideals of "better"? What does it mean to understand real political processes, or how do we describe the subject matter of empirical political theory? I think one compelling answer to that question was largely provided by Arthur Bentley over a hundred years ago.

BENTLEY'S PRAGMATIC THEORY OF GOVERNMENT

Bentley's approach to political reality was empirical in attending to the nature of existing government. His work was first ignored in academic political science and has overall received scant attention in political philosophy. But his ideas were taken up by legal scholars, historians, economists, and political scientists, at different times in the 1930s, 1940s, and 1950s and may be receiving a new turn in the early twenty-first century.[30]

Bentley criticized the work of early twentieth-century political scientists for their focus on narrow description of the formal rules and structures of government as an institution separate from other social activities, especially real-life political processes. He viewed such descriptions as incomplete in leaving out the roles of interest groups and contested practices that made up political life. In his 1908 *The Process of Government: A Study of Social Pressures*, Bentley developed a pragmatic perspective (he collaborated with John Dewey toward the end of both their lives, although not on political philosophy[31]) for describing government and political life as a dynamic, interactive process that extended widely beyond the formal apparatus of state.

THE PROCESS OF GOVERNMENT

Social Causes for Social Events

Bentley begins *The Process of Government* with a critical discussion of claims that human sympathy as the moral foundation for Western society has advanced historically. He points to instances of contemporary cruelty and refers with approval to Peter Kropotkin's reference to altruism among animals and primitive peoples.[32] He examines the work of leading early twentieth-century political theorists, such as Albion Small, Herbert Spencer, and Rudolph von Jhering, to clear the way for what is distinct about his own theory. Bentley attacks posits of human feelings or desires as causes of social action and institutions. He reasons that such posits are not directly observed, but inferred from what is observed, in order to explain what is observed. It is instructive to consider some of the details of Bentley's critique, because the intellectual heirs of Small, Spencer, and von Jhering remain unaware of the circularity of their methodology.

Bentley painstakingly exposits Small's elaborate system of social causes but concludes:

> What Professor Small's theory comes to is that certain rough groups of social activities are first taken; that it is inferred next that there must be desires or wants corresponding to each; that these main desires or wants are set up, six in number, as the springs of social action; that all specific desires as found from day to day in individual men are brought under these six classes, no matter how they quarrel when fastened together; and that finally it is asserted that because the six great desires have been named, we are given in them a classification of social activities which is for that reason valid.[33]

Bentley finds a similar circularity in Spencer's claims about the workings of sympathy in society, summing up:

> I challenge anyone to read these and point out from them where Spencer finds any "sympathy" as a feeling thing which is not itself merely his own bald inference from the external facts this sympathy is supposed to explain.[34]

After conscientiously consulting the original German phrasing in his presentation of Jhering's focal notion of "Zweck" [purpose or goal] Bentley nicely expresses exasperation:

> [Jhering] never learned to posit the simple answerable question: "How are these masses and groups of men doing these things in these ways?" which is the only scientific question. . . . He asked: "Why are these men doing these things and not some other things?" and not, "How are these processes of men working?" He asked, "Why does a society of men set up certain laws and then why do these men obey these laws?" and not: "How do these socially and legally organized men function along? What are the various elements of their functioning? And how do these elements fit into one another and condition one another?" He might as well have asked why is gold gold and not silver, and why is silver silver and not gold, instead of simply studying all the gold and silver phenomena under as many conditions as possible, and trying scientifically to make out their similarities as distinguished from their differences.[35]

Bentley then calls for a descriptive account of how society functions, insisting that the social contexts of individuals be included in this account, along with their distinct perspectives:

> [Jhering] had an assumed individual to start with. As he progressed he found himself compelled to assume and personify a society to set over against this individual. His entire theory consisted in a desperate struggle to bring his two assumptions into harmonious relations. And of course the harmony he established was as fictitious as the assumptions upon which he established it. If instead of setting the concrete individual over against the concrete society, he had taken the individual point of view and the social point of view merely as points of view, that is, each as covering the whole range of the social life of men, he would have had both his individual and his society capable of being broken down, that is of being analysed, without the interpolation of fictitious "Zwecke."[36]

Bentley's point is that if we can understand how individuals do things in society, it is unnecessary to set up the individual and society as opposed realities. Rather, we keep society as the ultimate social reality that can be understood from both individual and social perspectives or points of view. That is, for Bentley, the proper subject matter for the political scientist is society, as a concrete organization of human life. Thus:

> If all this process of government were some "external" thing waiting to be pushed by feelings, or now and then pushing feelings in return, that would be one thing. But such is not the case. It is "internal," it is human, as much as anything we know of is internal and human.[37]

There are two main theoretical aspects to Bentley's critique of individual feelings (and desires) as primary causes of social and political events and conditions. First, his argument against the claim that individual feelings are causal factors for social institutions is a kind of behaviorism insofar as he refers to such feelings as unobserved "soul stuff." But one could be a behaviorist in reducing feelings to physiology and behavior and still use individual physiology and behavior in final social explanations. The second and more interesting aspect of Bentley's critique is his insistence on a social science method that looks for causes of social phenomena *within* social phenomena. He writes:

> The interpretation that will hold scientifically will ignore these feelings. It will watch the social situations build themselves up, one unfolding itself out of the other. It will look to the future only through these unfolding situations. It will not put a grainspook in the wheat-field, nor a brain-spook in the class war or the reform of government or the social movement. It will see every bit of social activity as psychically functioned, and it will see nothing concretely psychical that is independent of society and yet dominating it. It will calmly, "positively," in the Comtean sense, grasp social facts just for what they are, study them for what they are, analyze and synthesize them for what they are, and leave all the mental "spooks" for men and women so hard pressed with the actual doing of things that they need convenient catchwords and symbols to save them the trouble of pushing their thinking back into a region that would inevitably send forth great disturbance for the day's work they have in hand.[38]

RACE AND SOCIAL CONSTRUCTION

While Bentley did not have a distinct concept of social construction, he carried his insistence on social causes for social phenomena into criticism of eugenics advocacy, which targeted its circular reasoning. He thereby made short shrift of the work of Karl Pearson and Frederick Alan Wood, who posited superior and inferior hereditary "stock" as causes in ethnic and racial group differences in intellectual achievements and morals. While Bentley did not quarrel with anthropometric or other such physical measurements of racial and ethnic difference, per se, he objected to subjective measurements of psychic traits and posits of "soul stuff" accounting for them. Bentley comes closest to developing an idea of racial difference as socially constructed, that is, resulting from events and attitudes within society, when he makes fun of Pearson for asking, "Have we a reserve of brain power ready to be trained?" Bentley continues, "And he sadly answers: 'I must confess to feeling that an actual dearth is upon us.' And all this because Kaffirs and negroes, as a social fact, have not developed, as a social fact, great complicated social organizations."[39]

Bentley sums up chapter 1 of *The Process of Government* with what holds up today as a remarkably progressive attack on essentialism, or the idea that human beings have fixed traits that are both independent of society and determine their positions within it. He puts it:

> I am not denying that men are in fact distinguished from one another by epithets relating to their intelligence and moral qualities; nor that different adults act differently in situations which we describe to ourselves as substantially the same; nor that this method of statement is useful in its own time and place. What I am asserting is that the attempt to erect it into a causal interpretation of society on the basis of fixed individual characters which can adequately be described and defined apart from the society they explain, is a hotbed of confusion and irrelevancy.[40]

In chapter 9, "Individual Endowment and the Race Type" (of *The Process of Government*), Bentley dismisses a social causal role for psychic aspects of racial difference by referring to his more general analysis of feelings. Even though Bentley thought that "the physical endowment of the individual" could be scientifically measured (part and parcel of living in the heyday of antropometric racial studies), he claims that "most of it is capable of adequate statement only in terms of masses of men living together under given conditions."[41] That is, individual physical racial differences can only play a social explanatory role in terms of the organization of groups in specific societies. Regarding the use of physical racial differences to explain such group organization, Bentley writes:

> I am not denying that there may be actual differences in nervous complexity (and so capacity) between physical races of men just as there may be between individuals. I am not denying the significance of the skulls of Pithecanthropus and of the Neanderthal man. The whole point concerns the interpretation of social activity and organization in terms of such differences. Against the exaggerated emphasis that is placed on slight shadings of capacity stated in anatomical or physiological terms, I am appealing to a whole world of social facts, and asking [for] their analysis on their merits.[42]

Bentley understood that physical racial group differences within a given society cannot be assumed to have a causal role independent of other social factors. For Bentley, "race" as a characteristic of individuals refers to racial group membership. And, differences among racial groups cannot be understood scientifically in terms of either physical or psychic race—not even when ideas of physical race include inherited psychic capacities—but must be referred to other social facts, to human interaction. Bentley's treatment of race is a good example of this thesis that society cannot be explained by nonsocietal factors external to it.

THE POWER OF IDEAS

Bentley also attacks the assumption that ideas and ideals, as factors external to social functions, have the power to shape history. He first deals with obvious cases of political speeches that are mere rhetoric or transparent hypocrisy, observing that the platforms of winning political parties have little effect on how winning candidates act after elections. He dismisses even sincerely held articles of faith or belief, such as the ideal of a "City of God" or socialist principles, because their presumed causal effects are not verified by history. Bentley also challenges for its lack of historical evidence, John Stuart Mill's claims that great social change is preceded by changes in opinions and modes of thinking and that "human progression" depends on intellectual development. Others are criticized for attempting to interpret human societies based on dominant ideas, especially Franklin Giddings for his thesis that the ideals of unity, liberty, and equality were primary social causes at the beginning of the twentieth century.[43]

Given Bentley's general insistence that social interpretation do more than extract a concept from known facts and use that concept to explain the same facts, it is not surprising that despite some guarded approval, he has little use for the notion of "social will." He approves of the implication that those who use "social will" are cognizant of society as an entity beyond the individuals making it up. But he finds the use of society as personified to explain social processes at best tautological: "To talk of the will of the state is nothing more than to talk abstractly of the state itself."[44] Returning briefly to Rawlsian ideal theory, and nonideal theory as striving toward the conditions that would approximate those of ideal theory, Bentley's critique of external psychic factors posited as causes of societal events raises the question of the purpose of both ideal and nonideal theory. If ideal theory is perfected, that in itself does not entail that it will have an effect on even a well-ordered society. Within nonideal theory, descriptions of how society can be changed so that it is closer to the circumstances of ideal theory will not by themselves result in social change. Bentley would probably claim that if there were a well-ordered society to which ideal theory could be applied, or even if the prescriptions of ideal theory were somehow realized, ideal theory could not serve as an explanation for the more just nature of the society in question.

The Subjects of Empirical Political Theory

How should the subjects of empirical political theory be described? The answer is complex. A causal account of the successful implementation of a social plan, while it would need to refer to individual or group activities and available resources, would also need to refer to the plan implemented, as a goal, standard, or ideal. Feelings, ideas, and ideals held by members of society and used by their leaders to motivate them are themselves part of society or social functioning, so that reference to them would have a legitimate place in empirical political philosophy, as well as social science. Bentley does distinguish between social process, as observable events, and social content as perception or understanding of social process from an individual perspective.[45] Thus, as long as content is understood as *from* an individual perspective within a social context, it does have a distinct place in Bentleyan interpretation, even though it lacks causal power. However, the line between observable social and political events and individual beliefs about them is not that easy to draw, because events are often described by and to participants in the language of their standing beliefs. Human action is not mere physical movement but movement that is only intelligible to other humans given shared beliefs and in the case of group efforts, shared goals. People often behave according to social scripts that are based on fictional stereotypes about others. What Bentley viewed as "content" overflows individual minds. In terms of even practical political theory, the power of Rawlsian ideals should not be underestimated. Not only has some of the best work in political philosophy after 1971 issued from the House of Rawls, but the idea of stakeholder participation in planning has trickled down in quite practical policy construction, such as the ethics of disaster.[46] However, this kind of "off-label" usage is more literary than philosophical, because ideal theory was not created to apply to existing reality, much less apply to deliberation about practices so particular or concrete.

As I have tried to emphasize in this discussion of Bentley's critique, his important contribution is to remind us that psychic factors and biological facts do not *by themselves*, as factors external to society, cause societal events. When viewed as embedded in social structures and processes or functionings, they can be viewed as playing causal roles and, as we shall see in chapter 2, Bentley does take that view in his positive account of how government actually works and what it is.

Of great interest for the project of this book is Bentley's overall focus on social action and events as the main subject matter of political reality. Such a focus has implications for effective approaches to societal change, as well as for understanding specific existing societies. For instance, it is how a law is obeyed in reality or interpreted by the courts, rather than what has been formally written, which is important for understanding what the law is. But we still subscribe to the fiction, of which Bentley was well aware, that our laws accurately describe our society under those laws, for example, the assumption that formal equality for racial minorities is equality in real life. We will soon see in chapter 2 how Bentley's positive claims about explanations and theories in social and political science explanation support an understanding of how injustice can peacefully coexist with just written law.

BENTLEY AND SEN

Bentley has a metaphysical view of government that might be best understood if we briefly return to Sen. For Sen, the institutions and rules (*niti*) seem to have a separate existence from "the world that actually emerges" (*nyaya*). Apart from insisting that any conception of justice would not have causal efficacy in itself, Bentley would recognize no empirical distinction between *niti* and *nyaya* or between rules as written down and what happens in people's lives, or between "institutions and rules" and "actual realizations in the societies involved." According to Bentley, *the institutions and rules are nothing more than the actual realizations as associated with them or called by their names*. This is the useful lesson from Bentley, to be carried out in theory and projects of applicative justice.

However, before going forward with this lesson, it should be noted that Bentley's notion of government as process can be theorized further in ways that exceed the present interpretation. The present interpretation relies on two main commitments. First, causal efficacy should not be assigned to external political factors that cannot be directly related to activities within society. Second, descriptions of real-life practical political behavior that may or may not be associated with laws naming it should be included in descriptions of government. That is, descriptions of formal aspects of government, consisting of laws for (or over) society and laws about the structure of government itself are only part of descriptions of government and cannot on their own be considered comprehensive descriptions of government. For example, the US income tax laws *are* the written laws themselves plus actions of compliance or violations of written laws and government response to those actions; the famous principle of the division of powers *is* both that principle and descriptions of the real activities among the legislature, executive, and judiciary at any given time.

The limits that so far seem reasonable to impose on Bentley's analysis are caution about absolute social reduction and the option of rejecting a metaphysical pragmatic reduction. Bentley sometimes writes as though written law and abstract principles are *nothing but* the actions associated with them but that would be to take his reduction too far. A Bentleyan reduction of written law and abstract principles to human action associated with them—that is, the action has the name of the law or principle, should be understood as resting on a hypothesis about human nature, rather than a metaphysical analysis of social causes. The human nature hypothesis would be that human beings do not act in fulfillment of predetermined "blueprints" for their actions, but according to their wants, needs, and desires and what they are at liberty to do or refrain from doing. Their doings and refrainings may be symbolically associated with blueprints, but it cannot be assumed that actions are accurately and fully described by blueprints. The party platform is presented as a blueprint for what a president will do after the election, but the winner is not only free to do things entirely differently, but usually does.

There have been other interpretations of Bentley's notion of government as process, which are strictly metaphysical in that they engage ideas of change as opposed to permanence and events as opposed to things for units in true descriptions of reality. This metaphysical approach or worldview was probably shared by Bentley,[47] but it is important to note that the aspect of his reductionism taken up here is not logically incompatible with a view that there is permanence through change in the world and substantial things in contrast to events. It could be argued that Bentley's reliance on the non-blueprint actualizing nature of human beings with liberties in society is a permanent characteristic of human behavior. Similarly, there is nothing in a Bentleyan approach to laws and their actualizations that precludes positing as substantial the physical instruments through which laws are recorded, or for that matter the stuff of which monuments are made. I am not saying that I hold such a metaphysical view, but merely wish to focus on the political world as a subject, without being concerned about quite independent metaphysical issues. A pragmatist theory of government or political life need not imply a pragmatist ontology. It should, by the way, also be noted that what Bentley calls "government" is often more accurately termed "political life."

The foregoing distinction between a metaphysical worldview favoring process and reduction of legal writing to legal activities, in light of human nature, would not be necessary to insist on, in considering Sen's focus on practical affairs as opposed to ideals. The reason is that Sen does not, as noted, reduce ideals or laws to real life actualities, but simply emphasizes the importance of real life actualities or eventualities. There may be an assumed causal connection between *niti* and *nyaya*, in Sen's thought, such that *nyaya* imperfectly actualizes *niti*, while it should actualize or eventualize it better. If that is true, Bentley avoided this kind of normativity in insisting that *nyaya* is all that is politically real.

While ideal theory ignores *nyaya* and Bentleyan reduction does away with *niti*, a more comprehensive political injustice theory would allow for both *niti* and *nyaya*, without a meta-normative expectation or imprecation that *nyaya* express *niti*. Rather, we have to consider both *niti* and *nyaya*, both political content and political life, as human action. Injustice is a starting point, but unlike Sen's approach, applicative justice theory as a specific form of empirical political theory proceeds from a more thorough rejection of ideal theory than an awareness that what happens does not fulfill ideals. Rather, ideals as content, and what happens, as reality, are part of the same integral whole of political life.

2

LIMITS OF LAW AND GOVERNMENT

The state is that great fiction by which everyone tries to live at the expense of everyone else.—Frédéric Bastiat[1]

In chapter 1, we considered the need for an accurate description of government or political life for the subject matter of an empirical approach to the correction of injustice. Bentley's analysis of government as process and his insistence that societal events and conditions be explained by other societal events and conditions is a more productive empirical methodology than inferring external causal factors from observed societal processes. As well, Bentley's restriction of what people say and believe, to content with no causal power in itself, accords with a long history of good ideas about justice (including ideal theory) followed by or coexisting with injustice. There is little or no historical evidence that good ideas or aspirational beliefs, including acceptance of an ideal theory of justice, could cause changes in political life. Bentley's ideas about what does cause change in political life therefore merit further examination. However, Bentley's subject is law and government that he analyses as coextensive with the whole of society and the scope of an analysis that broad raises questions about the limits of government: How expansive is the process of government and how expansive should it be? Limits to just government, as well as "states of exception," need to be considered in this regard. While seventeenth-century state of nature concepts are no longer credible, it may be more important than ever to consider the nature of human life without government. Moreover, classic models of democratic participation and representation may no longer be relevant to contemporary democratic consumer societies and that has a bearing on the nature of government process as political life, including its limits. In the present chapter, I will take up these perspectives and tensions and then attend to positive aspects of the theory of applicative justice in the discussion of equality in chapter 3.

BENTLEY'S VIEW OF LAW AND GOVERNMENT AS PROCESS

Bentley held that the behavior or action of people in groups—and not what they think, write, or say—is of primary importance for understanding law and government. That view does not entail behaviorism in a psychological sense and neither did it work that way for Bentley. For Bentley, psychic processes are intact, integral parts of social processes, while the psychological behaviorist seeks to reduce individual psychic events to observable behavior. Bentley, the sociological behaviorist, sought to reduce systematic statements of law, such as the US Constitution, to all that it is done in their name, especially actions that further the interests of dominant groups. Bentley's sociological reductionism relates law to government process and identifies groups with their interests. Group leadership is suffused throughout a group and public opinion is a vital part of group interests.

According to Bentley, law is nothing but an abstract description of the active process of government. However, the connection between law and government goes back and forth. In this passage, Bentley emphasizes the function of law to express a culmination or result of government process:

> Law matches government every inch of its course. The two are not different things but the same thing. We cannot call law a resultant of government. Rather we must say it is government that same phenomenon—only, stated from a different angle. When we talk about government we put emphasis on the influence, the pressure, that is being exerted by group upon group. When we talk about law we think not of the influencing or pressure as process, but of the status of the activities, the pressures being assumed to have worked themselves through to a conclusion or balance. Of course, the pressures

> never do as a matter of fact work themselves through to a final balance, and law, stated as a completed balance, is therefore highly abstract. Law is activity, just as government is. It is a group process, just as government is. It is a forming, a systematization, a struggle, an adaptation, of group interests, just as government is.[2]

We will soon see how Bentley's emphasis here on the instability of law as government process is more important to his analysis than the function of law to express the results of government process.

For Bentley, government *is* process. Bentley describes government as a vast human interactive "cloth . . . out of which individual patterns are cut." His example of federal response to misdeeds by Standard Oil Company conveys the complexity of the raw material that he asserts is the proper subject for the political scientist:

> The morning paper tells me that the Standard Oil Company has been indicted on some thousands of counts for violating the federal laws. A few months ago it told me that many employees of one of the executive departments of the government were scurrying over the country gathering facts about the way in which that company had conducted its business with the railroad companies. Before that it told me of a resolution put through Congress ordering such an investigation. Still farther back I could have read of the excited activities of many men which came to a climax in the passage of the law under which these indictments have been found. If I wait a few months more I shall read of the trial in the court, of the punishment which will perhaps be imposed, and in part of the effect which the punishment has, or, alternatively, which the indictments even without punishment have, on the company's business methods. I have reason to think also that I shall soon hear a certain leader of a great portion of the people announce fresh steps to be taken toward the introduction of improved methods of controlling such corporations as the Standard Oil Company; and that this will sooner or later be followed by a renewed assertion by another popular leader that the present methods of control will be applied so vigorously as to secure the desired change in conditions without further legislation. If I care to I may read many criticisms of everybody and everything concerned, both in current periodicals and in books of all degrees of remoteness from the hottest spots in the conflict.[3]

We can see from this example that Bentley's process of government includes: laws, reactions to their violations, the legislature, courts, executive agencies, relations between government officials and corporate employees, and publication, approval, and criticism of all of the foregoing. In the "narrowest sense," Bentley recognized the existence of government as "a differentiated, representative group, or set of groups . . . performing specified governing functions for the underlying groups of the population." But even in this narrow sense of the apparatus of the state, which is what most people today still mean by "government" or "the government," Bentley specified that government was "not a certain number of people, but a certain network of activities."[4]

Bentley acknowledged that law in a narrow sense of statutes and precedents may correspond to government in a narrow sense of the apparatus of the state. But he held that although this aspect of law may seem to stand apart from the government apparatus, it is in reality coincident with it. Thus, law dissolves into the contentions or agreements among the interest groups that are government:

> The government itself can only be interpreted, or adequately stated, in terms of the interest groups it represents; and law is merely another manner of statement of those same interest-group facts, so that the correspondence is in fact exact. The interests that function through government, and that are government in the sense that the governing body is only their instrument or tool, are the same interests that hold law in place and bring changes in the law.[5]

What are interests? As Dean Mathiowitz notes, interests for Bentley are not the psychic possessions of individuals that motivate them to join groups, although the activities of a group, as its interests, may be the basis of identities for group members.[6] Groups are evident through their activities that are undertaken in contestation with the activities of other groups. In other words, groups are their activities which are also their interests: "There is no group without its interest. An interest . . . is the equivalent of the group."[7] The group (or group activity/group interest) cannot be understood objectively according to a prior set of social or economic concepts, but requires observation over time, as it interacts with other groups. Interests, like groups, emerge constantly and also dissolve in response to external pressures. The dominance of groups varies with a variety of factors depending on their circumstances: numbers of membership (more members increase dominance, although there are dominant minorities), intensity (e.g., race, ability, education, moral vigor), technique (e.g., force or reasoning), and habit background (but only if taken up in the present).[8]

Leadership as an integral part of group activity is differentiated and suffused throughout groups and in interactions between groups, and leadership influences public opinion concerning the group. Bentley specifies considerable complexity in leadership:

> The leadership of the chairman in the executive committee, of the executive committee in the party, of the convention in the party, of the party among the underlying groups and interests which it represents—all these kinds of leadership are not phenomena of different, but of the same, nature, when one cuts down to essentials. The party gets its strength from the interests it represents, the convention and executive committee from the party, and the chairman from the convention and committee. In each grade of this series the social fact actually before us is leadership of some underlying interest or set of interests.[9]

Public opinion expresses group interests in ways that mirror group leadership:

> There is no use attempting to handle public opinion except in terms of the groups that hold it and that it represents. Public opinion is an expression of, by, or for a group of people. It is primarily an expression of the group interest by the group itself, but where it has become a differentiated activity representing an underlying group we may say it is expressed by the opinion group for the underlying group.[10]

Bentley's "behaviorist" reduction of law to government process, which is interest group process, is an empirical alternative to the blueprint model of law. One does not have to accompany Bentley all the way. It is possible to get off the train for a while at any number of stations, such as the presidency, congress, the actions of lobbyists, the interests of major corporations, the present strength of labor unions, and/or any number of discourses and and counter discourses. But despite the speed of his reductions, Bentley attunes us to the human interactions that constitute decisive but changeable power and authority in democratic society.

Recognition of the complexity of the process of government in terms of contending interest groups reminds theorists to avoid hypostatizing their terms or forgetting the inherently heterogeneous nature of political reality and the absence of a rational ruling center that stands above political society.

Nevertheless, at certain junctures, we need to part company with Bentley for normative and limiting reasons. While it's useful to have an account of law and government that reduce both to concrete reality, we also need to know where they end. Law and government are, after all, only one of many human projects or influences.

THE LIMITS OF LAW AND GOVERNMENT PROCESS

Bentley's analysis goes too far in assimilating to government, not only political parties and interests that seek to influence government in his most narrow sense of the apparatus of state, but some political, as well as nonpolitical activities that are not part of government process. If law as government, behavioristically understood as all political activities, were as broad as Bentley suggests, the result would be an inescapable form of totalitarianism, theoretically leaving no distinction between just and lawful political and nonpolitical activity and crime and unjust action. In his primary concern with "process," Bentley was aware that his analysis resulted in ambiguity concerning the inclusion of unjust activities, such as lynching, in government process. The following (disturbing) passage indicates his theoretical ambivalence:

> Lynching, it may be noted, is from one point of view an embryonic governmental activity itself, while from another point of view it is an offense against the government; each point of review represents a group attitude, and according as conditions cause one or the other attitude to prevail does lynching spread, or is it suppressed.[11]

Bentley was correct that during the era of lynching, many government officials, as well as prominent black leaders, did not speak out against lynching.[12] So in that sense, lynching was a government activity. However, to say that as blithely as Bentley does is very different from showing how the lack of action by those in government, who could have stopped lynching, resulted in unjust government complicity with the practice. We can see here that Bentley may have been too enamored of the idea of government as process to put limits on what counts as government, much less legitimate government. As a political scientist, he was right to stick with description as far as feasible, but some actions call out for normative evaluation, as well as description, if not from political scientists, then from political philosophers, activists, and members of the public. Bentley's oblivion to government injustice is part of an absence of normative ideas of justice and injustice throughout his analysis.

The State of Exception

While Bentley is not an ideal theorist who requires the background posit of a well-ordered society, his description of government process does rely on an underlying assumption of satisfactory normality. But we know that normal government is rarely satisfactory to all who are affected by it. We also know that normal government may be curtailed or interrupted by "states of exception," in which normal rules for legitimate government functioning are excepted or contradicted in response to some stated emergency. Contemporary theorists and activists differ over whether such states of exception are merely a different form of the same government or a new illegitimate regime. The pivotal concept in these disputes has an uncanny resemblance to medieval and early modern ideas of divine voluntarism. The historical question was whether God, as the creator of natural law and necessary truths, could will their contradiction—that is, suspend the constitution and violate its principles and foundational individual rights. As the source of rational and moral order, God would be bound by previous expressions of his will. But God, as omnipotent, could will against such order. (He was "The Decider."[13]) Descartes is commonly regarded as a champion of the voluntarist position because of passages like this:

> I do not think we should ever say of anything that it cannot be brought about by God. For since every basis of truth and goodness depends on his omnipotence, I would not venture to say that God cannot make an uphill without a downhill, or that one and two should not be three. But I merely say that he has given me such a mind that I cannot conceive an uphill without a downhill, or a sum of one and

> two which is not three, and that such things involve a contradiction in my conception.[14]

The principle philosophical opponents of voluntarism were natural law theorists who believed that God was constrained by the laws previously willed by him, which meant that he was not omnipotent.[15] Voluntarism posited a God who could legitimately do anything, even actions that struck mortals as contradictory or in violation of natural law. If we substitute the idea of legitimate government for the idea of God, there is a parallel problem of whether government has the power to change the rules on which it was founded that justify its existence. Does the legitimacy of government continue if government actions contradict its presumed legitimacy or does its power as government allow it a continual opportunity to determine its own legitimacy? Or, is government that is supposed to benefit those governed but instead arbitrarily harms them, still legitimate government?

The fundamental problem with the idea of divine voluntarism lies in its posit of God as an ideal entity in two senses of "ideal": what is ideal does not exist, from an empirical perspective; what is ideal is good. The contemporary concern with the legitimacy of a government in a state of exception that it has declared similarly turns on whether government is something beyond its empirical actions in the first sense of ideal and whether a specific government is legitimate, in the second sense of ideal as good.[16]

A Bentleyan perspective would enable us to reduce the first sense of government ideality to government functioning, that is, to the process of government. Contemporary critics of the state of exception use an empirical ideal that government should benefit those governed. Benefit from government, like harm from government, can be reduced to government process, including actions by the apparatus of the state. But evaluative comparison of government harm with government benefit is difficult to situate in Bentley's analysis. For Bentley, government is what it does and evaluation of what it does, has no existence apart from what government does, or how it functions—such evaluation is merely part of "content." So long as government in a declared state of exception retains its power or continues with its process, the question of its legitimacy cannot be raised on the level of Bentley's analysis. Thus, a Bentleyan perspective would accept government in a state of exception as just another form of the same government before the state of exception. Bentley's framework becomes problematic, here, because it blocks consideration of the structure and process of government in light of the human devastation and havoc that governments have wrought while in self-declared states of exception.

Giorgio Agamben claims that World War I marked the beginning of a now-permanent state of exception, as a new form of government in erstwhile democracies. Agamben addresses this historical situation with appropriate grave concern in *The State of Exception*. When malevolent government in a self-declared and self-justifying state of exception takes both the source of law, which should be the will of the people, and the implementation of the law, which should be constitutionally prescribed, onto itself, to determine as it wills, the result is "a killing machine."[17] What can we say about the apparatus of state or government as a "killing machine," on an empirical basis, that is, without positing government as a metaphysically totalistic, evil entity, The Devil of Our Time? We can recognize such a government by the harm it does and even reduce it to that harm, as something to be avoided and opposed by all possible means. We can seek to understand causes of such states of exception for the sake of prevention and correction and morally condemn the harmful actions of government operation under a state of exception. And we can insist that the government generating these harms is not a legitimate government according to our legal, moral, and historical awareness of what legitimizes governments. In all such cases, given the power of government in physical force, what can be thought and said is usually much more than what can be done. (Although modern surveillance technology combined with punitive resources may restrict what will be said privately, as well as publicly.)

In Bentley's terms, assessments that governments functioning as states of exception are not legitimate states would be part of political "content" but not part of political process. However, content is important in this regard and could motivate group action, but only if there has not already been a radical difference in the process of interaction and contention among groups as interests, that is, if resistance has not been immediately blocked (i.e., censored) along with the government's self-declaration that it is in a state of exception. Resistance and objection to government as a state of exception becomes more complicated and difficult, after an ideology and system of surveillance and punishment accompanying the declaration by a government that it is already in a state of exception, is a reality. Resistance then moves from normal interest-group conflict and contention to oppositional discourse or an underground movement.

Furthermore, the "state of exception" is not the only kind of bad government. History is replete with examples of governments that have privileged some groups at the cruel, brutal, and inhuman expense of others, without declaring themselves to be in states of exception. The allowance for slavery in the first version of the US Constitution and its legal practice for almost two centuries thereafter was not predicated on exceptional circumstances. The expansion of the American colonies by the slaughter of indigenous groups and appropriation of their lands, under the doctrine of Manifest Destiny, were in no ways undertaken in conditions akin to defense in declared war or preemptive responses to emergency. Similar observations can be made about European colonial expansion in the modern period.

The declaration of a "state of exception" is usually reserved for a suspension of rights of those who previously had rights, as a justified response to war or other emergency conditions. African slaves, American Indians, and those colonized did not have preexisting recognized rights under those governments who launched aggressive action against them. Also, wherever and whenever Euro-American justification was offered for such aggression, explicit reasons of exception to Enlightenment ideals were not claimed. Instead, the inferiority of victims (e.g., slaves) and the greatness of aggressors (Americans who had a "Manifest Destiny") were proclaimed. It could be said that *identities of exception* were ascribed.

Writers are often vague about who the casualties of states of exception are, but the implication remains strong that the paradigm abuses are against those who previously had recognized rights. Examples of states of exception adduced in the Agamben literature include government during the period of the Emancipation Proclamation (US Civil War period), President Roosevelt's New Deal, the Third Reich, union strikes in Great Britain, an earthquake in Italy, and periods of financial crisis in Germany and France.[18] (Placing in the same category those who opposed Roosevelt's safety net programs and Holocaust victims should be understood to reflect how uses of the state of exception were invoked by governments, rather than a claim that these victims belong in the same category based on their suffering.) Nevertheless, while most "enemy combatants" in the early twenty-first-century War on Terror do not have rights under the jurisdictions detaining them, their treatment is often objected to as abusive results of "a state of exception," with reference to their international human rights.[19] For instance, Slovoj Žižek and others have referred to US prisoners on Guantanamo Bay as stripped of all life and reduced to "bare life," or *homo sacer* as described by Agamben.[20] Such reference to international rights, like reference to the rights of citizens when their national governments oppress them, invokes a higher authority than national government as actual and normal process. It calls for moral intervention that places absolute limits on legitimate government. (To return to the earlier example, God cannot will absolutely anything, and voluntarism is mistaken.) Such limits would either already be clearly stated before the declaration of a state of exception or somehow imposed after government abuses during the state of exception. In either case, if the government in question does not "stand down" from its violation of rights, it is not surprising that some theorists would talk about revolution, even when revolution is highly implausible as a practical matter.

Agamben argues that the state of exception is a fictional posit, used to justify increases in arbitrary government power, in states otherwise governed by laws protecting the rights of citizens. For Agamben, on one side is Carl Schmitt's criticism of the idea a state of exception is a fiction, because a state's declared state of exception is not an exception to an abiding legal state, but a new legal state, or even a continuation of the old one. In opposition to Schmitt, according to Agamben, is Walter Benjamin's revolutionary and real state of exception that deposes the fictitious state of exception.[21] The "state of exception" as used by dictatorial governments, which is not a real exception, seeks to capture into its legal order, *anomie*, or what Benjamin calls "pure violence," which is outside of the law. But according to Agamben, Benjamin's divine or transcendental or revolutionary violence would serve the purpose of deposing unjust government by acting within its own, real, and justified state of exception.

Agamben warns that the question of who will capture the realm of anomie, the bad state or just revolutionaries, is as decisive for politics as "the battle of the giants for being" is for metaphysics. The grandeur of this invoked drama goes far beyond Bentleyan normal government process and the give and take of contending interest groups seems vulgar and pedestrian, by contrast. But from the standpoint of African Americans subject to lynching, what Bentley speculates may be an "embryonic" government activity could be a candidate for Benjamin's kind of "pure violence." That no state of exception had to be declared for lynching to occur underscores the necessity of prior rights that are violated for there to be a state of exception. There was no state of exception declared for lynching to be permissible, because blacks did not have prior rights that were recognized. By contrast, Benjamin's idea of a real state of exception seems to have been posited for the sake of those who he imagines would be justified in committing pure violence. He is interpreted to imply that certain oppressive states of exception *should* be met by violence. And so, there may be violence in a government-declared state of exception, there has been violence against those whose rights have not been recognized without a government-declared state of exception, and aggrieved parties may be imagined to have their own justification for declaring a state of exception, in which "pure violence" is permissible. This is a lot of violence.

Human beings have a long history of violently resisting injustice. But we need to distinguish among wars, civil wars, and revolutions. Revolutions are now exceedingly rare in well-developed societies and may be impossible within powerful and wealthy nations. It is very difficult to imagine successful revolutionary movements in such nations, given powerful state force. At any rate, those who act from their own states of exception, because their rights have been violently violated, to depose governments operating under fictional states of exception—fictional because they have instituted a new, permanent form of rights-violating government—are not part of the process of existing government. Yet, the actions of even revolutionaries still concern that part of human life which is about government or who should rule and how. Only anarchists who succeed would be able to do away with government in its entirety, and that is not the issue here. Agamben's subject of life, "the use and human praxis that the powers of law and myth had sought to capture in the state of exception"[22] needs to be protected as something outside of government, but not necessarily outside of human society, in general, or even outside of a particular society with a repressive government.

IDEAS OF HUMAN LIFE WITHOUT GOVERNMENT

Bentley's perspective has the advantage of offering an expanded, empirical view of government as social process. But the disadvantage of his analysis is that government seems to permeate the whole, or too much, of society. It has been noted that even Bentley identified a narrow range of government process that was limited to official actions of governing. Answers to the question of whether and how "life" in Agamben's sense can practically oppose oppressive government partly depend on what is meant by the scope of government, on how much of society it includes. A range of responses are possible, from John Locke and Peter Kropokin on the notion of society as sufficient and completely independent of government, to Michel Foucault who describes modern government control and surveillance as "biopower," or extensive regulation of all aspects of human life. In addition, Hannah Arendt's "life of the mind" suggests a less material approach. Even brief consideration of these views leads to reflection on current historical circumstances.

Locke's State of Nature

John Locke's idea of the relationship between life and government was part of his rationale for representative parliamentary government in England. Locke wrote for the benefit of the new land-owning class that came to power after the Glorious Revolution of 1688–1689 enthroned William and Mary. He shared their interests and was their main intellectual leader.[23] (Locke would be an *organic intellectual* according to Antonio Gramsci, although today we reserve that honorific for progressive leaders of our own era—see chapter 6.) Although the institution of the British parliament had roots in the eighth century,[24] it fully came into its own as a stable, powerful institution, only after 1689. Locke told the story that justified the ascent of his patron's aristocratic (but not noble) rising socioeconomic class that limited the rights and power of English monarchy.

Locke posited a state of nature before the existence of civil government, where and when humankind was able to cooperate and sustain agriculture, industry, and even a monetary system. The inhabitants of the state of nature enjoyed, "a state of perfect freedom to order their actions, and dispose of their possessions, and persons as they think fit, within the bounds of the Law of Nature, without asking leave or depending upon the will of any other man."[25] But government was specifically necessary for protection against foreign enemies and to avoid the inconveniences of the partiality of criminal punishment executed by victims and their heirs. The purpose of government was to protect the private property of its citizens, where "property" meant life, liberty, and estate (material possessions).[26]

Locke maintained that the general justification of government was benefit to those governed, who had to consent to its existence. As a result of that original consent, the inhabitants of society retain certain rights even in the presence of government, including the right of revolution against a government that is not fulfilling its purpose. If a society is destroyed, so is its government, but if the government is destroyed, society endures and may set up a new government.[27] Also, the state of nature as the regulatory structure of society, co-exists with government in at least three senses: individuals do not inherit citizenship but must consent to it, even if that consent is tacit, or implied by the use they make of their property rights;[28] property rights originate in a state of nature and are therefore both antecedent to government and ongoing with it;[29] heads of state or whole governments exist in a state of nature in relation to one another.[30]

Locke's restrictions on government delineate what could be called "life," in a political realm that can oppose government in the narrow sense. Individuals under government retain the freedom to do everything that is not forbidden by law, "a liberty to follow my own will in all things, where the rule prescribes not."[31] Government cannot render citizens worse off than they would be without government, because as legitimized by the consent of those governed, men are not "so foolish that they take care to avoid what mischiefs may be done them by polecats, or foxes, but are content, nay think it safety, to be devoured by lions."[32] Legitimate government cannot deprive citizens of their rights of life and freedom because, according to the law of nature, life and freedom are given by God and all individuals have only stewardship over them.[33]

Locke's idea that freedom consists in the right to do what the law does not prohibit remains an accurate description of practice in contemporary liberal societies, in that same narrow sense of government.

His insistence that the state of nature and society exist as something distinct from government makes sense only if government is understood in a narrow sense as the apparatus of the state. But, some contemporary institutions, such as powerful global corporations, now have so much influence over government as to be part of it. As well, societal domains under government regulation and administration (e.g., utilities, education, business entities, the monetary system, entitlements and safety nets, and that old standby, weights and measures) that are accepted for convenience and public benefit now make it difficult to identify a Lockean part of society that is distinct from government. Society and government inter-permeate one another in reality. However, if Locke is understood to be referring to power, his distinction holds for the groups that have the most influence over government. In our own oligarchy, as in Locke's, this segment of society is made up of rich property owners. In a democracy, power would remain with the people, but to draw on recent rhetoric, the 99 percent is not the 1 percent.

Locke's claim that government exists to benefit citizens and that it cannot deprive citizens of God-given rights are normative prescriptions and there would be incursion on "life," as distinct from government, where and when rights are violated. In our time, such incursions are not monolithic, nor do they permeate every aspect of even nonprivileged human life. The common people still have some breathing space, as well as influential political advocates. Still, when it benefits them, people in general are apt to overlook not only the convenience-organizational presence of government in their lives but its violation of the rights of others. There is no bright line between government that leaves material life alone, although free speech doctrines may leave the life of the mind alone, most of the time. The result is that Locke's notion of society as distinct from and independent of government does not apply to our time. In its narrow sense, government can be abolished in the form of regime change (which elections regularly bring about) but in the wide sense, it is difficult to see how government could be abolished and society still stand.

Michel Foucault views the inter-permeation of society and government in terms of a shift during the eighteen to nineteenth centuries in the nature of government power. Instead of a sovereign right to grant life and take it away, the government became a support for myriad forms and arrangements of human life in society: "The ancient right to *take* life or let live was replaced by a power to *foster* life or disallow it to the point of death."[34] This biopower became visible in new forms of social organization and institutions of social regulation, over sexuality, race, education, crime, health, medicine, madness, morality, and the family. At different times, the law identified itself with one or another of these vital technologies, as surveillance and control of human beings became more systematized, detailed, and complex. Foucault's genealogies of major modern social institutions in *The History of Sexuality*, *Madness and Civilization*, and *Discipline and Punish* are well known for their emphasis on the "social construction" of aspects of human life otherwise assumed to be natural or in some way external to society.

Kropotkin and Engels on Society without Government

Locke's account of life without government in the state of nature and society as coexistent with government was based on the fiction of the social contract. The ideal of contract or consent by those governed supported the legitimacy of strong British parliamentary government. In principle, if the social contract had really been between all of the people and their government, Locke's doctrine would have been an early-modern form of anarchism. Peter Kropotkin's nineteenth-century anarchist views are more democratic, perhaps because he hoped to inspire and motivate new forms of social organization in the revolutionary spirit of his time. Kropotkin began with the premise that throughout Western history, self-serving central rule by predatory minorities had been opposed by majorities in favor of local self-rule, expressed for instance by medieval guildsmen and nineteenth-century utopians and labor organizers. Kropotkin called his form of anarchism *individualization*, envisioning voluntary associations that would plan and implement all phases of economic and social life. Individualization was opposed to centrism and capitalism as protected by the central government; it would require a rearrangement of society into geographically defined, self-sufficient communities of laborers, craftsmen, and agricultural workers. (Kropotkin was vague about how these communities would be administered within themselves and what would happen to minorities within them.[35])

Kropotkin's vision was eclipsed by Friedrich Engels's Marxist post-revolutionary utopia: "The government of persons is replaced by the administration of things and the direction of the processes of production. The state is not 'abolished,' it withers away."[36] Neither Kropotkin nor Engels provided a descriptive account of existing life outside of government. Both were engaged in constructing ideals that could motivate and justify revolution or revolutionary change, despite Kropotkin's optimistic belief that the history of humankind was an evolution of cooperation, and the inevitabilities of historical dialectic that were in the background for Engels. Kropotkin's ideas have found expression in small numbers of semi-isolated communes, with peaceful cooperative origins; Engle's vision of the state "withering away" remains a vision. But we need something more than alternative lifestyles or a vision to "sever the nexus between violence and law," so that, as Agamben put it, law is no longer tied to life.[37]

Arendt's Life of the Mind

Hannah Arendt provides an account of life outside of government in terms of thinking: The self is inherently twofold and for that reason must be logically consistent. Conscience is an awareness of internal contradiction that is intolerable to live with. The condition for thinking is solitude, which makes thinking a natural obstacle to totalitarianism. Arendt claims that people are not left alone or by themselves under totalitarian regimes, which stifles morality: "The frequently observed fact that conscience itself no longer functioned under totalitarian conditions of political organization, and this quite independent of fear and punishment, is explicable on these grounds."[38] However, Arendt did not recommend a scholarly life of solitude, because logos, or thought and speech with others, unites the twofold self into one. In logos, a (united) "one" can engage in dialogue as a way of uncovering the truth behind the different opinions of speakers. This process results in a common world—but only for philosophers who are able to suspend logos and regard the common world with *wonder*. About the philosopher, Arendt writes:

> His distinction from his fellow citizens is not that he possesses any special truth from which the multitude is excluded, but that he remains always ready to endure the pathos of wonder and thereby avoids the dogmatism of mere opinion holders.[39]

If thinking is deliberately undertaken as a process leading to dialogue, which may eventually evaluate existing government, it is a form of life, as Arendt signaled by the title of her last work, *The Life of the Mind*. Still, there is a daunting problem of connecting conclusions and questions from the life of the mind to political life. Disembodiment is not an ideal and even if it were, it would be useless in a world where government is material and its most oppressive influences are material, for example, as attributed to Marx and Engels, "the state is a body of armed men." But the life of the mind is a distinctively human form of existence that unfolds outside of government. So long as its processes and products are understood not to be causal factors external to any general process of government—for reasons based on Bentley's critique, as discussed earlier—there is no strong impediment to locating "life" in Agamben's sense, or part of it, exactly there. As well, those who live the life of the mind, even though they may be disconnected from material political process, can still be considered part of the wide political process, as I will suggest in the final section of this chapter.

It is ironic that although there has never been a world government, universal human ideals of equality first originated in twentieth-century international discourse, from the "life of the mind" that resulted in the 1948 United Nations Universal Declaration of Human Rights.[40] But perhaps that source outside of government was the only possible origin. Ideas and ideals of equality will be the subject of chapter 3, but here it is important to note that for instances of *homer sacer*, brought to that condition by oppressive government, the only "content" on the basis of which to oppose oppression is something like universal human rights discourse. The process for implementation of such rights remains ad hoc, unformed, and unpredictable. This content is currently based on absolute or objective ideas of human equality. (There is another, comparative way to view such content, so that it can be connected with real political life—an approach that will be developed in subsequent chapters.)

Bare Life within Government

Agamben's idea of the relationship of government to *homer sacer* seems strange at first, although it makes perfect sense: Those whom government casts out of society it draws deeper into society. Outcasts are drawn back into the most painful and degrading forms of society. Prisons, torture facilities, and concentration camps are all places with highly structured systems of control by governments and there is a greater government presence in those places, than anywhere else in society. This process of official expulsion from one place, followed by punitive incorporation into another, can start early in a person's life. A black youth expelled from school for trivial reasons based on more broad social exclusion of poor African Americans may be directly removed to a correctional facility.[41]

In some distant past, physical exile from civil society to woods, islands, or open waters was practiced. Today, those who are exiled or expelled (e.g., deportees or subjects of extraordinary rendition) are sent to other governed societies or if they are political refugees, seek entry into them. Some people may live extremely isolated lives in small rural communities or as feral individuals, but they are only out of political life because the state tolerates their physical absence, is not threatened by their mode of existence, or has not yet noticed them. Voluntary expatriates with money, skills, or leisure, deliberately move from one society under government to another. But, generally, in the early twenty-first century, human life outside of governed society is not any more possible outside of any given society than within it.

If present government ultimately has its hooks on all forms of human life, then opposition to government would have to be a process from which such hooks can be removed, or else cannot penetrate. Agamben is accurate in describing politics as "contaminated by law, seeing itself, at best, as constituent power (that is, violence that makes law), when it is not reduced to merely the power to negotiate with the law."[42] The problem with the law and contemporary government according to Agamben and many other critics is that the process of government expulsion that draws victims further into or under government is constantly and ubiquitously imposed on people who are already suffering from injustice.

RECENT CHANGES IN POLITICS AND THE PROCESS OF GOVERNMENT

The difficult question remains of what can and should be done in response to oppressive aspects of states of exception. In that context, politics becomes particularly important for criticizing existing law and acting to expand, contract, or otherwise change it for the progress of justice. But what is the relationship of such politics to the process of government?

When aspects of the workings of government in the narrowest sense are believed to be unjust because they violate the rules of government procedure and government officials have approved such violation, analysis of such "states of exception" requires a gap between government and its victims and their advocates who oppose it. That is, oppositional political action would be external to government. The basis for such political opposition would probably have to be constructed in parts of national or international society that in Locke's state-of-nature sense remain independent of government. The discourse and practices that constitute progressive and liberatory politics are the medium for applicative justice. But in the early twenty-first century, an idea of such politics requires more than simple adjustment of Bentley's main insights or concern about changes in the meaning of government processes under or during states of exception. Agamben concludes *The State of Exception* with a nostalgic evocation of politics as independent of government: "To show law in its nonrelation to life and life in its nonrelation to law means to open a space between them for human action, which once claimed for itself the name of 'politics.'"[43] Of course, Agamben is focused on politics in a state of exception, which means that the main problem for him is the nature of government—he assumes that if politics is not possible, then government is at fault. Matching this focus on problematic and faulted government, other theorists have focused on changes in the nature of those who are governed in contemporary, perhaps post-democratic, Western societies.

The result of this change of subject is that the generic "men," to whom Bentley referred as members of groups that were the basic units in political processes, may no longer be available. The difficulties already encountered in forming a concept of life or society that is outside of government suggest that these political "men" have already been too coopted or coerced by government to oppose it. But the real problem may be more diffuse, a matter of apparently voluntary dispositional changes in the political subject. From a more optimistic perspective, new forms of grassroots expression and oppositional academic content may constitute new political sectors in formation, even though they both lack official political mechanisms for influence and structured forms of group representation.

The Silence of the Masses

In 1982, Jean Baudrillard's *In the Shadow of the Silent Majorities* presented a still relevant caricature of the inert democratic masses in democracies, which had ceased to voice political opinions, such that the political structures of representative democracy could no longer represent their interests. Thus:

> Bombarded with stimuli, messages and tests, the masses are simply an opaque, blind stratum, like those clusters of stellar gas known only through analysis of their light spectrum—radiation spectrum equivalent to statistics and surveys—but precisely: it can no longer be a question of expression or representation, but only of the simulation of an ever inexpressible and unexpressed social.[44]

Baudrillard interprets the silence of the "silent majorities," not only as a refusal to speak, but a refusal to be spoken for, that is, to be politically represented. "No one can be said to represent the silent majority, and that is its revenge."[45] Baudrillard does not say exactly what harm is motivating such revenge; he appears to believe that the position of the silent majorities is the result of their complete absorption in private life, as consumers.

About 60 percent of the eligible American electorate votes during presidential elections; otherwise, about 40 percent regularly vote. In other established democracies, voting ranges from 70 to 90 percent.[46] Consideration of the apathy Baudrillard theorizes may include ignorance on the part of those who do vote, on the one hand, and the fact that the American figures of 60 percent and 40 percent are not negligible, on the other. Overall, the wealthy are more likely to vote than the poor, which is especially problematic in a time of increasing economic inequality.[47] We could embellish Baudrillard's analysis and say that the withdrawal of the silent majorities from active civic life, which extends beyond voting, is the result of an intensive process of seduction by the marketplace. This materialism enables enough members of the former and potential electorate to lead lives that are "good enough," so that in comparison to their satiating consumption or everyday problems, political participation is neither appealing nor compelling. Perhaps the electorate has been partly bought off by goods it helps produce for the marketplace, which it also consumes with wages from its labor. This would be a sustainable system, except that the profits made by the masters of the marketplace are never enough. Competition among the masters and greed for greater profits cause periodic turbulence in the system, sometimes to the point of collapse.

It might be that money worries make the apolitical masses vengeful, or else they have a sense that something important is missing from their lives. In either case, their revenge is not only taken coldly, but silently and very secretly, because Americans and others in rich Western societies tend to present themselves as cheerful, gratified people. However, such background information would be beside the point, according to Baudrillard, because apparently nothing can be done to change or control the new apolitical masses. (This suggests that the silent majorities Baudrillard writes about are not so much vengeful as presently and for the foreseeable future, resentful.)

According to Baudrillard, the masses are fascinated by electronic spectacles of hyper-reality and portrayals of only very extreme events, such as media reports of terrorist destruction and dramatic government responses to them, can get their attention. But that attention does not motivate political action, because news and entertainment overlap in content and modes of presentation. Being entertained or fascinated is a self-contained condition.[48] The masses live in a bubble. The political interests of these inert and passive groups are not expressed and they have no visible leadership or internal organization. They can furnish raw material for statistical study of certain aspects of their lives and circumstances, but the individual subjects of statistics are cyphers. Baudrillard writes:

> The referendum (and the media are a constant referendum of directed questions and answers) has been substituted for the political referent. Now polls, tests, the referendum, media are devices which

> no longer belong to a dimension of representations, but to one of simulation. They no longer have a referent in view, but a model.[49]

In other words, the silent majorities cannot be studied by social science metrics because the products of measurement serve mainly to construct models for social scientists. Simplified charts and graphs may be presented to the public from time to time, but they are received apathetically, as a mild curiosity within a rich mix of entertainment and news. Baudrillard does not propose an alternative practice for social scientists. Maybe they should do more participant-observer or ethnographic research? But not only may they reject such methodology as unscientific, but the end results would have to compete with other genres that already have advanced technologies, such as video games, television shows, and movies with special effects. The art of getting the masses' momentary attention(s) or lulling them into their default mode of complacent comfort has already been perfected in the marketplace. Good literature has a small readership and public humanistic higher education barely survives from one recession or state budget to the next.

To the extent that Baudrillard's enigmatic picture of our contemporary political reality is accurate, the capacity of traditional democratic political processes to bring forth liberatory change has diminished. But how far back in the past would we have to go to find a referent for Agamben's notion of "the political"? The eighteenth and nineteenth centuries were times of aggressive colonialism and slavery; the medieval period was dominated by the Catholic Church; slavery was an institution in ancient Greece and Rome. Let's consider a political time that we already know partially by description.

At the time Bentley wrote, it was plausible that the representative structure of government could function to represent a plurality of interests that were expressed by legislative, and enacted by executive branches of government. The group relationships involved in representation were subject to all kinds of irregularities in the hurly-burly of political life, but these could be viewed by many observers as normal irregularities resulting from the interactions and accommodations of group interests. There were, of course, critics and victims of a political system that, as already noted, Bentley knew included lynching,[50] but lynching was not broadly recognized to be a disturbance to normal democratic life. When *The Process of Government* was published in 1908, women did not have suffrage. Furthermore, in the early twentieth century, there was no robust academic or recognized scholarly opposition to injustices of this nature. Thus, in Bentley's time, there was lively, normal political activity for white men, but the majority of the population was not part of political life and the life of the mind as productive of a standpoint opposed to injustice had no institutional foundation.

New Forms of Political Process

In contrast to the accepted, business-as-usual irregularities of Bentleyan governmental normality, at this time, new forms of progressive political processes now occur in journalism, physical demonstrations, and academic critique, not to mention segmented-by-audience electronic media. It is too soon to tell whether such projects will be effectively liberatory or merely provide occasion for new forms of government to defend itself or both—that is, too soon to tell which group interests will dominate. But we can note some interesting changes in the nature of political process.

New forms of journalism, such as WikiLeaks, National Security Administration documents obtained by Edward Snowden, and posted pictures of prisoner abuse at Abu Ghraib during the second Iraq war have emerged in opposition to new forms of government misdeeds and surveillance in the US state of exception that has followed the post–9/11 War on Terror. Government and military officials are secretive about their immoral actions that do not serve national security and are embarrassing and shameful if the public finds out about them. The invasion of such "government privacy" through theft or whistle-blowing, immediately followed by free electronic publication to a world audience, should be recognized as a new "technique" of oppositional political journalism. However, it is not clear whether scandals of this nature have a liberatory effect or change the indifference of the silent majorities. The political careers of individuals found responsible might suffer, but that does not mean there will be changes in policies that enabled such behavior.

Large-scale demonstrations like Occupy Wall Street in 2011 in Zuccotti Park in New York City and its iterations throughout the country, and before then, the Hispanic/Latino protests against new legislation against undocumented immigrants, in April and May 2006, received large-scale media attention. But there was also backlash through local police action against the Occupy participants and strengthening of the Minuteman Project along US-Mexican borders.

The Occupy and Mayday demonstrations and others like them are iconographic, because the participants have the identities they are valorizing (members of the 99 percent and Hispanic/Latino immigrants) and also symbolize political issues or circumstances that they are protesting (unequal distribution of wealth, harsh immigration policies against undocumented immigrants). But whether even newly iconographic public action can do more than express some popular opinion and entertain a large electronic audience is not yet evident. Extreme economic inequality persists and beginning in fall 2013, an unprecedented immigration crisis of tens of thousands of unaccompanied minors from Central America, began. Public awareness has undoubtedly expanded, but that does not amount to public demand for change—as the silent and inert masses keep up with news, they also just continue to absorb it.

But if the silent and inert masses continue not to vote in increasing numbers, does their absence from political life matter? Critics assume that people do not vote because they are distracted or apathetic. But maybe they do not vote because they have lost confidence in the willingness and ability of elected officials to represent their interests. Maybe they believe that their political power has been appropriated by the alliance of government and wealthy corporations. Some observers believe that the age of social media is enabling opportunities for political expression that are revitalizing democracy as a form of government for the common people. Hashtags and Facebook postings have a viral ability to galvanize multitudes.[51] Also, not only is consumer survey technique finer grained than when Baudrillard wrote *In The Shadow of the Silent Majorities* (e.g., "Please take this brief survey about your recent car wash") but every story posted online by a major news source now has a commentary section following it. The degree to which all of these invitations and opportunities for individual expression will coalesce into political power or amalgamate into a giant mass of congealed electronic "cookies" is an intriguing subject for speculation.

ACADEMIC SPEECH

Within the academy, criticism of political injustice has emerged as a robust dimension of scholarship in the humanities and social sciences. Sometimes it surfaces to a *New York Times* Opinionator piece in "The Stone" or a "Ted Talk," but more often than not, it seems to be read and heard only by the captive audiences of students in higher education and other academics. This rich variety of ideas for making the world better has no structured outlet in any government process that could make the world better. The interests of the academic group are apparently mainly confined to the career interests of individual intellectuals. And those individuals make their livings and receive honor and praise within institutional structures that are not of great interest to the public, except as a means of certification for middle-class employment (for high school graduates whose families want and are able to finance their college degrees).

When academics write, talk, and publish their thoughts about politics, they are engaged in a political process, but insofar as they lack structured connections to the apparatus of government, academics may seem to have nothing to represent *to*. As representation, it is also undetermined who or what is being represented, whose concrete interests are being served. When specific social groups, such as women, racial and ethnic minorities, LGBT, handicapped people, the poor, and immigrants, are the subjects of academic analysis, perhaps those are the groups being represented in this untethered or free way. But most real-life members of these groups remain unaware of their academic representation and may not even see themselves as members of the groups written and talked about by academics. Furthermore, intellectual representation is almost always about potential political content in abstract ways, rather than potential government or political process—scholars gravitate toward theory rather than practical policy—although often without a clear sense of this division. Under the rubric of "critical theory," many liberatory humanistic scholars continue to describe psychic entities as political causes and fail to distinguish between normative and descriptive analyses. Nevertheless, publication of academic political discourse is not without ad hoc audiences in the marketplace of ideas. Policy recommendations by academic experts do have political life, in unrecorded and unpredictable influence on individuals on all levels of government. Also, some academics work directly for government entities, serve on special government panels, or are consulted by government entities as "experts."

When a political process has been accessible to them, philosophers have, on rare occasions, produced political content. Plato's unsuccessful contributions to Syracuse, Locke's ideology and political activism (he escorted Queen Mary back to England on a ship from Holland after the Glorious Revolution), and John Stuart Mills's service in parliament provide positive examples, while the actions of Pol Pot in Cambodia and Slobodan Milošević in the former Yugoslavia dishonor our discipline. Overall well-meaning, but confused about what they are doing and its effectiveness, philosophers and other theorists throughout the humanities, do not, as authors of political content, constitute a group with interests, which is engaged in political life, as part of government process. But such theorists are political subjects or agents in at least an ideal sense. This kind of representation without structured constituency, or membership in or access to, a governing body, is for the time being, an activity in the life of the mind.

Arendt refers to Aristotle's departure from Athens so that "the Athenians should not sin twice against philosophy" (by repeating Socrates's execution) as the beginning of a tradition that separated philosophers from political life: "The only thing that philosophers from then on wanted with respect to politics was to be left alone; and the only thing they demanded of government was protection for their freedom to think."[52] These wishes have only partly been granted. Philosophers, broadly understood, have so far retained their freedom to think (except for the unfortunate McCarthy era of which Arendt must have been aware). But although they may be left alone (for the time being), their logos (thought and speech) is closer to being part of politics, because many philosophers no longer wish to be left alone to think but welcome opportunities for public participation.

Added to changes in political agents in a time of diminished political participation is that radical change in technique of communication. The ancient expectation of face-to-face discussion and persuasion by participants in the same place at the same time survived through the era of print. However, such simultaneity is no longer necessary for political communication. The effect on politics of all available information made accessible to everyone all the time, or at any time, may encourage solitary thought, as Arendt described, perhaps building up a suppressed demand for dialogue. Or else, all of this information will simply be absorbed or ignored by more specialized subgroups of the masses. Among intellectuals, only academics retain the political privilege of face-to-face interaction with their peers (at conferences) and a known audience (in the classroom), although the latter, less and less. This may turn out to be a case of one-eyed political elite in a society of the blind, or just another detail in the ongoing irrelevance of the academy to political life. Maybe the academy with its oppositional politics will take its place as an institution resembling the church. Regardless of its real life influence, at this time, the academy does furnish political opposition, albeit in the form that Bentley called "content" (what people think, believe, write, and say). Bentley was an intellectual, but not an academic. Had he been an academic, he might have recognized the life of the mind as a life of content that surpasses and has a little more power than mere opinion.

I began this chapter with exposition of Bentley's analysis of law as coincident with government process of the interactions of interest groups throughout all of society. Recognition of the lack of a normative dimension in Bentley's analysis and the need to find a place in such an analysis for oppositional liberatory politics motivated a contraction of Bentley's idea of government to the apparatus of the state. In the process of that contraction, reference was made to Agamben's treatment of the state of exception and his attention to the value of life outside of government and the difficulty of reclaiming it during states of exception. Locke's idea of human rights in society, as independent of government, was brought in, as a way to think about human life apart from government, but to apply Locke's distinction now would be anachronistic. Baudrillard's treatment of the absence of those represented in representative government was considered, but optimism was rekindled via reference to new forms of political or proto-political process in academic critique and electronic discourse. (Chapters 5 and 6 will be about discourse in terms of content.)

Perhaps Bentley's analysis conveyed a background of satisfactory government doing business as usual, rather than content or evaluation of such process, because he was primarily concerned with legal and government process as raw material for political science and he wanted political science to be more like political sociology. It might also have exceeded Bentley's relatively comfortable social location. (Bentley's father was a banker, and after his PhD from Johns Hopkins, his main employment before writing *The Process of Government* was as a newspaperman for the *Chicago-Tribune*.[53]) Still, any form of political life, as continual resolution and emergence of conflicts between group interests is, regardless of normative interpretations of it, contingent, difficult to predict, and impossible to control from preconceived ideals—it is history. In contrast, it is important to recognize that political content can, for theoretical purposes, be held distinct from descriptions of political process. Content, especially that produced by academics, is better controlled by its authors and agents than process, which depends on real-life interaction. Chapter 3 will address a vital form of such content for processes of law and government believed to be just, namely, the idea of human equality.

3

IDEAL EQUALITY AND REAL INEQUALITY

All animals are equal, but some animals are more equal than others.
—George Orwell, *Animal Farm*[1]

Everybody is a book of blood; wherever we're opened we're red.
—Clive Barker *Books of Blood*[2]

Equality has been a humanitarian idea since antiquity, but the word or concept is loose, tethered on one end to equality according to law and on the other to spiritual equality. Equality in law, or formal equality, has been the goal of many progressive and liberatory movements, but once achieved it seems not to fulfill what progressives had in mind. In the American struggles concerning race and gender, formal equality with white males, as achieved for women and nonwhites by the early 1970s, was but a starting point for academic liberatory feminist and anti-racist scholarship. Middle-class women and racial minorities have had more opportunities and better lives after nondiscrimination laws were passed. But in studies of ongoing sexism, racism, and higher rates of poverty, everything proceeds as though formal equality has been no more than a necessary condition for embarking on a new wave of liberatory polemics, social analyses, ideologies, and aspirational proposals.

Indeed, it is a great puzzle that there can be both formal equality and persistent intergenerational socioeconomic and status inequalities for nonwhites, gratuitous violence against young black men by police, hate crimes against blacks that are justified by white supremacist ideology dispersed through the US population, domestic violence against women that could be prevented by local police but isn't, and the ongoing dominance of white men in political and business institutions. Most who study such discrepancies are not content to believe that the inequalities will automatically correct themselves as a matter of time. Political and social "backlash" against *Roe v. Wade* has continued decades after the 1973 US Supreme Court ruling and the Court itself has restricted positive programs for racial integration in higher education, beginning with *Regents of the University of California v. Bakke* in 1978. Such backlash may lead to devaluation of formal equality. But if formal equality is dismissed as not worth very much in reality, progress in equality becomes relegated to ethical discourse alone or unpredictable results of activism. Also, law continues to have an important labeling and symbolic function and large changes in law are intensely ceremonial in ways that unify large parts of the national population.

Based on the discussion in chapter 1 of the Bentleyan reduction of the form of government as law, to processes of what people do in the name of those laws (which includes what they do not do), the discrepancy between formal equality and real inequality can now be accounted for: Equality in formal, written law is only part of "equality." There is no contradiction between legal equality and unequal treatment in society, if we understand that law is not a blueprint for action in society, but a symbolic name or description that human behavior mirrors only partially and imperfectly. How people behave, whether in compliance with legal equality or not, is part of the same whole political process that includes law.

Liberatory scholars need to be disabused of thinking about good law as either a blueprint for action or a set of rules and principles arrived at in the right way, which citizens automatically obey and express in their fundamental institutions. This view sets up unrealistic expectations, so that when compliance and application are lacking, effective political response seems impossible. People give up if they have assumed that all paths to progress in justice end with the right blueprint and they have got that blueprint, but little or not enough has changed.

A Bentleyan model of law as patterns of group interactions that constitute government holds more promise for the possibility of liberatory political change. On that model, the idea of human equality is a matter of content or what some of those active in political processes believe to be true. While political processes can be studied by observing human behavior, the study of political content is more amenable to political philosophy. Political process involves habitual group action, whereas content is a matter of individual thought and speech. From a practical perspective, in the spirit of John Stuart Mill's comparison of thought and speech to action,[3] content is easier to change than process.

Discourse (thought, speech, and writing) about equality could also become more precise. Humanist scholars generally, including political philosophers, rather easily accept principles of human equality as though there were a foundation for them in human similarity, and they often fail to distinguish between normative and descriptive statements about justice, which are based on their vague ideas about equality. Given these confusions, it might be better to approach equality in comparative ways, such that the subject is whittled down to how members of only some groups are treated equally in desirable respects. The purpose of this chapter is to develop these alternate perspectives on law and equality so that they can be put together for thinking about progressive change or applicative justice.

Human *in*equalities in society, for example, of race, gender, wealth, ability, religion, ethnicity, and so forth, play out in many ways for different groups, depending on their economic and social status and histories of the distribution of power. It may never have occurred to anyone to assert human equality if not for the experience and perception of injustice involved in human inequalities in society. As well, assertions of equality have been believed important to voice against assertions of inequality. For the past several hundred years or longer, the idea of human equality has been most obviously associated with racial difference because real and extreme practices of social inequality based on racial difference were historically rationalized by assertions of fundamental human inequality between whites and nonwhites. The type of equality proclaimed against such evident social inequality is normative—often moral and sometimes legal.

This chapter begins with discussion of the relations between statements of racial equality and human equality. Ideas of human equality in the history of philosophy are then quickly examined, toward a negative result. A consideration of fairness then follows and after that, the idea of applicative justice without a foundation of either fairness or equality is proposed. Finally, egalitarian rhetoric is related to distributive justice.

RACIAL EQUALITY AND HUMAN EQUALITY

Almost all complaint and criticism regarding the American and global disadvantage of nonwhites compared to whites proceeds on the underlying principle that whites and nonwhites are morally equal, and that both nonwhites and whites have equal intrinsic worth as individuals. This racial equality principle (REP) is normative: Whites and nonwhites are morally equal and have intrinsic worth as individuals, and everyone should act according to that general equality.

Progressives recognize that not only is it possible to violate REP but that REP is frequently violated in many different places. Ideas, policies, and practices that violate REP are considered obviously unjust. Why is REP a good or suitable or adequate foundational principle for racial justice? A logical reason would be that all human beings are morally equal and that nonwhites, as well as whites, are human beings. To say that all human beings are morally equal introduces a general equality principle: Everyone owes everyone else respect for core human rights, entitlements, or privileges; everyone should act accordingly; and everyone is entitled to such treatment from every other person. Acceptance of this general equality principle (GEP) would seem to provide an important justification for claiming it unjust to violate REP. That is, if all human beings are equal and nonwhites are human beings, then nonwhites are equal to whites. Hence, this GEP hypothesis emerges: The way to secure (or make a case for) racial equality, theoretically or philosophically, is to first make a convincing case for human equality, because the added premise that nonwhites are human beings makes it possible to deduce REP from GEP.

Closely associated with GEP is an idea or intuition concerning human dignity, usually attributed to Immanuel Kant, entailing that all "subjects"—we will see later how Kant was not speaking of all human beings—have intrinsic worth or dignity:

> In the kingdom of ends everything has either a *price* or a *dignity*. What has a price can be replaced by something else as its *equivalent*; what on the other hand is raised above all price and therefore admits of no equivalent has a dignity.[4]

Kant's idea of intrinsic human worth with its associated idea of dignity is for him the reason that moral principles are to be accepted *categorical-*

ly, without requiring prior or consequential justification. He distinguishes categorical from hypothetical imperatives in this way:

> All imperatives command either *hypothetically* or *categorically*. The former represent the practical necessity of a possible action as a means to achieving something else that one wills (or that it is at least possible for one to will). The categorical imperative would be that which represented an action as objectively necessary of itself, without reference to another end. . . . Now, if the action would be good merely as a means *to something else* the imperative is *hypothetical*; if the action is represented as *in itself good*, hence as necessary in a will in itself conforming to reason, as its principle, *then it is categorical.*[5]

A derivation of Kant's idea of human dignity seems to have been propounded in a universal form in the preamble of the 1948 United Nations *Universal Declaration of Human Rights* (UDHR), which states that all human beings have inherent dignity and equal rights: "Whereas recognition of the inherent dignity and of the equal and inalienable rights of all members of the human family is the foundation of freedom, justice and peace in the world."[6] The UDHR preamble also asserts that if such rights are not recognized, immoral or oppressive actions are taken against those whose rights are not recognized, because the rights of free speech, security, and rights to satisfaction of basic needs are the highest aspiration of the masses, the oppressed, or as the United Nations styles it, "the common people":

> Whereas disregard and contempt for human rights have resulted in barbarous acts which have outraged the conscience of mankind, and the advent of a world in which human beings shall enjoy freedom of speech and belief and freedom from fear and want has been proclaimed as the highest aspiration of the common people.

That is, the common people aspire to their rights because if their rights are recognized, they will be safe from "barbarous" actions that outrage "the conscience of mankind." It is interesting that UDHR does not state outright that the barbarous actions are morally wrong or unjust, but instead suggests that they are shocking. (That it is the conscience of mankind that is outraged also suggests that mankind in general is responsible for such actions.)

It should be emphasized that the UDHR preamble departs from Kant by not categorically proclaiming human dignity and resulting rights (as a claim[s] standing on its [their] own without instrumental justification), but hypothetically (in Kant's stated sense of a means for something else). The UDHR preamble makes it quite clear that if such rights fail to be legally protected, peace will be disturbed: "Whereas it is essential, if man is not to be compelled to have recourse, as a last resort, to rebellion against tyranny and oppression, that human rights should be protected by the rule of law" (UDHR). That is, not only do those without rights aspire to them for their own safety, but if they continue to be denied such rights, they will rebel.

In sum, Kant posits moral equality and dignity for (some) human beings as a categorical moral principle not requiring justification in terms of its effects. By contrast, UDHR extends the idea of such equality to all human beings and also extends it to include rights to material goods, as well as respect. But UDHR does not categorically assert the existence of such rights or the obligation to respect them; instead it warns that failing to recognize and respect such rights will lead to the rebellion of those who are treated in ways that disregard their rights. UDHR thereby takes a hypothetical or instrumentalist approach to human rights, with an eye to the consequences of not recognizing them. The only prior justification offered is membership in the "human family." Although this vague reference reminds readers that they owe certain kinds of action to family members and by extension to all humankind, it does not explain how we are all one family or what our "human family" is. Thus, if we read UDHR carefully and take it literally, it is compatible with the belief that human rights are an instrumental device (hypothetical according to Kant) for avoiding revolution against those of its readers who have the power and authority to behave as though all human beings are equal, but are not yet behaving that way.

Apart from UDHR, GEP is not often explicitly stated, although it tends to be implicitly invoked when it is violated. Reactions to violations of GEP often depend on inchoate ideas of fairness, and fairness is, since John Rawls's 1970 *A Theory of Justice*, a primary conception of justice for political theorists. We must be fair, because we are equal. Beyond this, GEP is vague. GEP does not tell us what equality *is*, beyond an implication that treatment should be the same for all human beings in certain respects—that is, that human beings should be treated equally.

As a principle of justice, GEP would be something more positive than a conception of justice or the instantiation of a commonly held ideal of justice. GEP would need to have more positive content than fairness. Fairness is, after all, a matter of procedure, which does not preclude an equal ability to inflict barbarous acts, as in a Hobbesian society. And we don't want that.

Justice is a social and moral ideal that is also defined by positive law. As a social and political ideal, justice has been a traditional subject for philosophers in the Western tradition. But Western philosophers have not traditionally proclaimed GEP as a principle of justice. As noted, GEP first appeared in the UDHR preamble and, although it was prepared for the United Nations by a group of humanist experts that included philosophers, UDHR was not a direct product of academic philosophy per se.[7] Moreover, UDHR does not, strictly speaking, proclaim human equality, but an equality of human rights. Although the justification for equal rights would presumably be human equality, it is logically possible that human beings could both have equal rights and not be equal as human beings. Indeed, the UDHR preamble's consequentialist reason for respecting rights is not that all human beings are entitled to such respect, but that if rights are disregarded, peace will be disrupted when those whose rights have been disregarded are badly treated as a consequence, so that they rebel. In and of itself, the implication is that rebellion is a bad thing, which, as noted, suggests that UDHR is a declaration from the perspective of those against whom rebellion would occur, and not from the perspective of those who would rebel.

UDHR was written in the aftermath of World War II. Its authors sought to morally condemn the possibility of a repetition of Germany's anti-Semitic Holocaust and address apprehension on behalf of world leaders about what would happen during impending processes of decolonization. (W. E. B. Du Bois vainly attempted to have some mention of the rights of Africans incorporated into the UN's founding documents.[8]) Consideration of this "What shall we do?" aspect of UDHR suggests that UDHR was not written on behalf of those whose rights were, or might in the future be, disregarded, even though its authors may have been concerned about them.

Sometime after 1948, it generally became morally incumbent on intellectual, cultural, educational, and political leaders in democratic societies to recognize an equality of human rights. There have been contentious interpretations of what "rights" are, whether they are real, and if so, in what precise way. In addition, rights are often violated and require struggle and litigation to be recognized, efforts that are not always successful. The moral obligation to recognize an equality of human rights is conditional according to UDHR because, as noted, it is not an absolute or unqualified obligation but a pragmatic necessity "if man is not to be compelled to have recourse, as a last resort, to rebellion against tyranny." If rebellion after barbarous acts that "outrage the conscience of mankind" has not and will not likely occur, then presumably the recognition of such rights is not as urgent. Apart from the public protests leading to the US civil rights legislation in the mid-1960s, which was more of a social and political movement than a real rebellion, the UDHR warning has not proved prescient. In over half a century, violations of universal human rights as proclaimed in that document have not reliably disrupted the political tenure of those directly responsible for such violations. If "world peace" means the absence of rebellion within the richest and most powerful nations and the absence of world war, then world peace is unperturbed by human rights violations.

What becomes essential in real world politics is not the recognition of human rights, but their "protection by rule of law." Nevertheless, apart from disagreements about the nature and reality of rights, if it is plausible that all human beings have the same rights, then for all practical purposes—especially since the recognition of equal rights requires that they be protected by law—it can be inferred that all human beings are equal in whatever it is that grounds or gives rise to their rights. One could also make the more controversial claim, not about the source of rights but about protecting them, namely that all human beings are equal in being equally entitled to the protection of their rights by the laws and actions of existing governments, both national and international. And, one could take this further by insisting that such government entities are obligated to use force to protect those rights. But the question of obligations incurred by the violation of human rights is not the primary philosophical subject presented by UDHR. Rather, the subject and problem is an objective idea or fact of human equality in the democratic Western tradition, in the sense that such equality would presumably ground the normative claims generated by positing and recognizing the rights of the oppressed who now, as in 1948, consist mainly of members of racially nonwhite populations.

HUMAN INEQUALITY IN THE HISTORY OF PHILOSOPHY

UDHR does not refer to selected groups of human beings, but to "all members of the human family." It is this phrase that implies that the rights posited are *universal* human rights, so that any principle of equality inferred from the recognition or acceptance of these rights would be a principle of universal human equality. It might be expected (however vaguely) that the political philosophers in the Western tradition that had given rise to democratic constitutions in national governments, as well as UDHR, had already proclaimed varied doctrines of universal human equality. With the impractical exceptions of Cicero, Saint Paul, and Saint Thomas Aquinas, they have not. It is not surprising that philosophers who assumed fundamental human hierarchy as the foundation of their moral theories, for example, Plato and Nietzsche, would not proclaim or argue for universal human equality. However, it is surprising that liberatory and "enlightened" historical figures such as Kant and John Stuart Mill did not have a principle of universal human equality. If they had such a principle, or if such a principle could be inferred from the things they wrote, then the exclusion of nonwhites from the range of their moral variables would not have been logically possible—although it may have taken a while for everyone to realize this. They could not, with GEP, have been subject to accusations of having designed or been in tacit agreement with what Charles Mills has identified as "the racial contract," which excluded non-Europeans from the conditions of a flourishing human life, or even from bare life itself.[9]

Logically, a commitment to universal human equality blocks commitments to racially biased practices and racial inequality in a general sense. In the historical absence of both REP and GEP, social and legal justice on the grounds of race and gender has proceeded piecemeal, without explicit foundational demand for universal human equality. For example, freed male slaves got the right to vote in the United States before women did, and African American and women's liberation has been advanced on the basis of those social identities. But the theoretical or philosophical, egalitarian foundation has never been constructed. It has been called upon literarily, religiously, and rhetorically. But those activists who could have made good use of an intellectually authoritative version have had to pluck their version of it out of thin air. Theoretically and philosophically, universal human equality would be a much simpler and stronger basis for the assertion of rights than the bases of particular social identities. It is therefore important to register how key political philosophers in the Western democratic tradition have avoided analyses of universal human equality. It should also be determined whether an assertion of universal human equality could be universally convincing. That is, GEP may have been lacking for the wrong reasons, such as racism and sexism, but this does not mean that GEP is true or could be true, or that it could effectively motivate justice.

If we consider how ideas of universal human equality espoused by Cicero, Saint Paul, and Aquinas are empty,[10] and the lack of commitment to universal human equality in the apparently egalitarian writings of Kant and Mill, the conclusion is that GEP has not been of serious interest to key political philosophers from whom we should expect it and to whom we like to think we can turn as a source of it. This leads to questions about the nature of equality that apparently need to be answered in the larger project of a positive GEP that could imply or motivate REP. The unavoidable conclusion will be that: *The question of what human equality is, is less important than the question of which group or type of human beings has members who are treated equally, in preferred or privileged ways, and which group or type of human beings have been denied such treatment.* The evidence, here, consists in how Cicero, Paul, Aquinas, Kant, and J. S. Mill, all of whom are vaguely believed to have subscribed to universal human equality, did not.

Cicero is often lauded as an early cosmopolitan based on his "model" of human relations as a series of concentric circles, with those nearest and dearest in the central circle followed by more distant relations, friends, acquaintances, and so forth, all the way out to a perimeter of faraway strangers. Cicero's cosmopolitanism is held to lie in an ideal of bringing the outer circles closer to the center, even though he does seem, in an unalterable way, to place the highest value on the ties to family members, close friends, neighbors, and countrymen. Although Cicero's focus is on how we should behave toward others, there is nothing in his circle model that suggests universal human equality in any objective sense.[11] Cicero is also often referred to as a proponent of ancient natural law in the Stoic tradition, which has been held to proclaim human equality. But, for Cicero, that equality is a matter of possession, and it comes only after private property has been possessed and given its due respect within a community. Cicero's moral sense of equality is expressed by a spirit of "fellowship" that is more a matter of kindness and courtesy than justice, because it has nothing to do with redistribution or retribution. Thus:

> These possessions common to all men are, it seems, of the kind which Ennius applies to a single instance, but which can be extended to many: The friendly soul who shows one lost the way, lights, as it were, another's lamp from his. Though he has lit another's, his own still shines.[12]

Not only are kindness and courtesy compatible with real inequality—one can be very kind and polite to subordinates—but norms of kindness and courtesy, like cosmopolitanism, concern how we should act in the world as it is. Kindness and courtesy need posit little or nothing of importance that is objectively shared in our common humanity—they may just make interactions among unequals smoother and easier. Cicero's ideas about natural law cosmopolitanism did not preclude him from owning slaves or believing that there was anything wrong with slavery.[13]

Christian philosophers had a doctrinal commitment to equality insofar as they held that all human beings had souls and were thereby eligible for an afterlife of reward or punishment. Still, secular slavery was not generally considered to be incompatible with Christian doctrine before the nineteenth century[14] and the church itself owned slaves throughout Europe until at least the Renaissance.[15] Saint Paul and Saint Thomas Aquinas engaged in remarkable intellectual juggling of their belief in human equality and acceptance of slavery.

Paul, in Galatians, states that religious faith results in a new identity in which all are the same:

> For you are children of God through faith in Christ Jesus. For as many of you who were baptized into Christ have put on Christ. There is neither Jew nor Greek; there is neither slave nor freeman; there is no male and female: for you are all one in Jesus Christ.[16]

Paul's "one" could mean "united" rather than "the same," but there is a clear implication that the social divisions entailing human inequality will be erased, on a spiritual level, through religious conversion. However, there is no indication that this erasure will double back into equality in secular reality.

Aquinas addresses slavery as a wrong, quoting Seneca on a distinction between "the whole man" and the part enslaved. In what he called matters "that belong to interior acts of the will," Aquinas wrote:

> Even the slave is not required to obey his master, because obedience is required only in terms of external bodily action. Also, given the internal nature of the body in reproduction or nourishment, the obedience of the slave is not required and neither is it required in "contracting marriage or observing virginity, or such like."[17]

Aquinas thus aims to preserve the human equality of slaves, spiritually and privately, but at the cost of a ludicrously naïve underestimation of how enslavement itself shapes the entire life of someone who is the property of another. The injustice of the secular inequality of slavery is thus not taken seriously by Aquinas.

By the late eighteenth century, human inequality became an explicit and more dramatic secular doctrine in Western thought, after the variations in human culture and physical appearance that were encountered during exploration and colonization were "organized" within the new science of biological classification. The racialist and racist speculative anthropologies of Hume, Kant, and Hegel authoritatively posited Africans, American Indians, and Asians as exceptions to Enlightenment statements of universal equality. For instance, Hume dismissed the possibility of nonwhite achievement. Kant not only equated stupidity with being black, but denied that nonwhites could appreciate "the beautiful" and "the sublime." Hegel drew a portrait of the terminally savage minds of the inhabitants of "Africa proper."[18] These writers and many others made up profoundly antihumanist racial hierarchies in the process of describing and justifying human differences in power.

The accepted Enlightenment inequalities were not restricted to new ideas about biological racial hierarchy, but extended to exclusions based on gender, wealth, and often religion, as well. Females, the poor, nonwhites, and Catholics (in the Anglo-American tradition based on John Locke's political philosophy[19]) were not in the groups who were the subject of discourses of human equality. Moreover, exclusionary lines were even more finely etched around only those white, wealthy males who displayed certain kinds of intellectual and moral virtues.

It is appropriate to focus on Kant in terms of such exclusion. The "end-in-itself" formulation of his categorical imperative endures as a standard for human dignity if it can be made egalitarian in a universal way, such that all humankind can be guaranteed membership in a "kingdom of ends." This would be a universal application of "Act in such a way that you treat humanity, whether in your own person or in the person of another, always at the same time as an end and never simply as a means."[20] But this general proscription against using other people or allowing oneself to be used looks like a promising ideal of universal human equality, only until we remember what Kant means by the expression of an unqualified "good will."

A good will is the only thing in the world that is good without qualification, according to Kant. However, by a "good will," Kant did not mean benevolence, but rather a "principle of volition" in accordance with duty. For Kant, any action done as duty, out of respect for the (moral) law, must pass the test of my ability to generalize that action, so that "I should never act except in such a way that I can also will that my maxim should become a universal law."[21] Morality thus has a stringent requirement of abstract reasoning, according to Kant. And it is exceedingly unlikely that, for instance, even everyone who is allowed to vote in contemporary democratic nations would be able to regulate their actions according to reflection on a generalization of their action that positively passed the test question, "Can I will that the maxim of my action should become a universal law?" (Talk about a literacy test!)

The result of considering Kant in his intellectual context is that the categorical imperative yields a notion of a "good will" that is not in accord with ordinary ideas about benevolence. Moreover, Kant's possessor of a "good will" is necessarily required to perform cognitive gymnastics that are beyond the ability or interest of those who would need to be included in a normative, universally egalitarian principle (GEP). The best that we can derive from Kant in this regard is a fuzzy idea of human dignity and intrinsic worth that could probably be derived from a number of sources that lack such august philosophical authority or presumed justification, such as, for instance, the inclinations or impulses of benevolent people.

Mill is perhaps the most egalitarian nineteenth-century philosopher on the subject of formal gender equality, as well as representative government. However, throughout *The Subjection of Women*, where Mill's arguments for female suffrage and legal personhood are utilitarian for all humans, they are also instrumental to the service of patriarchy. Mill's justification for granting women civil autonomy is that they would be better wives and mothers. And in a more general political sense, Mill restricts certain principles (mainly those against censorship) espoused in *On Liberty*, by qualifying that they are "meant to apply only to human beings in the maturity of their faculties" and not to "those backward states of society in which the race itself may be considered in its nonage." He goes on, "Despotism is a legitimate mode of government in dealing with barbarians, provided that the end be their improvement and the means justified by actually effecting that end."[22] In other words, although utilitarianism specified "everybody to count for one, nobody for more than one," on an individual level, utilitarian autonomy was for the mature only and on a global level for "advanced" societies only.[23]

FAIRNESS, FOUNDATIONS FOR EQUALITY, AND THE IMPORTANCE OF LAW

Before approaching the nature of equality in GEP—everyone owes everyone else respect for core human rights, entitlements, or privileges; everyone should act accordingly; and everyone is entitled to such treatment from every other person—it should be acknowledged that GEP is *normative*: everyone *owes*, everyone *should*, and everyone is *entitled to*. GEP can be universally agreed upon, as advised by the writers of UDHR, but that in itself is no guarantee that everyone *will* respect core human rights, entitlements, or privileges, *act* in accordance with that respect, and in turn *receive* that to which they are entitled. Indeed, history tells us otherwise. So GEP remains an ideal. Because we haven't realized it yet, it makes sense theoretically or philosophically to ask why we are seeking it: What is the objective or factual nature of the normative ideal of universal human equality?

Fairness as a conception of justice does not seem to answer that question. Rawls's veil of ignorance as a standard for planning a well-ordered society avoids the question of the objective nature of human equality because its main objective is to offer a standard for blocking the dominance of certain interests in the formation and change of basic institutions in a well-ordered or law-abiding society. Still, the question, "Why should fairness be a standard or an ideal?" easily arises. If the answer is, "Because human beings are morally equal," then some foundation for this is needed, again, because an assertion of moral equality is already normative—it means that human beings should be respected and treated in certain ways. Indeed, Rawls himself begins with moral equality:

> Moral persons are distinguished by two features: first they are capable of having (and are assumed to have) a conception of their good (as expressed by a rational plan of life); and second they are capable of having (and are assumed to acquire) a sense of justice, a normally effective desire to apply and to act upon the principles of justice, at least to a certain minimum degree. . . . One should observe that moral personality is here defined as a potentiality that is ordinarily realized in due course.[24]

Some human beings may not have Rawls's features of moral equality, for example, the cognitively disabled, those who are unjust themselves, and those who have been so severely oppressed as to lose or not develop a sense of justice. In addition to the lack of universality of Rawls's features of moral equality, the features are only effective if they give rise to entitlements. Thus, Rawls writes: "We see, then, that the capacity for moral personality is a sufficient condition for being entitled to equal justice."[25]

To say that X is entitled to Y is to make a normative statement that X should get Y. Why should those who have moral personality get equal justice? We remain in the position of needing to ask, "Is there or can there be a factual foundation for universal moral equality?" Of course, any such foundation will not *logically* entail moral normativity (because, as Hume taught us, an "ought" cannot be logically derived from an "is"). But an irrefutable universal factual foundation would make universal moral equality more compelling as a normative ideal.

There are a number of unconvincing candidates for objective universal human equality, unconvincing because they have been known to those who have acted unjustly: biological similarities; shared species identity; common basic needs; distinctive human subjectivity; being an actual or potential object of sympathy or compassion; the intrinsic goodness of human happiness, pleasure, and flourishing and the intrinsic badness of human suffering, pain, and destruction; a common creator of all humankind; shared evolutionary ancestors; a shared conception of individual good and a sense of justice. As posited commonalities or equalities, none of these putative foundations for a moral GEP have effectively checked choices to treat humans unequally, when the actions ensuing from such choices have not been blocked or punished.

Besides the practical ineffectiveness of these candidates for equality, it is unlikely that the factual holy grail of human equality will ever be found, because all of the candidates, in necessarily referring to what is distinct about human beings, necessarily refer to human inventions and constructions in social life that are full of exceptions. For instance, not only would moral equality based on homo sapiens species membership require argument in its own right—as Rawls seemed to be aware[26]—but inter-species genetic engineering will soon, if it has not already, complicate human species identity. Distinctive universal human subjectivity is impossible to confirm and can only be imagined. Sympathy and compassion are not universal. It can always be argued that some human suffering is good or necessary or justified. God is no longer a viable foundation for liberatory projects in a secular society and neither is it clear how evolution could be.[27]

Fortunately, the normative aspect of human equality is not exhausted by morality, because legality is also normative. Unlike moral norms, legal norms as expressed in positive law have government force to punish those who violate them. The force of the law makes its real life application categorical in a Kantian sense. Although law can of course be changed and resisted, when it is in operation it needs no justification outside of its legal system and its operation is not specifically instrumental. That is, although the justification of law may be instrumental, many people obey the law simply because it is the law. And in its implementation, law is enforced because it is law.

Existing laws well enough protect certain subjects equally, usually preferred groups of citizens in states where there is social inequality. The ground for this equal treatment becomes unimportant after a legal system purporting to rest on it has been established. Thus, in the beginning, founding documents may proclaim universal human equality based on universal creation by God, and reference to that universal equality may be offered as justification for the creation of certain legal rights. But rhetorical justification is not a factual foundation. Furthermore, in unequal societies, as soon as the rights are created, it may also be immediately obvious that members of only some groups are entitled to those legal rights, because the rights are qualified by clauses in founding documents or laws for applying them. It then becomes easy for government officials to determine who gets equal treatment, for example, only free, property-owning adult white males are entitled to vote. The result of such a sequence of legal principles and practical rules is that the importance of the claim that "all men are created equal" is not due to the nature of their equality but to the fact that "men" may be understood to mean "adult, free, property-owning white men." Thus, in reality, a very specific identity is a precondition for equality and whatever is meant by "equality" extends only to those who have the specified identity.

The search for a factual foundation for GEP is a wild goose chase. The search rests on the assumption that if the facts of human equality are discovered, then all will be treated equally, or that most in a position to violate normative rights will no longer do so. But "equality" doesn't *work* that way. Historically, within the most free and democratic nations, the idea of equality has never been anything beyond a justification for a certain kind of preferred treatment for members of certain subgroups of humanity. As an important foundation for the equality of nonwhites with whites, universal human equality is a boondoggle. The GEP hypothesis can be taken as disconfirmed on empirical grounds, because its factual basis is difficult to establish and in human history, equality has never been universally extended.

APPLICATIVE JUSTICE WITHOUT FAIRNESS OR EQUALITY

The challenge for progressives since at least the eve of the French Revolution has been to extend that protection of subjects considered equal in positive law to new groups of potential subjects or citizens. That kind of extension or application of legal equality has also been the only effective mechanism for moving from a vague principle of human equality to racial equality. Human equality may very well be a nebulous idea, but it is not nebulous to insist that nonwhites be treated the same as whites are treated in a system where legal equality has been conferred on whites (all whites receive the same political benefits), but not yet extended to nonwhites, in whatever respect.

Those who seek to retain the racial identities that were first imposed on selected populations, as part of ideologies and technologies of oppression, understand an important practical truth. They understand that if they do not have a socially intelligible means of identification in a "nonideal society" that only hypocritically asserts "color blindness," then they will have no basis on which to insist on their inclusion in the privileged circle of human equality.

The identities of those excluded from received forms of justice become the identities in whose name *applicative justice* is sought. Applicative justice is simply the extension of received functions of ordinary justice under positive law, to those who have been denied them in modern democratic societies.[28] What is in reality practiced and sought by members of subordinate groups has been an ongoing application or extension to them of the legalities that benefit dominant groups. In other words, the disadvantaged in nonideal societies and their advocates have been struggling for what can only superficially described as *fairness*. To call the goal of that struggle "fairness" is superficial, because fairness will not do the work of an impossible factual basis for equality. One can always ask why fair treatment is an entitlement, which requires an answer in terms of factual equality. Unlike the idea of fairness, the idea of applicative justice merely extends how one group is treated to another group.

The idea of fairness is very abstract. Consider again Rawls's thought experiment of those behind a veil of ignorance choosing basic social institutions in a condition of ignorance or unknowingness about which groups in society they represent. The imagined exercise requires that an anonymous representative put herself in the place of another, because in not knowing who or what I am, I have to imagine major possibilities that are socially advantageous or disadvantages. But, as discussed in chapter 1, it may not be possible for the representative to conduct this exercise in imagination so that what she imagines is an accurate representation of who she may represent. Although the Rawlsian thought experiment seems "fair," as in "You cut the cake and I will choose which piece I want," it has the same vagueness as the Golden Rule. "Do as you would be done by" will not accomplish a just result if treatment that is acceptable to me is not acceptable to you, or the reverse. Also, as noted in chapter 1, on the naïve interpretation of deliberators behind the veil of ignorance, deliberators may not know what it is about their interests that they should be ignorant of, so as to be fair. A more sophisticated interpretation of Rawlsian deliberators as partial persons may simply posit their ignorance or unknowingness. But in real life, whole persons with privilege may be in positions to decide what is fair for those less well off, but not have sufficient knowledge or experience to do that. The many white Americans who believe that existing formal equalities for nonwhites are sufficient for egalitarian justice are examples of that failure of fairness.

By contrast, if we begin with a concrete perceived injustice and require that a comparative just legal practice be extended to the victims of that injustice, the problems with Rawlsian institutional fairness do not arise. For example, suppose that X group of children regularly get adequate nutrition, in compliance with a law, L. Y group of children do not get adequate nutrition and because they are children and presumed entitled to adequate nutrition, their situation is considered unjust. To correct this injustice, no abstract concepts need be referred to, beyond advocacy of an extension of L, which is working well enough for X, to Y.

For a "bigger" example, and a lesson in the abstract uses or misuses of "fairness," in the United States, the legal struggle for justice in the opportunities available to nonwhites is made difficult by a persistent reluctance of the US Supreme Court to consider nonwhite race any differently from white race in discrimination lawsuits. All considerations based on race are held to be suspect, presumably on the grounds of constitutional amendments outlawing discrimination. The judicial doctrine of *strict scrutiny* thereby precludes the use of disadvantaged racial identities as a sole justification for affirmative action.[29] Discrimination against nonwhites must be proved according to stringent legal criteria and the present effects of past discrimination do not meet those criteria. Achieving applicative justice for nonwhites in a society with a history of overt discrimination and the present systemic results of that history requires that it be proved how the extension of justice to nonwhites in the wider historical and ongoing systemic sense—which is an effect of that history—will not be unjust to whites in the narrow present. The present legal test of "fairness" thus requires that there be no sacrifice from members of groups who have historically benefitted from racial discrimination and continue to benefit in the form of "privilege." This test looks fair in the present but it is unfair if fairness is impossible without taking the past, with its present effects, into account. Similarly, the present doctrine of "color blindness" (equal treatment regardless of skin color) sounds "fair," but its real meaning is normative—we should be color blind. But there is no guarantee that everyone will obey that rule. Instead of trying to convince people that there are present effects of unjust historical events and conditions, or that the society is not color blind, progressive time and energy may be more usefully directed toward attaining for subordinate groups the specific privileges that are already equally distributed among members of dominant groups.

However, for rhetorical purposes, it is "fair" that nonwhites who claim justice for themselves appropriate pseudo-foundational notions of universal human equality that have privileged whites. The rhetoric of human equality, whether it is based on a common creator, notions of intrinsic worth, the value of subjectivity, or the entitlement to justice of rational beings capable of asserting their interests in an ideal society is too well established as a reason or justification for justice to be left solely in the possession of those who have historically been "more equal than others." But for the unjustly disadvantaged, taking up this rhetoric is only effective to the extent that it is persuasive. As rhetoric, its uses are not part of political process, but what Bentley called political content, or what people believe and say that does not necessarily motivate action by them or others. That is, egalitarian rhetoric is not part of political process on the level of action, unless it finds its way into actual policy that is followed. In addition to its rhetorical uses, the idea of equality can work as a background heuristic for theoretical proposals in philosophy and economics. We should now consider some examples, and then briefly consider Sen's emphasis on inequality as a theoretical starting point.

EGALITARIAN RHETORIC AND DISTRIBUTIVE JUSTICE

In recent decades, what have been presented as egalitarian theories of justice show little concern with the vagueness of equality as a general abstract idea, but instead proceed with the construction of specific principles of equality as matters of distributive justice. Mainly at stake has been the question of what kinds of differences should be used as the basis for just distribution, a question that was the title of Amartya Sen's 1979 Tanner Lecture, "Equality of What?"[30] and further explored in his 1998 Nobel Lecture[31] and his 2009, *A Theory of* Justice.[32] Sen was joined by others, such as G. A. Cohen in two 1989–1990[33] articles, in agreement with John Rawls's criticism of utilitarianism for failing to consider inequalities within a society and instead focusing on the maximization of utility for the whole.[34] Such maximization can result in a stability or increase for the whole society, while the majority becomes more poor relative to an elite (e.g., the contemporary issue of income inequality in the United States[35]). Until the 1980s, both utilitarians and social choice theorists rejected the possibility of measuring or comparing individual utility because it was assumed to be based on subjective states of mind that were in principle unknowable. In addition, the formal mathematical aspects of social choice theory, as developed by Kenneth J. Arrow, resulted in his *impossibility theorem* that demonstrated the impossibility of simultaneously satisfying both individual preferences and social choice or optimal choice for everyone in the society.[36]

In continuing with Rawls's objection to utility, Sen points out that income or wealth may not be the best measure of social well-being, because people have different capabilities to use money, based on individual or environmental factors. For instance: someone who needs dialysis will have less well-being than someone without that problem, if both have the same amount of money; a poor person in a wealthy society will experience less well-being than someone with the same amount of money in a poor society. Capabilities for Sen are abilities to benefit from certain goods of life. Thus, possession of food is different from a state of being well nourished, and being able to be well nourished is a capability. By 1998, Sen had apparently successfully demonstrated his claim that comparisons of well-being in terms of capabilities bypassed the problems of Arrow's impossibility theorem, even if the comparison of capabilities were only partial.[37] The most important contribution of capabilities discourse is its promise of an objective standard of well-being, apart from subjective states, because those afflicted or very poor might not experience their lives as miserable, even though their conditions are miserable in comparison with others. The idea of capabilities also bypasses the subjective nature of "preferences" as used by utilitarians.

In his 1989 article, "Equality of What? On Welfare, Goods and Capabilities," Cohen develops a disambiguation of Sen's idea of capabilities, which can mean either what a person can do or what goods do for the person, with the additional concept of "midfare," as an objective state. According to Cohen, midfare is what a good does for a person so that utility has the value it does. If we understand "utility" to be a positive state of mind, then, as Cohen puts it, midfare "is posterior to having goods and prior to having utility." Thus, he continues, "We must look, for example, at her nutrition level, and not just, as Rawlsians do, at her food supply, or, as welfarists do, at the utility she gets out of eating food."[38]

We can see from this brief discussion of some of the ideas in play with Sen's "capabilities approach," that equality is not the issue. Rather, the issue is how to think about the kind of help that those who are obviously disadvantaged require. Sen announces this focus at the beginning of his chapter on equality and liberty in *The Idea of Justice*, when, reprising his comments in *Inequality Reexamined* (1992),[39] he writes:

> [E]very normative theory of social justice that has received support and advocacy in recent times seems to demand equality of *something*—something that is regarded as particularly important in that theory. The theories can be entirely diverse (focusing on, say, equal liberty or equal income or equal treatment of everyone's rights or utilities), and they may be in combat with each other, but they still have the common characteristic of wanting equality of something (some feature of significance in the respective approach) . . . the really critical question is "equality of what" rather than whether we need equality at all in any space whatsoever. . . . The demand for seeing people as equals (in some important perspective) relates, I would argue, to the normative demand for impartiality and the related claims of objectivity.[40]

Philosophically, Sen's remarks here would seem to bring us back to fairness. However, we have seen that, historically, fairness is possible only within limited domains and nowhere in his writings does Sen claim that equality of capabilities, or *his* normative theory of social justice, is universal over humankind. Indeed, the capability approach is comparative, through and through, as opposed to absolute, transcendental, perfect institutional justice.[41] And, as the previous passage indicates, the idea of equality is mainly a heuristic device for Sen. We can see this in the way Sen qualifies the importance of equality when he considers the importance of procedural concerns:

> The subject of fair process and a fair deal goes beyond individuals' overall advantages into other—especially procedural—concerns, and these concerns cannot be adequately addressed through concentrating only on capabilities.[42]

To put it simply, according to Sen, distributional justice, even the distribution of human capabilities, may be less important than procedural justice. Why is procedure so important? That is, what is the value of procedural justice, apart from its ability to protect and enhance human capabilities, especially if understood as the kinds of states Cohen calls "midfare"? Or, should equality be expected from procedural justice and what would that look like? Here, the danger of the idea of equality might lie in making two individuals or groups the same in one respect, to the undeserved detriment of one of them. But it should be recognized that the active nature of capabilities, as what persons are able to do or the states they are in, cannot be separated from what Sen called "fair process," when punishment or rights are at stake. Punishment, either in the form of incarceration, execution, fines, or requirements of losing litigants to pay up, directly impairs capabilities. Taking something away from one group of people to be redistributed to another may interfere with the wealth and freedom of the first group and violate their rights to "process." But that is the easiest kind of case, in which there is a background of just process.

As rhetoric or heuristic, the abstract general idea of equality serves to inspire and it adds authority to a position. But in reality, equality can only be grasped in limited, specific ways. And insofar as equality means only "the same in some respect," it has its harms and dangers. What this seems to leave us with is comparison through and through, and that alone. Furthermore, if it is assumed that redistributions of capabilities, including midfare, is a matter to be kept separate from procedure, for the sake of not encroaching on freedom, it seems to be further assumed that procedure is already just, fair, or equal, or that unlike distributed or redistributed inequalities, there are no constraints of scarcity in procedure. However, procedure is well known to be carried out in unequal and unjust/unfair ways and it has material requirements, the scarcity of which may distort fair process. For example, in the United States, tightly booked court calendars are an incentive to pressure defendants to plea bargain, rather than insist on a trial, and on the other side of injustice, overcrowded jails and prisons may pressure release of even dangerous felons.[43]

In *Inequality Reexamined*, Sen's starting point is inequality. He introduces "the distinction between achievement and the freedom to achieve," as an "aspect of inequality assessment." This is more promising than reliance on general "equality," as though that could be clearly defined and justified. As with justice and injustice, we can begin with inequality and aim for remedy or correction in a limited sense, where it can be shown that there is sameness between two individuals or groups, which merits equality that is lacking. We are back here to something like Aristotle's claim that equals should be treated equally, but with the understanding that the grounds on which people are equal may vary widely and be subject to dispute. Moreover, once procedure, or what Sen calls "fair process" is brought into consideration of inequality, given inequalities in procedure, a comparative approach would seem to be necessary for correcting inequalities in procedure also. In other words, it is difficult to see how fair process or just procedure does not get distributed in the same way that food and education might. But procedural justice is not usually thought about as something that can be distributed. The distinction between distribution and procedure within theories of justice will therefore be the main subject of chapter 4.

A slightly different version of this chapter was published as Naomi Zack, "Philosophical Theories of Justice, Inequality, and Racial Inequality," Graduate Faculty Philosophy Journal, Special Issue on Race in the History of Philosophy, New School University (2014): 353–68.

4

THE DISTRIBUTION OF PROCEDURAL JUSTICE

> All social values—liberty and opportunity, income and wealth, and the social bases of self-respect—are to be distributed equally unless an unequal distribution of any, or all, of these values is to everyone's advantage. —John Rawls, *A Theory of Justice*[1]

As we saw at the end of chapter 3, Amartya Sen said that "the subject of fair process and a fair deal" goes beyond individuals' capabilities and advantages, into procedural concerns.[2] In *Development as Freedom*, Sen emphasized the idea that development requires an increase in political liberty, the removal of "unfreedoms."[3] There is a distinction between procedural justice as something that people need and procedural justice as it is in place in societies where some get it and others do not. Sen's focus in terms of capabilities is on procedural justice as what people need. The perspective on procedural justice that I would like to examine is how procedural justice is viewed by optimistic progressives in societies that are assumed to have a very solid tradition of procedural justice that has not yet been extended to all groups. In this context, there seems to be a certain sacrosanct aura around procedural justice that may be misplaced.

Deference concerning procedural justice seems to be based on an assumption that procedural justice is already just and fair and has been applied to everyone, including those with diminished capabilities. Procedural justice thus has a connotation of moral goodness that is intuitively respected and revered. It is often referred to as something that holds the political world together, is universally accessible, and can never fail to deliver what is right. Procedural justice is believed to be omnipresent as the right way legal matters are conducted. But to understand this requires a clear idea of the distinctive nature of procedural justice.

The first part of this chapter is an analysis of how procedural justice is distributed, so that the concept of procedural justice could be reduced to the concept of distributional justice, albeit with some intact residue that refers back to procedures. When just procedures are viewed as distributable goods that some get and others do not, it is easier to understand their redistribution as the result of a usual push and pull within government process, rather than the success of an intense moral struggle to get political goods through the application of preexisting just procedures, plus expressions of moral outrage at the injustice of how they are being withheld. That is, procedural justice as a distributed good can be viewed as part of Bentleyan political process, whereas procedural justice as content is an idea without causal efficacy. The second part of this chapter is an account of how certain key legal victories in the US civil rights movement were the result of Bentleyan processes of interest group contention, rather than moments of moral enlightenment attained by the proper application of procedural justice that preexisted its application. These examples will show how applicative justice pertaining to procedural justice has been a matter of distribution.

THE DISTINCTION BETWEEN PROCEDURAL AND DISTRIBUTIONAL JUSTICE

Theoretical considerations of justice in organized, law-governed societies usually distinguish between procedural and distributional justice. Although most writers focus on one or the other and do not commit to hard and fast distinction or definition, the following seems to be a general consensus. Distributive justice involves the division or allocation of goods among different groups and subgroups, with individuals as ultimate end recipients. The goods are usually assumed to be material, but services such as education and medical care are also distributed. In contemporary consumer societies, such distributed goods have monetary value. Distributional justice is thus largely a matter of who gets what and how much it costs. Usually, those who focus on distributive justice aim for greater equality in the distribution of goods, because of existing distributional inequality. Their main concern is often the satisfaction of human needs.

This present consensus about the meaning of the term "distributional justice" is a recent modern notion. When scholars begin with the tradition originating with Aristotle, they note that distributional justice did not originally refer to the distribution of goods, but to a giving out of honors and rewards that treated members of elite groups in a hierarchical society equally. This type of distribution was meritocratic according to virtues and accomplishments believed to be part of the character of the members of an elite group. However, the meaning of distributional justice as who gets what of the goods of life, according to some principle of fairness based on ideas about human equality, works better for contemporary democratic societies, where it is assumed that inequalities in distribution are matters of human conditions, rather than human identities. In democracies, we should be able to assume that the poverty of those who are poor is a matter of their external economic circumstances, rather than their character or hereditary incapacities. As Samuel Fleishacker explains, when it was believed that there was something intrinsic to the poor that did not mean their poverty was unjust, older ideas of distributive justice made more sense.[4] Of course, these ideas persist in blame of the poor for their poverty and distinctions between the deserving or worthy poor and those who do not deserve help. It is difficult to successfully argue in contemporary US society that the poor should be helped because they suffer from their poverty and cannot help themselves.

Perfect and Imperfect Procedural Justice

Procedural justice, in contrast to distributional justice, is a matter of how political society, especially government, is organized, and the effects of that organization on how individuals are treated by government. It includes rules for government structures, divisions of government powers and limitations on them, and the duties of government officials. In democracies, procedural justice requires reasoned public discussion and debate, transparent (publicized) government decision-making processes, and opportunities for all groups and individuals who are affected by government decision-making processes to participate, have influence, or express their views. This last is a relatively new requirement, inspired by Rawls (although perhaps based on the naïve interpretation first put forth in chapter 1) and taken up by those who are concerned with injustice in the organization of a society that has sexist, racist, or classist outcomes.[5] Continuing with the received view of procedural justice, it is presumed that just procedures are fair, which is to say that equals are treated equally, without bias based on factors irrelevant to the respects in which they are equal. For example, if all citizens have the right to vote, then nonwhite citizens ought not to be deprived of that right because of their race or skin color. Above all, the outcome of processes of procedural justice should appear just according to some criterion that is independent of the rules governing the process. For example, if the procedure for a fair trial is followed and a guilty defendant is not convicted, or an innocent defendant is convicted, the verdicts cannot be called "just" for the sole reason that procedures for a fair trial have been followed. In general, it is presumed that procedural justice can be formulated independently of distributive results, based on the value of liberty, which has been presumed to be overarching, since the formation of modern democratic states. Procedural justice is assumed to safeguard the liberty of subjects: just procedures do not deprive people of liberty arbitrarily or without just reasons; the innocent are not supposed to be convicted and the guilty are convicted and punished; probable cause is required for stopping and detaining individuals.

A fair trial requires procedures that make it highly unlikely that the guilty will be acquitted or innocent convicted, but a definition of a fair trial becomes tautological if all it does is refer to those aims. Cognizant of this problem with tautology or triviality, Martin Gustafsson has shown how the distinction between Rawlsian perfect and imperfect procedural justice breaks down. In imperfect procedural justice, the procedures are fallible, for example, sometimes the guilty will go free and the innocent will be convicted, whereas in perfect procedural justice, the procedure is guaranteed to lead to a just result, according to an independent criterion (in this example, actual guilt or innocence, determined in some way). However, whether a procedure leads to perfect or imperfect justice depends on how the procedure is specified. The limiting case occurs when the result is given in the specification of the procedure, making the result achieved trivial. Gustafsson contrasts this triviality with the triviality of what Rawls called pure procedural justice, for example, procedures using chance to determine results. In pure cases, the justice of the results, and not the specific results themselves, is trivial.[6] This means that for all practical purposes, perfect procedural justice is impossible. Indeed, as Gustafsson reports, Rawls himself said "perfect procedural justice is rare, if not impossible, in cases of much practical interest."[7] What's more, procedural mechanisms for legal appeals and the ability of even the highest courts to reverse earlier decisions suggest that allowances for the imperfections of procedural justice are a robust part of legal systems.[8]

For imperfect procedural justice, or since that is all we have, procedural justice, the independent standard is distributional justice. Except when a more general principle of procedure is evoked to justify a specific principle, the validity of a principle of procedural justice cannot be based on other principles of procedural justice, which will themselves require independent standards, but on some principle of distribution, such as equality, merit, or desert. However, in real, imperfect societies, laws have developed without strong motivation for either equality of distribution or unbiased procedures. Furthermore, and of significant importance for progressive theorists, the distinction between distributive and procedural justice blends into more concrete systems of social organization and hierarchy, such as free enterprise capitalism, a class or caste system, a racial system, a gender system, or some mixture or intersection of these. Those who write about justice, abstractly, in terms of procedure or distribution may seem to be inhabitants of a different societal universe from those who study social systems in terms of who is oppressed. However, theoretical projects to improve or change such concrete systems usually require engagement with abstract, as well as real life, aspects of procedural, as well as distributive justice, so the prima facie distinction cannot be overlooked.

Calls for "justice" that are comparative, as based on some already being treated justly, often evoke principles of fair procedure. For example, objections to police racial profiling often refer to the doctrine of probable cause that requires police officers to observe evidence of criminal behavior before stopping members of the public.[9] That doctrine, as a practice of procedural justice, is not applied to those who are racially profiled (as criminals) compared to those who are not racially profiled (as criminals). The comparative approach thereby identifies how procedural justice is alive and well for some segment of the population but not for another.

Calls for justice that require an overhaul of the entire system, for reasons that it is inherently classist, racist, masculinist against women, or heterosexist against homosexuals and lesbians, use a rhetoric based on presumably shared and fundamental notions of human equality, from which new forms of what are now understood to be procedural and distributional justice would be derived.[10] However, the invocation of ideals of equality, which would require new principles of procedural justice, starting from scratch "after the revolution," is a project removed from the present concern about the distinction between procedural and distributive justice. In reality, we start from systems in place and focus on the distinction between those who are well served by them and those who are not. The gap between these well- and ill-served groups can be theoretically explained and practically addressed, in terms of what is distributed to both groups, where liberty and just procedures are part of what is or can be distributed.

The Flexibility of Procedural Justice

If Bentley's reduction of law to practice in reality is followed as a method of empirically based analysis, then we need to look to the reality of how people behave regarding particular laws, for an adequate understanding of what those laws are. Human societies, regardless of their just or unjust distributive and procedural legal structures, have always had elite groups that compared to everyone else, not only have more material goods, but are allowed flexibility in how procedural justice is administered to them. Elite membership may translate into either an ability to evade procedural justice when its results would be disadvantageous, or have it scrupulously applied when the results are advantageous. The first is simply unjust; the second is just for members of elite groups but unjust for those who do not get advantageous procedural justice. It is unjust if members of elites are treated the same within that group and members of other groups are also treated the same as members of their group, but the standards for justice are different for different groups. However, actual justice varies with jurisdiction and the situation is complicated in the United States, because even though all state constitutions are committed to upholding the federal constitution, there is considerable variation in procedures and statute law in different state jurisdictions.

Different distributions of social goods, according to racial identity, resulted from legally enforced racially segregated schools for black and white school children before *Brown v. Board of Education*. Not only were schools for whites better, which was unfair distribution of a social good, but insofar as segregation was intended to exclude blacks from white society, it was also an unfair distribution of social dignity. There is a similar problem now in a system where public education is funded by local property taxes, because residential segregation by income results in less educational resources for children who go to school in poor neighborhoods, compared to schoolchildren in affluent neighborhoods.[11] In contemporary school segregation, the inequality problem is not the direct result of law, but as President Eisenhower called it and others since have been content to let lie, "de facto."[12] The current situation is a complex effect of laws concerning distribution: how people acquire wealth, the distribution of education based on local resources, college preparation based on available resources, the final distribution of adult income based on highest degrees obtained. Like the earlier case, white children benefit from the procedural justice of having standard or superior educational facilities readily available. If access to good education is a matter of procedural justice, then the comparatively nonstandard education available to nonwhite children is unjust. But it's not clear that equal access to education is a matter of procedural justice instead of distributive justice.

Contemporary air travel provides a simpler example. Everyone who flies with a commercial airline is subject to at least a superficial search of their person and possessions, and a more invasive search of both, depending on the results of the superficial search. After 9/11, it has seemed fair that everyone who travels by commercial air transport is subject to search. But those who own planes, and their guests, can simply board without being subject to search. (This elite treatment is different when passing past superficial searches has accorded some frequent flyers a "prescreened" status, so that their superficial searches are even more superficial.) The private plane owners are treated the same within their group and everyone else is treated the same within their group. But the "everyone else" group is not treated the same as the private plane owner group. (In this case, correcting the injustice might require extending searches to private plane owners and their guests, and as of this writing, the Transportation Security Administration [TSA] is proposing to do just that.[13])

The education and air travel case both come down to unequally distributed goods (adequate or excellent education or unimpeded travel). Differences in state law pertaining to procedural justice require federal intervention toward uniform law, or voluntary compliance. Differences in the application of procedural justice within the same jurisdiction are the strongest instances of procedural injustice. When such correction of injustice amounts to a claim, right, or demand by those treated unjustly, for some specific redress that is already possessed by those who have already been treated justly according to existing rules of procedural justice, procedural justice can be viewed as a form of comparative distributional justice. What is called for to be differently or more inclusively distributed is, in this case, certain procedures. It is rarely, if ever, the case that aggrieved parties demand a wholescale change in an existing system of procedural or distributional justice. Rather, their demand is for a specific application of existing justice to them—a good education, a fair trial, unimpeded travel. (The alternative, as in the TSA example, would be to impose bad education, unfair trials, and intrusive travel searches on everyone. But few who live in democratic societies would want that, even though they are often eager to see justice done by punishing those who they believe are guilty.)

Procedural Justice Distribution

When abstract theorists of justice specialize in either procedural or distributional justice, they usually acknowledge the other kind of justice. Thus, Rawls acknowledges distributional justice through the difference principle, which holds that increases in inequality must benefit the least materially advantaged more than they would benefit under strictly equal distribution.[14] And, as recently discussed, Sen recognizes procedural justice as a supplement to the implementation of a capabilities approach. In each case, what the theory in question does not directly address seems to be deferred to the other kind of justice. If just distribution is a necessary condition for just procedure and just distribution requires just procedure, any combined theory of procedural and distributive justice at first looks circular on a theoretical level. However, if procedural justice is assessed by distribution and distributive justice refers to that same kind of assessment, both forms of justice can be viewed as matters of just distribution. Also, concerning the apparent circularity, the whole system of justice need not be addressed in order to correct particular instances of either procedural or distributional injustice. There is no good reason not to view procedural justice as a social good that is subject to distribution. This view also accords with common usage, as when we say, "He got a fair trial."

Often procedural justice has little practical use for correcting injustice, unless it can be viewed as a social good that is subject to distribution. Parts of the Rawls literature going back to the 1970s support this distributional nature of procedural justice and we should now consider those discussions. Ideals of general systems of distributional equality often persist in the imagined form of transitions from capitalism to democratic socialism.

One objection to egalitarian redistribution has been that systemic equal distribution could only be maintained by infringing on liberty. Andrew Lister believes that Rawlsians can rather easily handle this objection to distributional equalization, which he attributes in different forms to Robert Nozick and Will Kymlicka. Lister cites Cheyney Ryan and G. A. Cohen for the substance of his response that if the institutions are just, then unequal results will not be unjust. According to Lister, the institutions will be just if "they protect people's basic liberties, secure them fair equality of opportunity, and permit inequalities only if they raise the lowest social position."[15] Notice that Lister (or Rawls) is not talking about complete egalitarianism, but an already well-ordered society, and that it is stipulated only that the lowest position be raised, not that it be abolished. The problems are that unqualified procedural justice may jeopardize the well-being of the already disadvantaged, whereas unqualified distributional justice may jeopardize the liberty of the already advantaged. The question is how to qualify each so that together they result in the least amount of injustice.

Concerning procedural justice, it is stipulated that just institutions will not have unjust results. This raises the question of how one can know that designed institutions will be just, in a contingent world of political process, where laws have to be complied with and implemented. Historically, one approach to such issues has been mitigation of the effects of law in courts of equity. But equity has usually worked to soften the harshness of law and not extend its benefits to members of groups who have been excluded in its implementation or prevented from having it implemented for them. (The denial of access to voting or prevention of voting of African Americans is a prime example of an injustice concerning legal implementation that cannot be addressed as a matter of equity.[16]) Ryan and Cohen's stipulation that just institutions will not have unjust results may conflate written descriptions of institutions with institutions in reality. (Their stipulation is either a tautology or else it is false.)

If institutions are described as just but their reality is unjust, we cannot say that there are just institutions in the society. Lister and Cohen may be relying on an ability to distinguish between inequalities caused by unjust institutions and inequalities caused by actions for which individuals are responsible. This would be to assume perfect procedural justice, which is "rare if not impossible," as we have noted even Rawls said. How are we to determine which inequalities are the responsibilities of the disadvantaged? Suppose, as liberatory discourse since the last third of the twentieth century has taken great pains to explain, that individual responsibility is constrained by wider social structures. For example, the responsibility of a poor nonwhite child for her academic performance (assessed fairly), may be mitigated by the under-education of her parents and the examples of her peers, as well as less money spent on learning materials by a school in a poor neighborhood.

Nozick's Wilt Chamberlin Example

Let's now consider G. A. Cohen's famous 1977 Wilt Chamberlain article. The setup is Nozick's: An egalitarian society is brought into being. Wilt Chamberlain is a huge gate attraction and he signs a contract whereby fans will pay an extra twenty-five cents to see him play and this money goes directly to Chamberlain. Chamberlain will get $250,000 a season, which is much more than the average income. (In the early 1970s, after he signed on with the Lakers for $250,000 a year, Chamberlain was the highest paid athlete in the world, although in 2015, the highest paid athlete in the world is Floyd Mayweather, at $300,000,000 per year!)[17] Nozick addresses whether this is unjust and argues that the new distribution, while unequal, is not unjust, because it is the result of lawful voluntary actions: The fans were entitled to spend their money and the transfer does not affect the legitimate shares of those who have not participated in it. Furthermore, according to Nozick, it would be unjust to redistribute Chamberlain's new wealth.[18]

Cohen argues against Nozick, as part of a defense of socialism. We should note here that socialism is a theory of distributional justice, whereas Nozick's concern with liberty seems to be a matter of procedural justice, because his central claim is that it would be unjust to redistribute because redistribution would infringe on liberty. Cohen claims that in a socialist system, the unequal power enjoyed by Chamberlain might lead many of those who paid the extra twenty-five cents to rethink their choice. Cohen goes on to present examples where infringement of the liberty of some will increase overall net liberty, for example, the increased liberty of adults, who as children, were given subsidized milk with money appropriated from millionaires (who today would be billionaires).[19] With that example, Cohen shifts the argument from rights to utilitarian sums, which Nozick's deontological commitment to liberty would presumably not countenance. Nozick would be willing to sacrifice more liberty in the future for the protection of individual liberty in the present.[20]

Cohen and Nozick's disagreement turns on the comparative merits of Cohen's consequentialism that seeks to maximize the same thing that is at stake in a deontological or duty moral system, versus Nozick's insistence on directly performing the duty or preserving the value (presumably in every case, but in his example, a specific individual case). The issue is whether we should maximize individual liberty and preserve individual dignity for a large number of people, or not do anything to limit the liberty or have the dignity harmed, of any specific individual. This in itself blurs the distinction between procedural and distributional justice. Cohen's maximization of liberty treats liberty as a distributional good. However, Nozick's reliance on Kantian individual dignity does not rise to procedural justice, either, because it offers no guidance for when, as a general rule, the dignity of an individual may be sacrificed in a just process. We need a general rule, because many just processes require some sacrifice of individual dignity to arrive at just outcomes (e.g., the trial of an innocent person, even if acquitted). Liberty may be absolute, but it cannot be unlimited. Many libertarians would agree with John Locke who cautioned that "liberty is not license," before he asserted that "all men may be restrained from invading others rights, and from doing hurt to one another."[21]

Property Rights and Freedom

Cohen's millionaire might argue that the money taxed away from him was his property and that he had a right to retain his property. That right would only be intelligible in a system that generally upheld private property rights, so that he could compare his unjust treatment with the treatment of those whose private property rights were respected in situations other than taxation. In more general terms, the millionaire might claim that the procedure of taxation unfairly deprives him of liberty. Indeed, the keystone of procedural justice is supposed to be individual liberty. Rawls writes:

> It has seemed to many philosophers, and it appears to be supported by the convictions of common sense, that we distinguish as a matter of principle between the claims of liberty and right on the one hand and the desirability of increasing aggregate social welfare on the other; and that we give a certain priority, if not absolute weight, to the former. Each member of society is thought to have an inviolability founded on justice or, as some say, on natural right, which even the welfare of everyone else cannot override. Justice denies that the loss of freedom for some is made right by a greater good shared by others. The reasoning which balances the gains and losses of different persons as if they were one person is excluded. Therefore in a just society the basic liberties are taken for granted and the rights secured by justice are not subject to political bargaining or to the calculus of social interests.[22]

Thus, a theory of justice begins under an (imagined) condition of liberty and the liberty of each individual is absolute in comparison to the welfare of others. Furthermore, this individual liberty is equal: "In justice as fairness . . . persons accept in advance a principle of equal liberty and they do this without a knowledge of their more particular ends."[23] However, according to the most general principle of justice, liberty according to Rawls is to be equally distributed:

> All social values—liberty and opportunity, income and wealth, and the social bases of self-respect—are to be distributed equally unless an unequal distribution of any, or all, of these values is to everyone's advantage.[24]

Rights to the acquisition, possession, and alienation of private property have, of course, been strongly associated with liberty in this sense, even though the distribution of absolute, equal, individual liberty is not matched by an equal distribution of private property. What makes the distribution of liberty, as an absolute right, just, is that it is equally distributed—everyone is to have the same degree of absolute liberty. However, Nozick's defense of the property rights of the ungenerous millionaire assumes that his property rights are absolute in the way that his individual liberty is absolute, so that he can claim that infringement on individual private property rights is equivalent to an infringement on absolute liberty. Such valorization-by-association with absolute liberty, of private property rights, overextends the scope of exercising the right to private property, to exercising liberty.[25] But, the liberty to own private property does not entail the same liberty in exercising one's ownership of that property. (I am free to buy a Yamaha Kabuto steel snare drum but there are restrictions on when I can play it, owing to my neighbors' need for sleep.)

In support of the distinction between liberty and private property rights, Cheney Ryan criticizes Nozick's claim that interference with private ownership involves restrictions on individual liberty. Ryan notes that the institution of private property has itself continually interfered with the liberty of the majority, for instance in the early modern enclosure of common lands by rich land owners. He argues that more general than private property is the institution of holdings that have had various accepted restrictions on liberty already built into them. Ryan's examples are resources used by an entire community and teaching positions that cannot be sold. Ryan also distinguishes between private possession and private ownership, because private ownership is normative and its protection presupposes a preexisting system of ownership.[26] Possession, in contrast to both private ownership and holdings, requires only occupancy or control over the object possessed.

Private property rights are one form of social organization that enables exercise of liberty, but there is no convincing argument for their absolute status and they are not coextensive with liberty. The millionaire would have to provide an argument making private property an integral and necessary part of liberty, before he could claim that taxation violates his liberty. However, he would not want to pursue that argument if he thought that liberty as an absolute had to be equally distributed, because that could support a redistribution of his property if he had more than others. Liberty may be a core and absolute value, but private property ownership is relative and contingent.

Suppose that liberty is an absolute value to be equally distributed, as Rawls claims. That liberty is not equally or fairly distributed undermines its relegation to procedural, rather than distributional justice. Furthermore, if all do not have an equal share of liberty, then liberty is not universal and procedural justice cannot be envisioned as a neutral safeguard of everyone's liberty, apart from distributive justice. The problem of unqualified liberty resulting in unjust distribution, while unqualified equal distribution infringes on liberty, does not arise if liberty is equally distributed but not identified with the distribution of anything else. This is because the distribution of liberty is less flexible for just results than the distribution of other material and social goods. Nozick's claim that the ungenerous millionaire ought not to give up his property, because his ownership of however much property he owns is coextensive with his liberty, is incompatible with liberty being an absolute, equally distributed value. Such conflation of liberty and ownership would and has resulted in putting a price on liberty—only the richest people have it. The result is that liberty is implicitly treated as a distributional good while those who fear the distributional equality of material goods protect inequalities in wealth with empty rhetoric about liberty.

If liberty is an absolute value that should be equally distributed, then its unequal distribution should constrain the distribution of other goods. On this view, a libertarian would need to yield to egalitarian distributions of those goods that were closely tied to the furtherance of liberty, for instance education. But she might be able to hold firm against egalitarian distribution of luxury items or goods that did not further liberty, such as alcohol, cigarettes, and non-nutritious food that tastes good. However if such a calculus were worked out, it would need to be based on the recognition that fundamental human values are subject to distribution, including fair or just procedures for dispensing reward and punishment.

The Psychological Value of Procedural Justice

So far, the perspective on the prima facie distinction between procedural and distributional justice has been implicitly limited to philosophical and political science perspectives within democratic nations—that is, nations with explicit democratic legal structures and written laws, although not necessarily with just societies. But from the perspective of social psychologists, considering international situations, procedural justice in its symbolic and ceremonial sense is important in itself. In recommending the transparent practice of procedural justice to the European Court of Human Rights, Eva Brems and Laurens Lavrysen go so far as to appropriate the concept for their own field of social psychology and write:

> The concept of procedural justice (sometimes called "procedural fairness") was developed by American social psychology researchers and has gained worldwide recognition. Its central empirical finding is that in people's contact with the law, they care not only about the outcome of their case, but also about the way in which it is handled. In fact, the perception of procedural justice (was the case dealt with in a fair manner?) is a more significant factor determining the perception of the legitimacy of the institution concerned, than the perception of distributive justice (was the outcome of the case fair?).[27]

Transparent procedural justice, even when outcomes are not favorable to defendants or litigants, by producing just results, has the psychological effect of engendering trust in administrative or governing bodies and supporting perception of their legitimacy.[28] But from the perspective of philosophy or theories in political science or economics, procedures are merely social mechanisms for deciding who will get what, given incompatible claims. There is nothing sacrosanct in a procedure itself, apart from its being a means to arrive at the best outcome, in a way that participants and observers consider appropriate. When procedures do not result in justice but are nonetheless valued, that value lies in the role of procedures as rituals. Such valuation fetishizes procedures, perhaps at the cost of demanding a more fair distribution of just procedures.

PROCEDURAL JUSTICE AND US CIVIL RIGHTS

Those who study law and legal principles often ignore politics. Within the current traditional informational discourse about US civil rights pertaining to African Americans, there is a tendency to briefly document injustice, but record legal changes as "milestones" in "timelines" of progress toward justice.[29] While this focus keeps history alive in readily accessible ways and supports optimism about the future, it cannot provide a full picture of the correction of racial injustice. The milestone-timeline model makes it seem as though the entire story of procedural justice and injustice can be understood in terms of successive written law and various victories and defeats therein. Changes to written law have been a major lever for wider changes in society, but the history of racial injustice in the United States reveals remarkable tendencies by whites to violate the letter as well as the spirit of just written law and to do so with impunity. Law, especially law about procedures, is broader than what is written and it cannot be understood apart from the rest of society, especially political process.

Insights that laws and judicial decisions are influenced by other factors in society and broader understandings of law as just one part of political process have been developed in sociological jurisprudence and sociology of law,[30] as well as politically contextualized legal history. Insofar as philosophers of law concentrate on law and political philosophers proceed from normative ideals in seeking to correct injustice by designing the right top-down model of legal justice, they have both neglected insights from this type of social science. Consideration of the political contexts of the Reconstruction Amendments, *Brown v. Board of Education*, and the Civil Rights Act of 1964 can show how written law alone is inadequate for an account of human life as affected by law. Effects on human life matter, because law is not just a beautiful, self-contained set of objects for contemplation, but correctly assumed to structure society. But just written laws may neither come into being for the sake of justice nor have the just effects on human life that they are assumed to have. It is important for theorists of justice and injustice to understand how this has worked, historically. The content of the Reconstruction Amendments and Civil Rights Act directly concerned procedural justice. *Brown* was a mix of procedural and distributional justice. All of these "milestones" and their implementation and judicial interpretation were influenced by external factors that, as we shall soon see, either had little to do with the content of procedural justice or contradicted it.

The Reconstruction Amendments and Racial Justice

The Reconstruction Amendments, passed after the Civil War (1865–1870) are often cited as milestones of racial justice: Amendment XIII outlawed slavery and involuntary servitude, except as punishment for crime. Amendment XIV stated that all persons born or naturalized in the United States were citizens of the United States and their state of residence; that no state shall make or enforce laws abridging the privileges or immunities of US citizens, deprive any person of life, liberty, or property without due process of law, or deny any person equal protection of law; and that when the right to vote is denied eligible persons, the representatives from that state will be proportionally decreased. Amendment XV stated: "The right of citizens of the United States to vote shall not be denied or abridged by the United States or by any State on account of race, color, or previous condition of servitude." Each of these amendments gave Congress the power to enforce them. In 1875, Congress passed a law against discrimination in public accommodations, in the spirit of the equal protection clause of Amendment XIV.[31]

The US Supreme Court's interpretations of the Reconstruction Amendments became part of the law attached to the amendments. During Reconstruction, the court interpreted the reconstruction amendments, ambiguously, sometimes withholding procedural justice from nonwhites and sometimes extending it. But after Reconstruction, the court generally interpreted the amendments on the side of white dominance.

When United States v. Cruikshank reached the Supreme Court in 1876, the issue was whether a Ku Klux Klan attack on black men attempting to legitimately occupy a state office violated their constitutional rights. The court ruled that the white defendants were private citizens and that other private citizens needed to rely on state governments to protect their rights, not Congress.[32] However, in two later cases, the court did rule against racial discrimination within states: In *Strauder v. West Virginia*, a statute restricting jury service to white men was struck down in 1879; in *Yick Wo v. Hopkins*, 1886, the Court ruled in favor of Chinese immigrants who were denied laundry licenses in San Francisco, although there was no explicit restrictive state law. Robert Cottrol, Raymond Diamond, and Leland Ware point out that this kind of willingness to examine practice on the part of the Court could have been very important for further liberatory interpretations of Amendments XIII, IX, and XV, but that trend did not develop.[33]

After Reconstruction ended in 1877 and federal troops withdrew from the South, former slaves were dependent on state governments to protect their rights. If that failed to occur, the Supreme Court was the ultimate resort for correcting a number of injustices: segregation, violence against black voters, mob murders (including lynching), peonage based on a sharecropper agricultural system in the South, and prisoner leasing (renting out prison labor to private employers). Segregation that was both mandated and enforced by law became a primary issue for African American advocates.

Criteria for black and white racial identity were also part of the late nineteenth-century public subject of race. Black racial classification as based on any known black ancestry, according to the "one-drop rule," was becoming the social rule of the land.[34] Adolphus Plessy had one black great-great grandparent and looked white. He was a member of the self-identified mixed-race community in New Orleans and his case was about the right of the railroad company to classify him racially, in addition to his attack on segregation on Fourteenth Amendment grounds. But it was the unsuccessful challenge to segregation that made *Plessy v. Ferguson* famous. Plessy's lawyers argued that segregation was prohibited by the Thirteenth and Fourteenth Amendment because it "stamped the colored race with a badge of inferiority." Justice Henry Billings Brown rejected that claim with a thought experiment that if the two racial positions were reversed, whites would not assume they were inferior.[35] *Plessy* left the question of criteria for racial identity in the hands of social opinion, where it remains to this day.[36]

At the turn of the twentieth century, 90 percent of African Americans lived in southern states under political structures controlled by whites. Public officials, including governors and senators, praised lynching and other violence against blacks. A new generation of professional historians, led by William A. Dunning of Columbia University, viewed Reconstruction as a "tragic era" and the Thirteenth, Fourteenth, and Fifteenth Amendments as a mistake. Social Darwinists used ideas of the "survival of the fittest" to support hopes that "inferior races" would die out; US Supreme Court Justice Oliver Wendell Homes Jr. supported the eugenics movement that aimed to restrict reproduction of "inferior" groups. Holmes wrote the majority opinion for *Giles v. Harris*, denying injunctive relief to five thousand black men in Alabama who were not allowed to vote because of a difficult literacy test.[37] William Graham Sumner, founder of *American Sociology*, proclaimed in *Folkways* that the law should not be used to correct social inequalities and that equality in law was not a viable principle. President Woodrow Wilson increased segregation among federal employees and made it more difficult for African Americans to enlist in the US Navy.[38]

Early twentieth-century Supreme Court decisions reflected the prejudice of the times but did not actually destroy the Reconstruction Amendments' constitutional foundation for legal equality. Congress had passed an anti-peonage law in 1867, in implementation of the Thirteenth Amendment. In *Clyatt v. United States*, 1906, the white defendant appealed his Georgia conviction for forcibly moving two black men from Florida to work for him to pay off their debts. Interestingly enough, although the court ordered a new trial for Clyatt, it did not revisit *United States v. Cruikshank* to further erode the Thirteenth Amendment. In *Berea College v. Commonwealth of Kentucky*, 1908, Berea College appealed a fine for violating Kentucky's segregation law. The court ruled that because Berea College was a corporation, it was a creation of the state, subject to the state segregation law (Berea was a private college, but not a private person—although corporations were considered persons then, as now, and Berea wanted to provide integrated education). In *McCabe v. Atchison, Topeka and Santa Fe Railway Company*, 1914, McCabe, based on the *Plessy* decision that "separate" required "equal," sought an injunction against the railroad because it did not provide sleeping or dining cars for black passengers, while it did for whites. The court agreed with McCabe's claim but did not order injunctive relief. In *Buchanan v. Warley*, 1917, the court, on freedom of contract grounds, struck down a Kentucky statute prohibiting whites from selling homes to blacks in majority-white neighborhoods.[39] The balancing act of the court that sometimes preserved the letter of the Reconstruction Amendments in a restricted constitutional law context, while not disturbing white supremacy in US society, continued through a number of education cases until decisions on the five cases that made up the unanimous 1954 decision in *Brown v. Board of Education* struck down *Plessy*.

The sometimes contradictory deference to the legitimacy of state law that violated the Reconstruction Amendments was a manipulation of the principles of procedural justice that required the court to interpret and apply the Constitution and its amendments. The seventy-three years between the end of Reconstruction and *Brown* cannot be captured by a historical timeline that is assumed to reflect continual progress in procedural justice for African Americans. Furthermore, this era of legal history shows that even the highest level of written law, namely constitutional amendment, cannot be understood in isolation from the society of its time and the highest judicial will to defer to the preferences of dominant groups in that period. We can say that the US Supreme Court justices were more interested in social convention than justice, or were themselves unjust, during this time, and leave it at that. Or, we can expand our ideas about procedural justice to include practices beyond written law that distributed procedural justice. A closer look at the context of *Brown* and the Civil Rights Act will show how contextual factors influenced both what came to be written law and judicial decision. Moral judgment does have its place in such matters, but a view of law as political process in the past is more promising for considering how to change political process in the present and future.

Brown v. Board of Education

In the decision of *Brown v. Board of Education*, Chief Justice Earl Warren referred to social science findings, in the context of what some have viewed as renewed postwar repudiation of racism and inequality and growing black resistance to discrimination and mob violence:

> Segregation of white and colored children in public schools has a detrimental effect upon the colored children. The impact is greater when it has the sanction of the law, for the policy of separating the races is usually interpreted as denoting the inferiority of the negro group. A sense of inferiority affects the motivation of a child to learn. Segregation with the sanction of law, therefore, has a tendency to [retard] the educational and mental development of negro children

> and to deprive them of some of the benefits they would receive in a racial[ly] integrated school system.[40]

Warren's words are commonly presented in historical writings on civil rights as a pivotal point in US race relations that epitomized a profound liberatory change in US society, both in cultural factors reflected in the court's decision and as an influence on subsequent history. However, neither the cultural climate attending *Brown*, nor its subsequent influence, support that view. *Brown* was not preceded by more egalitarian white public opinion about nonwhites, and neither did it resolve the issue of segregation. Practices akin to lynching continued unabated and school segregation persisted after it. As a result of contending interests, *Brown* primarily expressed international US government interests during the Cold War and if we consider *Brown* from that perspective, we are less likely to be stymied by what followed.

Concerning American antiblack violence after World War II, Mary Dudziak, while noting war-related black gains in employment, housing, and mobility, writes:

> A wave of violence swept the South as black veterans returned home. Lynchings and beatings of blacks, sometimes involving local law enforcement officials, were covered in the media in this country and abroad. The violence spawned protests and demands that the federal government take steps to alleviate that brutality and other forms of racial injustice. In one incident during the summer of 1946, Sergeant Issac Woodard was beaten with a nightstick and blinded in both eyes by the Chief of Police in Aiken, South Carolina. Woodard had been on his way home after three years of military service. The police chief was indicted for the incident, but was then acquitted "to the cheers of a crowded courtroom." Also that summer, Macio Snipes, the only black in his district in Georgia to vote in a state election, was killed at his home by four whites. In Monroe, Georgia, on July 25, 1946, Roger Malcolm, who was black, was jailed after fighting with a white man. Malcolm was released later that day. Malcolm, his wife, and two friends, all of whom were black, were then driven by his employer down a back road to a waiting mob. All four were killed.[41]

The National Association for the Advancement of Colored People (NAACP) had been active in the late 1940s and early 1950s, achieving substantial court victories in chipping away at segregation in higher education in states where there was only one white graduate school or law school that excluded blacks, and separate comparable facilities were not feasible.[42] However, the integration of graduate schools did not inflame the public as did fears and myths about the miscegenation believed certain to attend integrated K–12 education. Indeed, throughout southern states after *Brown*, K–12 integration required state and federal quasi-military intervention and hugely unpopular busing.

Real life comprehensive K–12 racial integration has never been achieved throughout the United States because local public schools are mainly funded by property taxes. Poor nonwhites, especially blacks, continue to live in poor neighborhoods and their children continue to attend schools that are not only de facto racially segregated, but with substantially less educational resources compared to nearby schools attended by white students.[43] At the end of the twentieth century, residential segregation remained higher for African Americans than any other group.[44] The authors of "The 2003 Harvard Civil Rights Project" wrote in their executive summary:

> At the beginning of the twenty-first century, American public schools are now twelve years into the process of continuous resegregation. The desegregation of black students, which increased continuously from the 1950s to the late 1980s, has now receded to levels not seen in three decades. Although the South remains the nation's most integrated region for both blacks and whites, it is the region that is most rapidly going backwards as the courts terminate many major and successful desegregation orders.[45]

Not only have K–12 schools been resegregating, but if law school graduates are the hope for future legal action against racial segregation in education, the lack of integration in the legal profession dims those prospects. As of 2010, lawyers in the United States were almost 90 percent white and black lawyers were less than 5 percent.[46]

If *Brown* did not express a sustainable change in US race relations and attitudes, then what did lead to, influence, or motivate the decision? Perhaps the best explanation is in terms of Derrick Bell's hypothesis that a convergence of black and white interests brought *Brown* about, with the white interests issuing from the US government's goal to be recognized as a preeminent moral, as well as military and economic global power.[47] This is not to suggest that African American efforts were not significant.[48] And neither should we overlook earlier interest in civil rights by the Truman administration, most notably Executive Order 9981 requiring desegregation of the US military.[49] Still, in 1947, the NAACP had been unable to get the United Nations to accept a human rights petition regarding treatment of African Americans, and the Civil Rights Congress' 1951 charge that the United States practiced genocide against African Americans was similarly dismissed. Both times, the US government was able to prevail in protecting the nation's international reputation.[50]

The Truman administration was very concerned about foreign reports of violent discrimination against African Americans in the Soviet Union and Eastern Europe, China, Japan, Southeast Asia, Latin America, Haiti, Great Britain, Holland, and many other places. However, the American racial power structure at that time, and at least through passage of the 1964 Civil Rights Act (as we shall soon see), dictated that whites take the initiative in addressing racial discrimination and not simply or directly respond to black complaints. President Truman formed a committee on civil rights that reported:

> Our foreign policy is designed to make the United States an enormous, positive influence for peace and progress throughout the world. We have tried to let nothing, not even extreme political differences between ourselves and foreign nations, stand in the way of this goal. But our domestic civil rights shortcomings are a serious obstacle . . . the United States is not so strong, the final triumph of the democratic ideal is not so inevitable that we can ignore what the world thinks of us or our record.[51]

The US State Department, on the recommendation of the president's committee, filed an amicus brief for *Brown*, which read in part: "[t]he United States is trying to prove to the people of the world, of every nationality, race and color, that a free democracy is the most civilized and most secure form of government yet devised by man." Dudziak notes that the Truman administration was able to claim *Brown* as a "blow to communism," and that was how it was reported in newspapers throughout the United States and the world.[52] The decision in *Brown* was not reported to the American public as a triumph of American justice over American prejudice and discrimination, for two reasons. First, it was not that kind of a triumph, and second, the majority of the American public would not have welcomed that kind of triumph.

The 1964 Civil Rights Act

Action toward racial social justice undertaken by whites with political motives unrelated to racial social justice was also evident in events preceding passage of the 1964 Civil Rights Act. During the early 1960s, as in the early 1950s, the American public was focused on relations with the Soviet Union and civil rights was a minor concern. Louis Menard reports that the Kennedy White House had initially considered reports of civil rights violations "human-interest stories." While the Kennedys were privately sympathetic to Martin Luther King Jr., sometimes offering discrete help when he or his associates fell into the clutches of southern judges, publicly they distanced themselves from the civil rights movement. Publicly, Kennedy approached civil rights as the leader of the free world, looking abroad, rather than speaking to Americans as the president of the United States looking at US society. His June 11, 1963, televised civil rights address to the nation, responding to demonstrations in Birmingham, Alabama, after Governor George Wallace's proclamation of "Segregation now, segregation tomorrow, and segregation forever," was abstract and indirect:

> We have a right to expect that the Negro community will be responsible, will uphold the law, but they have a right to expect that the law will be fair, that the Constitution will be color blind, as Justice Harlan said at the turn of the century. This is what we are talking about and this is a matter which concerns this country and what it stands for, and in meeting it I ask the support of all our citizens.[53]

Menard observes that "the 'we' in Kennedy's television address clearly referred to white Americans."[54]

Johnson inherited Kennedy's civil rights act and is largely credited with getting it through Congress, with the vigorous assistance of Robert Kennedy. Aspects of that process show how distant political motives were from the stated goals of civil rights legislation and how coincident with political contentions among whites. The two main issues that the passage of the Civil Rights Act turned on were women's equality and competition between Democrats and Republicans for votes. Contrary to received opinion, the addition of "sex" to Title VII of the bill was neither an attempt to jettison the bill, nor a joke, but the result of the efforts of Alice Paul, then head of the National Women's Party (NWP). Since 1923, Paul had been trying to get an equal-rights bill for women passed by Congress. Other women's organizations opposed equal rights for women on the grounds that they needed protection in the workplace. African American activists also opposed the sex amendment to the civil rights bill, maintaining as they had since the Civil War, that their oppression was worse than the oppression of white women. Anti-union conservatives who represented large employers of women supported it.[55]

In the early 1960s, the NWP mainly consisted of rich, elderly, white women. They wrote to white conservatives in Congress about their fears that the civil rights bill would result in "a mongrel race in the United States." Martha Griffiths, D-Michigan, told the House that the civil rights bill as it stood would leave white women out of civic equality:

> You are going to have white men in one bracket, you are going to try to take colored men and colored women and give them equal employment rights, and down at the bottom of the list is going to be a white woman with no rights at all.[56]

The competition for votes between Democrats and Republicans involved political control of the South. Republicans wanted both African American votes for their numbers and white Southern allegiance for their party's pro-business conservatism. They presented their own civil rights bills, often deliberately extreme in hope that Democrats would defeat them and appear to oppose civil rights. By June 1963, over one hundred civil rights bills were circulating in the House of Representatives. Democrats had a majority in both houses, but also a very strong Southern contingent, who opposed the bills.[57] Of course, the Civil Rights Act, with its sex amendment, eventually passed. But the political process beyond its content prevents interpreting the intent(s) of the act as whole-heartedly progressive or egalitarian, for either women or blacks. Concerning blacks, like *Brown*, the Civil Rights Act was understood to be an achievement of whites. While President Johnson was signing the act into law, he apparently did not notice that Martin Luther King was standing directly behind him (see cover picture). When informed of King's presence two days later, he is reported to have said,

"I'm sorry he was there. It was very unfortunate that he was there."[58] Johnson's remark suggests that he viewed procedural justice as a distributed good. His insensitivity to the cultural value of King's presence when he signed the act that represented culmination of a long and arduous struggle for African Americans suggests a crass pragmatic view that civil rights, as matters of procedural justice, could be distributed to blacks, or not. As with any other distributable good, the person or persons with the power to distribute or withhold it need not be subject to any higher legal or moral principle. The distributability of procedural justice according to this interpretation of Johnson's remark is both a cause and effect of injustice, because it objectifies just procedures. But unfortunately, it is to this day the real condition of US procedural justice regarding race.

Implications of the Distinction between Law and Practice

The distinction drawn here between written law and written law plus legal and political practice is not intended to suggest that ideals expressed by written law and widely known legal principles have little or no value when law and political practice contradict each other. In oppressive times and places, egalitarian and just written law and legal principles support hope and normative ideals. Martin Luther King Jr. was aware of the importance of ideals and hope, not only in his "I Have a Dream Speech," but in his speech accepting the Nobel Peace Prize in 1964, which contained many flights of oratory uplift, such as:

> I believe that wounded justice, lying prostrate on the blood-flowing streets of our nations, can be lifted from this dust of shame to reign supreme among the children of men. I have the audacity to believe that peoples everywhere can have three meals a day for their bodies, education and culture for their minds, and dignity, equality and freedom for their spirits.[59]

King had a dialectical talent for talking about injustice and its correction in the same breath. The immediate force of such rhetoric is impossible to assess in any historical interpretation and its inspirational importance and powers of consolation should not be minimized. However, by the same token, we do not know what the distractive effects of noble rhetoric might be, because it is easy for people inspired by exalted speeches to mistake speech about justice and/or written-law justice for justice in real life.

King was aware that justice for American blacks had not been achieved when he received the Nobel Peace Prize. In his acceptance speech, he explored why he had been awarded the prize, concluding that it was because he held peace to be a primary value and favored nonviolence in all of his efforts:

> After contemplation, I conclude that this award which I receive on behalf of that movement is a profound recognition that nonviolence is the answer to the crucial political and moral question of our time—the need for man to overcome oppression and violence without resorting to violence and oppression.[60]

Nonviolence as an avowed means to overcome oppression requires the kind of inspiration King was able to provide, as well as a commitment to undergo suffering, punishment, and even death, in the service of that overcoming. As noted in chapter 3, at its inception the United Nations proposed universal human rights as a way to keep the peace—the writers of UDHR specifically stated that without rights, violent rebellion was likely to occur, which was dangerous for those whose rights were already respected and protected. For those whose abstract rights are not respected or implemented, discourse about rights and the distribution of procedural justice is not only inspiring, but also purposive. It has a pragmatic dimension.

THE PRAGMATIC IMPORTANCE OF DISCOURSE

King and Mahatma Ghandi before him were not quietists. They established the now-received power of modern public demonstrations. But demonstrations themselves, when they are not supported with argument and discussion among all stakeholders, may not accomplish anything beyond the self-expression of the groups demonstrating. The allowance of such self-expression has a "steam valve" function that protects the interests of oppressors. Many demonstrations accomplish nothing beyond this "steam valve" function. Something more is needed to fulfill the expectation that nonviolent protest and the expression of moral right, even with powerful orators and charismatic leaders, will result in the correction of injustice. Strikes, boycotts, and public shaming are further tactics but even these, together with nonviolent demonstration, may not be enough to effect permanent solutions. If oppressive or negligent entities have sufficient power, the influence of demonstrations, strikes, boycotts, and so forth, may not be sufficient to result in lasting change. The oppressive or negligent entities can simply wait these things out, make token or symbolic concessions, or even change written law but fail to implement or obey it. All of that happened before and after *Brown*.

The reality of a gap or contradiction between constitutional rights, just judicial decisions, and law, on the one hand, and political practice, on the other, is not surprising on a broad Bentleyan construction of law. However, we are left with the question of what should be done or what can be done about such gaps and contradictions when law is just and action is unjust. Unjust actions may lead back to more statements, including laws, that proclaim justice, but we may still be left with a combination of static statement and action that does not match what was said. The result would be an unsatisfactory political model of a grinding succession of just laws and unjust practice that is corrected by more and more specific just laws and new forms of unjust practice, with no end in sight. Needed for a model of applicative justice is an idea of a different kind of activity besides the crafting and promulgation of written law and opportunistic injustice based on its loopholes or lack of implementation.

A legitimate and recognized sphere of ongoing dialogue and commitment by and for aggrieved stakeholders can balance endless cycles of legal change and noncompliance. Such discourse has had limited pragmatic success so far, but it is a principled alternative to violent rebellion, passive submission, or vain hope. It is something that can be done which supports self-respect and builds community. Chapters 5 and 6 address some of the complexities of oppositional political discourse that has the goal of correcting injustice.

5

DISCOURSE, PROPHECY, AND ATMOSPHERE

U.S. Mood on Economy Up, Race Relations Sharply Down"
—Gallup, January 19, 2005[1]

The democratic aspiration is no mere recent phase in human history. It is human history. It permeated the ancient life of early peoples. It blazed anew in the middle ages. It was written in Magna Carta.
—Franklin Delano Roosevelt, 1941 Inaugural Address[2]

The term "discourse" can encompass all human interactions. Voting, buying a hat online, and publishing an academic paper are all forms of discourse. Discourse also includes art, emotional expression, moral response, political demonstration, and violence. Here, "discourse" refers to a part of political life or government process, in holistic Bentleyan terms. Oppositional political discourse, made up of speech and action that add to and have the potential to interrupt combinations of just law and unjust practice, has a special place in injustice theory. Its content occurs in intellectual norms, rhetoric, emotion, moral outrage, and physical action, as well as political theory. Overall, oppositional political discourse is distinct from the speech and action of government officials, because it seeks to motivate them to revise their decisions and change their policies.

It is important to draw a line between verbal and active discourse, because speech is not action. Some speech is a form of action more powerful than physical movement (e.g., judicial decisions and whistle-blowing), so the distinction must be contextualized. In any given context, we can consider "speech" to be discourse that does not have practical effects on its subject matter (e.g., a political philosophy book, like this one). Verbal discourse will be the main subject of this chapter and active discourse, which includes real-life action, will be considered in chapter 6. This chapter begins with general consideration of contemporary injustice discourse, followed by attention to: academic discourse; public discourse and atmosphere; the tradition of black prophecy as developed by Cornel West; and a note on the use and function of symbols, which occur between speech and action.

DIMENSIONS OF INJUSTICE DISCOURSE

Many critics of contemporary injustice seem to envision a flat, two-dimensional plane of justice and injustice, which is applied to specific contexts, parts of society, or the whole of society. One dimension consists of laws and principles of justice and the second, noncompliance with those laws and principles. The critics correctly assume that justice is compliance with the laws and principles of justice and that injustice is noncompliance with the laws and principles of justice. However, laws and principles of justice are not rules that prescribe specific behavior of compliance and criteria for noncompliance. There is a gap between just laws and principles and how people behave regarding them. Anything can and has happened in that gap between just laws and principles and compliance, including long periods of time in which the just laws and principles are ignored and those with power violate them with impunity.

Noncompliance with law has to be confirmed and addressed by additional legal procedures. This is lucidly evident in a criminal justice system that operates according to rules that positively describe offenses and penalties, which are applied by law enforcement, prosecutors, judges, juries, and those who administer the prison and probation system. The judicial system also has civil procedures for alleging offenses and proving noncompliance, for example, violation of fair housing laws. Noncompliance by private and other nongovernment parties has to be prosecuted in legal action. Noncompliance with law by government officials generates objections that may be verbal (talk and writing), legal (investigation, court cases, and appeals to lawmakers), or physical (demonstrations, strikes, and protests). Officials who behave unjustly may be reprimanded or punished, but that is no guarantee that the injustice will be corrected, or that it will not recur. Altogether, it seems safe to say that compliance with just laws and principles does not follow automatically or voluntarily and enthusiastically from statement of the laws and principles, so that the correction of noncompliance almost always requires legal or political action.

The two-dimensional approach to just laws and principles, and compliance or noncompliance with them, naïvely assumes that compliance is or should be automatic, and that the judgment that compliance should be automatic means that compliance will be automatic. As a result, both noncompliance and the required mechanics of remedies are viewed as extraordinary events and procedures. This naïve view may omit or neglect consideration of events and beliefs that cause, accompany, and follow noncompliant events. Critics are prone to obsess over isolated instances of noncompliance that are in reality only symptoms or "tropes" of much larger problems or conditions. Consider, for example, the death of Michael Brown in Ferguson, Missouri, which followed the attempt of a police officer to stop him. A US Department of Justice Report eventually connected the racial bias that made Brown appear to be a criminal suspect, with a municipal practice of deriving revenue from fines following disproportionate arrests of black residents for petty crimes.[3] Correcting the injustice of apparently racially biased law enforcement action in the service of municipal revenue collection requires legal recommendation, litigation, and changes in policy. There is also a wider economic and psychic context supporting the system of injustice that contributed to Brown's death, which includes insufficient municipal funding and a racial status system that makes it normal for whites to commit acts against blacks that would be impermissible to commit against whites.

It seems unproblematic to say, hypothetically, that if whites were treated in ways that blacks are treated, it would not be permitted. But this is a counter-factual hypothesis, which is rarely tested, because whites are not generally treated as blacks are treated. This is why, as indicated throughout the present text, it is important that the syntax of justice use comparative normative terms, for example, "Blacks should be treated as whites are treated," or, and perhaps more exactly, "*Blacks should not be treated as whites are not treated.*" If we could get to a broad state of affairs in which blacks were not treated as whites are not treated, that might be sufficient for a system to be racially just (although it might remain unjust in other ways).

Even more generally, there is a cultural moral system that permits and does not punish the economic exploitation of blacks with the use of legal institutions, such as law enforcement. Focusing only on the racially biased aspect of the immediate events leading to Brown's death, i.e., the putative heart-and-mind racism of the officer who shot him, or on the local practice of racially skewed municipal revenue collection, will not yield sufficient understanding of the injustice at issue. The injustice is part of a wider system where cities are strapped for funds that would be spent on both black and white residents. The use of law enforcement to target blacks entails that blacks disproportionately pay for such services, including not only money turned over in fines, but the suffering unto death from biased punitive practices against them. It would take substantial legal and political work to change that system. Moral condemnation and public protest by those who perceive the injustice do not in themselves or together have the power to change the system or even effectively motivate those who could directly change the system. Racial bias and exploitation are just as much a part of the government process in this case as are written just laws and their underlying legal principles. There is, of course, an important expressive and communicative role for moral condemnation and public protest, but that does not make them sufficient to correct injustices that are an integral part of stable practice. For instance, the city of Ferguson could raise taxes. This is not to suggest that a financial revision of how cities collect money and from whom would completely address race-related injustice, because contentions over how sufficient funds would be spent or what services would be cut would then ensue. And the situation is further complicated by unemployment related to outsourcing in a global capitalistic system. But as we will see, understanding a complete situation resulting in a specific unjust event is not the same thing as implementing change in the part of the system that generated that event, for instance, reform of racially biased police practices.

The Asymmetry between Perceived Justice and Injustice

There is an asymmetry between justice and injustice that can mask how difficult it is to replace a system that results in injustice with a just one. Justice often consists in very large numbers of events that do not take place. Injustice, by contrast, can be defined by a much smaller number of events that issue from multiple sources and tributaries, which may not in themselves all be unjust. Thus, although justice can be understood as compliance with just laws and principles, understanding injustice requires complex navigation through thickets of needs, wants, practices, and ideologies. In this way, justice is like goodness, health, and beauty, with not a lot of difference in the conditions of those who enjoy each of them and myriad variations in the conditions that fall short of standards and ideals. Moreover, a racially just system would involve changes in behavior by many more people than the victims of injustice whose experience is sufficient to deem a system racially unjust. As a result, it is more difficult to change an unjust system into a just one than to create an unjust system.

Explanation versus Correction

The critic of racial injustice should be mindful of how much of the general economic, political, and social system and its institutional structures would have to be changed for the system to be racially just. Is it necessary, for example, to exchange capitalism for socialism, as some contemporary critics insist? Toward answering such questions, a distinction between explanation and correction is necessary. As theorists, we probably should begin with requirements for explanation that further understanding. But it is important to keep in mind that an understanding of racial justice and injustice is not the same thing as a determination of how to correct any specific injustice or type of injustice. Determination of the extent of system changes necessary for there to be racial justice in specific cases proceeds through analyses of different institutional levels. To continue with the Ferguson case, on a more general level, it is well documented that throughout the United States, many laws, such as drug laws and public loitering, are not enforced for whites, but are aggressively and often violently enforced for blacks.[4] Disproportionate stops and frisks of blacks are a degenerate application of the Broken Window Theory that was originally introduced as a way to build community, as well as forestall serious crime.[5] An account in terms of racism, as a hearts-and-minds condition of individuals, begins to add more depth to an analysis of injustice, but attention to psychological pathology and moral failing will not complete the analysis without consideration of economic practices of employment and profit-seeking within something like a "prison industry." And, examination of the prison industry will not complete the discourse without consideration of racism, again, but this time with awareness of how the *intersection* of economic motivation and social status based on race works to sustain unjust racially biased legal practices.[6] Such multidimensional consideration of racial profiling by police officers, as a form of injustice, would show how revenue-motivated racial profiling and degenerate applications of the Broken Window Theory are part of a larger economic structure of antiblack economic exploitation. Neither reference to comparative white privilege, nor Fourth Amendment protections against unreasonable searches and seizures or Fourteenth Amendment protections against unequal treatment by law officials, can alone or together accomplish such an explanation. If the protective constitutional structure is revitalized in application to such cases, it should be expected that new economic arrangements of race-based exploitation will arise without change in the broader system whereby racial status intersects with law enforcement discretion and carceral economics. And there are also eddies of sub-explanation, such as the fact that police officers may be required or expected by their superior officers to meet numerical quotas of stops and frisks.[7]

Without regard for these kinds of complexities and attention to relevant institutional structures, discourse about injustice is often immature, as if pointing out an isolated symptom is all that is required to understand and correct injustice. However, descriptions of the isolated symptom may be all that is required to design action to correct it, although whether or not the action does correct it is an empirical matter that will also require criteria for successful correction. Verbal discourse regarding injustice that is limited to complaint, blame, and vilification of those responsible for the injustice moves from the effects on victims of the noncompliance or injustice suffered by them to the guilt of perpetrators. Suffering and death are grieved and racism is excoriated—as they should be—but racists become increasingly difficult to pinpoint in a society with formal legal equality and so many who "just don't see color" or never "consciously" discriminate, at least not on racial grounds alone. Accusations of hearts and minds racism thus encounter a dead-end—they can't be proved if alleged racists deny that they are racists.

White Privilege Discourse

In contrast to what nonwhites experience compared to whites, whites appear privileged and so the liberatory discourse then shifts from blame and guilt to "white privilege." Whites who participate in that discourse painstakingly interrogate and articulate their many "privileges" on the grounds of race. But they may thereby reinscribe the very situation decried, because their discourse typically yields no concrete intentions or plans for change and does not motivate action. The broad, encompassing social situation may be called "white supremacist" by progressive members of all racial groups, but use of that epithet does not in itself serve to undo the conditions that are adduced to render it accurate, unless there is a comprehensive understanding of systematic factors holding those conditions in place.[8]

Worse than the superficiality of merely affixing the label "white supremacy" is obfuscation of violation of the rights of those, in contrast with whom, whites are deemed "privileged." Rather than stop with the view of whites as privileged—which they undoubtedly are compared to nonwhites—it is important to understand how (and where and when) their rights have not been violated and how they have been treated in ways that are compliant with justice. These justice-compliant conditions (e.g., police officers are not as aggressive to whites as they are to blacks in violation of their constitutional protections) are important to recognize, because contrasting noncompliant acts can be identified only relative to them. It should not be surprising in the United States that justice-compliant conditions are often ontologically negative, a matter of what does not happen to some people. There is a very strong tradition of both locating rights in what government officials may not do to others (e.g., murder, arbitrary searches and seizures, theft, censorship, interference with religion), along with the failure to extend those prohibitions to nonwhites. It is often overlooked how valuable not having something done to one may be, because discussions of constitutional rights are often critical of government officials on grounds that they have failed to take positive action that would have protected rights.[9] Liberatory discourse has become altogether more comfortable with demanding positive government action, in contrast to insisting that government officials stand down from certain intrusions. In current politics, it has been left to conservative Republicans to ask government not to do certain things and Democrats have been so caught up in the value of what they think government ought to do (e.g., single payer health care, support of affirmative action, or increased AFD funding) that they have neglected the value of government *not* doing certain things (e.g., aggressive racially biased stops and frisks, invasion of electronic privacy, harassment of homeless people).

The discourse of "racism without racists," white privilege discourse, and nonwhite grief and complaint can become a self-contained medium of expression for moral outrage, blame, defensiveness, and self-righteousness. Lacking in that medium is awareness and self-reflection about the status of the content of this verbal discourse as verbal discourse. We also need to distinguish between this content and who produces it—between what is said and who says it—because the racial identities of participants become a silent factor in the discourse, along with audible speech (or writing). Real people with racial identities engage in liberatory discourse, as an embodied activity involving their individual life projects and sources of satisfaction and employment (e.g., for academics). However, this material reality of their discourse participation is often overlooked by them, so that many present their contributions to the discourse of white privilege, as though their white racial identities did not silently play an active role in what they say, even beyond their explicit self-identifications as racially white. Thus, although many white academic participants in the discourse of white privilege proclaim their awareness of their own white racial identities, they usually do not stop to consider how that *explicit* awareness may augment the injustice they are seeking to correct: "I'm white, I'm unjustly privileged, the entire system protects my privilege, and there is no change in sight, because that system is white supremacist!" If they considered how their racial presence in the discourse of white privilege augments white privilege in reality, their good faith continuation in the discourse would require something more.[10] Perhaps admitting what people of color already know—that is, that they are white, is not enough without also signaling that this admission is meant to acknowledge the impossibility of being color-blind in contemporary US society and acknowledge that color vision picks out and picks on nonwhites. Or, there could be an intention expressed that the discourse of white privilege as undertaken by whites is only the first step in a process of racial reconciliation, whereby those who belong to an oppressor group based merely on their ineradicable appearances and family genealogies are *performatively* owning up to that fact about themselves. However, it is by no means clear that there can be reconciliation while injustice is ongoing. So maybe it would more realistic to suggest that the self-recognition of white racial identities at this time could qualify as a first step toward cooperation with nonwhites toward the correction of injustice.

ACADEMIC INJUSTICE DISCOURSE

Just law can coexist with unjust practice and both are parts of "empirical law" or what Bentley called "the process of government." Empirical law is constantly changing and some theorists are optimistic that verbal discourse has the ability to make written law more just, even though the same unjust practices recur or new ones emerge. These theorists, some of whom are or may aspire to become public intellectuals, hope that someday public political discourse on behalf of those who are treated unjustly will have the power to interrupt a cycle of just written law accompanied by continued unjust practice. That is, the "right" discourse perennially holds the promise of changing the beliefs, values, and goals of everyone in the public auditorium, so that the same kind of unjust practices do not perpetually chase the same kinds of just laws.[11] This search for "magic words" is futile for academics who are professionally confined to dry and abstract prose. Our verbiage does not have the power to move the multitudes who do not read or listen to it anyway. But even when multitudes are inspired and emotionally stirred by great orators, action that follows is unlikely to result in lasting change, without the support of powerful interests.

After the 1960s, academics began a robust practice of liberatory discourse about injustice that seems to grow more impassioned and intense each year. The quest for demographic diversity among students and faculty in higher education has weathered judicial defeat of explicit affirmative action policies, but only partly for the sake of justice. There are pragmatic prizes if the academy can justify itself by producing a racially integrated leadership and managerial class for business, politics, and the military. Top leaders throughout society realize that they need such racial diversity for broad consumption, voter support, and boots on the ground, and the expression of that need is evident in *amicus curiae* briefs submitted to the US Supreme Court as it has been torturously dismantling affirmative action, piece by piece, since *Bakke* in 1978.[12]

Academic political discourse has been deeper than polemics and debate, exactly because of its disciplined intellectual origins in different fields of study (i.e., discipline imposed by distinct "disciplines"). But it has been swimming upstream against a more rarefied and older academic tradition, particularly among many philosophers and their gate keepers outside of the profession. Even Hannah Arendt (see chapter 2) spoke approvingly of the life of the mind as cut off from real political activity that occurred in the realm of "opinion." In her 1970 interview with Adelbert Reif, Arendt addressed the phenomenon of college-student protestors, noting that they had brought social change through optimistic belief in their ability to make a better world, while at the same time discovering joy in civic participation. Arendt credited such protests with the success of the civil rights movement and progress toward ending the Vietnam War.[13] As discussed in chapter 4, it is doubtful that Arendt was correct that student protests caused the success of the civil rights movement. A historical analysis of the end to the Vietnam War is beyond the present scope, but what we already know about empirical Bentleyan analyses would warrant skepticism about Arendt's causal thesis there as well.

In the same interview, Arendt warned that demonstrations by student activists could be self-defeating in democratic Euro-American contexts, because in attacking their universities, they were attacking the very entities that made their protests possible.[14] American universities, especially large state schools that were the sites of the protests Arendt had in mind, have perforce developed very different financial structures since 1970. These schools have become increasingly dependent on private corporate and philanthropic funding, with state government funds now a much reduced part of their budgets.[15] While this structural change is not generally viewed as an incursion on academic freedom, it has been coincident with a very flat era of student protest and activism. Still, Arendt's notion of the "life of the mind" remains useful if we consider that the progressive/change-seeking output of professional academics since 1970 has been professionally accepted in the institutions that employ its participants. Also, much of today's liberatory academic discourse can be viewed as the legacy of earlier student protest, furthering a tradition that may have been founded when some of the 1960s student radicals became professors. This indicates that the connection between academic radicals and the hands that feed them is not as simple as Arendt thought. In the United States, everything now points to both the existence of real academic freedom and its real ineffectiveness.

Progressive academic writers ply a craft of formal speech that deals with contemporary injustice through complex theoretical frameworks, with requisite scholarly apparatuses and without translation into more simple views of the world; there is often also a lack of translation from one discipline to another or between subdisciplines in the same field. The audience is other academics and students. Neither specialization nor the limited and partly captive audience should be viewed as problematic because that is the nature of academic work, given broad social divisions of labor. But there is a problem with the delusional nature of so much of this work. The delusion consists of a naïve view of the power of academic speech to directly change reality. The rhetorical mode of address used by academics writing cultural criticism, political philosophy, social philosophy, or what is now called social-political philosophy (which combines the other subfield approaches), often proceeds as though its authors are making grand entries in a planetary cabala, where words have the immediate power to become their intended referents.

Those who do not write and speak cabalistically may subscribe to the Trickle-Down Good Ideas Theory that can be traced from Plato to John Stuart Mill to John Rawls. Subscription to that theory is immediately self-flattering, but it lacks reliable empirical support.[16] Although, after the US civil rights movement, there has been an uncanny coincidence of race-blind formal racial equality with the hegemony in political philosophy of Rawls's requirement that those who plan fundamental social institutions do so in ignorance of their own societal environments. As we saw in chapter 1, Rawls was quite explicit about this:

> I assume that the parties do not know the particular circumstances of their own society. That is, they do not know its economic or political situation, or the level of civilization and culture it has been able to

achieve. The persons in the original position have no information as to which generation they belong.[17]

Both race-blind racial equality and Rawlsian ideals are compatible with race-based real inequality. There are, of course, counter-examples, such as Katherine MacKinnon's work on sexual harassment in the workplace, as expressed in current law and institutional policy.[18] Nevertheless, even very good academic political discourse about justice and injustice cannot be relied upon to attract implementation or application in real life. This may be because there has not been sufficient time for the development of training programs for a new profession of "bridgers," who could translate good ideas in the academy for those who govern and make policy. An internal problem for such translators would be to decide where to anchor their bridges in fields—every humanistic field—where experts disagree. However, the current tradition of progressive academic writing and speech is less than half a century old and if and when such translators emerge, they will develop their own professional criteria for choosing among contending experts.

PUBLIC DISCOURSE, ATMOSPHERE, AND CLIMATE

Public media, as a democratic analogue to disagreement within academic discourse, supports the idea that expressing and airing views in day-to-day practices or special "national conversations" also have immediate practical results. It is not evident how there could be such results, when opposing views and opinions are treated with the same respect and have equal access to the same mass auditorium that lacks rules for evidence or valid argument. As with academic discourse, there is no structured connection to official decision processes. The only reliable result of participation in such unbinding referenda is that those who participate are able to express themselves and get attention that may benefit them in the marketplace of their related endeavors.

Public expression also serves to represent and create collective atmospheres of belief, attitude, and opinion. These atmospheres are implicitly known by a majority of people in the culture, even though such knowledge is difficult to validate. Ambiguities cannot be resolved by recourse to public opinion polls, because understanding the results of those polls requires creative interpretive skills that draw on what is already known about relevant atmospheres. For example, suppose that more blacks than whites believe that white privilege is real and that O. J. Simpson was innocent, or that more whites than blacks believe that white American police officers are not, in general, racially biased. Are the views of whites evidence of racial bias or racial oblivion? Are the views of blacks evidence of racial preference or paranoia? Moreover, such polls almost always have a large racial overlap of opinion: If 29 percent of blacks compared to 71 percent of whites believe X, then 71 percent of blacks and 29 percent of whites do not believe X. Does this mean that the percentages of each group that does not contribute to the discrepancy in belief recorded in the polls are in some degree of agreement?

Experiments in social psychology could be designed to answer such questions and others like them, but it is important to decide beforehand why the data is important and what it does and does not indicate. For instance, testing the claim that white privilege is a reality of contemporary life requires some prior definition of what is meant by "white privilege," which can range from injustice to social courtesies. In a widely discussed 2013 experiment conducted in Queensland, Australia, economists Redzo Mujcic and Paul Frijters found that the majority of free bus rides, based on conductor generosity, were dispensed to whites, with blacks least likely to receive this courtesy, compared to all other racial groups among commuters. Journalist Britni Danielle, writing for a general audience on *Yahoo News*, touted this study as evidence that "white privilege is real," without distinguishing between an amenity such as a free bus ride and recognition of one's rights by not being subject to arbitrary stops and frisks by police officers.[19] Conservatives reading Mujcic and Frijter's study might say that the bus driver may have been acting rationally based on past experience with unruly black passengers. From a progressive perspective, more specifics would need to be introduced to defend the claim that this study revealed white privilege, such as controls for the apparent social class and gender of passengers, as well as the preexisting racial climate among bus commuters in Queensland, as well as the broader racial atmosphere throughout Australia in 2013.

The 2015 Academy Awards

What is racial atmosphere and climate? A US example that is also global could help clarify these vague ideas, provided that it is understood beforehand that in this context, as in most public references to "race," "racial" means "pertaining to racism." From beginning to middle to end, the 2015 Academy Awards ceremony hit racist notes that slid by, unchecked, because it was an occasion of celebration. Neil Patrick Harris, the host, began with what might have been a critical remark about the lack of racial diversity among audience members and award winners: "Tonight we honor Hollywood's best and whitest, sorry, brightest." For those who were uncomfortable with the lack of robust racial diversity among audience members and award winners, his remark might have validated their unease. But those who would have been uncomfortable with more racial diversity may have been heard "best and whitest" as support for their social values. (The discourse of white privilege as a critique of contemporary anti-nonwhite racism is, as indicated, that kind of double-edged sword.)

Midway through the ceremony, Patricia Arquette called for people of color and members of the lesbian, bisexual, gay, and transgender (LBGT) community to support legislation for equal pay for women and to commit themselves to supporting women, thereby overlooking the women who were either or both people of color and members of the LGBT community. This kind of oversight may perhaps be excused by Arquette's ignorance of what academics have been for decades analyzing as "intersectionality." But Sean Penn's remark at the grand finale awarding for Best Picture to Alejandro González Iñárritu, the Mexican director of *Birdman*, was simply, explicitly, racist: "Who gave this son of a bitch a green card?" Iñárritu later brushed off the insult by saying he found it "hilarious," because "Sean and I have that kind of brutal relationship. I think it was very funny."[20] Iñárritu's attempt at a "save" for Penn does not address the impact of Penn's insult on other Mexicans and Mexican Americans, including those without green cards who struggle to remain employed in the face of anti-immigrant prejudice and discrimination. (That such a moment of maximum recognition was brought so low by a racist crack is not unusual in US culture, where the nastiest forms of racist insult are often let loose on people of color who have succeeded.)

As a spectacle watched by almost thirty-four million, the 2015 Oscars, despite ratings lower than recent years, was a global public event.[21] Symbolically, it has no peer for the display of beauty, talent, and artistic creativity. Its subtext inevitably has implications about current American race relations, which influence their future. The racial implications of the Oscars replays in millions of minds at countless other public celebrations and entertainment venues, as well as in private interactions (for a year at least). Such spectacles are forms of public discourse and what they represent or fail to represent about US racial demographics and the attitude of the dominant white group creates or augments a specific racial climate that in 2015 is part of a more general racial atmosphere of ambiguity and indeterminacy.

At the 2015 Academy Awards, for many critical observers, the issue or subject pertaining to race (insofar as it is understood that subjects of race are subjects of racism), was *recognition.*[22] The beauty, talent, and artistic creativity of people of color was not fully recognized. Some people of color did get awards and some audience members were people of color, so recognition, along with diversity, was not completely absent. But there appeared to be insufficient racial diversity for audience and award winners to be considered racially integrated. And that appearance was symbolic. However, the symbolic meaning is ambiguous: Were there people of color who were deserving of awards but did not get them because they were people of color? Is race a factor in who becomes a member of the Academy of Motion Picture Arts and Sciences? In the future, will the racial makeup of award winners become more or less representative of their proportions in the motion picture industry? If the proportion of people of color in the motion picture industry is not proportional to their presence in the population at large, why is that? The answers to these questions are undetermined in the symbolic spectacle of the 2015 Academy Awards. The observer does not know if recognition of the achievements of people of color in the movie industry will improve, stay the same, or get worse, and she does not know how to find out. The racial (i.e., in regards to racism) climate of the Academy Awards is cloudy, subject to many different interpretations, some of them conflicting. It is an epistemologically unstable racial climate, because people of color do not know what the weather is in that climate, as a basis for prediction, and neither do they know how to find out.

Racial Climates and Atmospheres

A racial climate is a common sense in a community or institution of the meaning of racial difference and how it is expressed between and among people of different races. There is a national atmosphere, there are climates in higher education, subclimates in particular, universities and colleges, and even sub-subclimates in departments; the same structure can be applied to geographical locations, down to sub-subclimates of neighborhoods, apartment buildings, and clusters of single family houses. Any given racial climate provides a subtext for understanding interracial interactions, and it also predisposes people toward some racist or nonracist beliefs and actions, in preference to others. It is not a coincidence that weather-words have been used after an officially successful civil rights movement that was followed by the legal attenuation of affirmative action policies, as well as other forms of what Vesla Weaver has so aptly called "frontlash."[23] Like the weather, predictions of future trends are not completely reliable. There have been steps forward and backward toward racial justice, and although explicit white supremacists are anomalous in public life, racism has become amorphous, difficult to detect, and difficult to prove, but undeniably present.

Posits of specific racial climates and general racial atmospheres in contexts of larger wholes need not be "imaginaries" in the postmodern sense of a shared default system of beliefs, images, myths, or reified ideas. Rather, at this time, the most striking aspect of racial atmosphere and climate is its indeterminacy with regard to racism. People of color do not know what is going to happen, which way the country is going, what will happen in higher education, or how they or their children will fare in their schools and neighborhoods. People of color do not know whether or not the whites they interact with approach those interactions with ethical commitments shared across racial differences, or with predispositions to interact on the basis of white dominance or racism. Ethical whites do not know how other whites will behave or what is expected of them by nonwhites. Whites who are predisposed to take advantage of their dominance are constrained by not wanting to appear racist, but they may not even know what is racist or whether they are racists. And if they are racists and know it, they may not know whether or not they will be found out and punished, or continue to get away with racist behavior.

The shared judgment throughout the American atmosphere of race in the early twenty-first century is that racism is morally bad. This judgment is a general principle that leaves the nature of racism undefined throughout the atmosphere and most of the climates and subclimates of race. The overriding shared judgment is a bitter and ineffective refuge for nonwhites, because it does not protect them from either First Amendment–protected racist expressions or actions that turn out to be indirectly racist. Energetic self-aware racist whites can try to evade the judgment that they are racist through coded language for racial difference, and the use of intermediate activities and traits as subjects of direct action. That is, something other than race, which nonetheless does a good job of picking out members of a specific racial group, can be used instead of the race of that group to maintain prejudice and legitimize discrimination.

The term "racial climate" has a history of meaning "micro-aggressions" based on race, small cuts, insults, and slights that can have a cumulative effect of individual harm.[24] In using the term "racial atmosphere," reference may be made to other issues of harm to people of color, such as ignorance of black history and contemporary racism or discrimination in career advancement.[25] The implication of these meanings is that the micro-aggressions add up to what is perceived as a general predisposition of white people to treat people of color in unjust ways. But, at this time, ideas of racial atmosphere and climate also work as metaphors for what is unknown about race relations and attitudes; they capture the vagueness and unpredictability of racial prejudice and discrimination that occur in a society where nonwhites remain disadvantaged, even though there is formal equality. This "vague weather" aspect of atmosphere and climate is an epistemological condition of indecision that may or may not constitute a lasting crisis, although some syndromes of political injustice should be viewed as crises.

A crisis is a period of indecision and uncertainty that requires a resolution before life can go on. Will blacks and other people of color achieve more equality with whites, or is the United States—and with it the world, because US racism is exported with business practices, tourism, and entertainment products—on the brink of a new era of explicit and direct oppression of people of color? Are most white Americans, whose race-neutral economic and social activities have racist effects on nonwhites, genuinely ignorant of how the system in which they operate works, or are they secretly but knowingly hearts-and-minds racists? It is not clear that this indeterminate aspect of present racial atmosphere and climates must be resolved now. We do not know if life can go on if it is not resolved or what it means for life to go on, or not. We do not even know if the putative crisis can be resolved at this time, because there is as yet no systematic and sustained, impassioned, liberatory discourse for our condition of ambiguity, a time with a black president and police killing with impunity of unarmed black youth, a time of voting rights for everyone but new restrictions and requirements that disproportionately affect African Americans.[26] Except for what academics write and say and how important they think their discourse is (among themselves), American discourse of racial liberation is at a standstill. And insofar as academic discourse is uttered and received in a closed system, with a semicaptive audience and no reliable means for it to affect the real world, that standstill remains at the disposal of history, where history is understood to be the unpredictable result of contingent events. However, if academic oppositional political discourse can be related to a longer historical trend, a more coherent and optimistic picture might emerge. Cornel West's ideas about the American black prophetic tradition appears to be a relation to such a trend.

CORNEL WEST'S PARADIGM OF THE BLACK PROPHETIC TRADITION

It is important to recognize Cornel West's protean background in consideration of his major philosophical claims. West has had a very productive career, publishing fifteen or twenty books and maintaining a schedule of two or three talks a week for decades. His academic credentials are impeccable. He studied at Yale University, taught at Union Theological Seminary, Harvard University, Princeton University, and most recently, back to Union. His academic positions have been in departments of religion and African American studies, but many philosophers of race have claimed him, also, and he has not completely repudiated that disciplinary ascription, although unlike other philosophers, he says about himself: "I'm a blues man in the life of the mind. I'm a jazz man in the world of ideas."[27]

West has been recognized as a public intellectual by people of all races and is one of the most well-known African American voices to contemporary youth, their parents, and civil rights–era grandparents. He regularly presents his thought in television and radio interviews,[28] with speech that like his writing is highly erudite, spanning the whole Western humanist tradition with an encyclopedic knowledge of black history, appreciation of black popular music, and insistence on Christian spirituality as a source of individual dignity. He has recorded hip-hop music, both solo and with a band called Cornel West Theory; he played the role of Councilor West in the movies *Matrix Reloaded* and *Matrix Revolutions*.

West's mode of address consistently has the cadenced grandeur of a prophet of his times.[29] His writing reverberates in his speech and after a while, in reading his prose, one hears him speaking. The content of West's discourse is literally reiterated throughout his publications, talks, and critical exchanges. Overall, he seeks to alleviate and redignify conditions of human suffering by proceeding from the experience of African Americans. His advocacy of socialism is motivated by an ethical interpretation of Marxism, combined with the ultimately altruistic selfless love of others exemplified by Jesus Christ. But his resultant "radical democracy" is grounded on the suffering of African Americans. West describes himself as a "Chekovian Christian," because human death and other tragedies are unavoidable, and he constructs and draws on the tradition of black prophecy to develop a dignified stance of hope in the face of such gloom and doom.[30]

Similar to many liberatory theories, West's paradigm of the Black Prophetic Tradition is both descriptive and normative. West has been developing this paradigm at least since the early 1980s and he is aware both of the nature of his own work as discourse and of historical vicissitudes in real life politics that result in uneven progress toward racial justice in reality. In his first book, *Prophesy Deliverance!: An Afro-American Revolutionary Christianity*, he wrote in 1982:

> The object of inquiry for Afro-American critical thought is the past and the present, the doings and the sufferings of African people in the United States. Rather than a new scientific discipline or field of study, it is a genre of writing, a textuality, a mode of discourse that interprets, describes, and evaluates Afro-American life in order comprehensively to understand and effectively to transform it. It is not

> concerned with "foundations" or transcendental "grounds" but with how to build its language in such a way that the configuration of sentences and the constellation of paragraphs themselves create a textuality and distinctive discourse which are a material force for Afro-American freedom.[31]

West's expressed intention in 1982—and nothing that he has done since then suggests that he has ever waivered from that intention—is to create a form of speech that can become a real causal force for black liberation in the United States. In other words, West is here explicit about his belief in the power of cabalistic rhetoric and the existence of "magic words." In this way, he is like many other academics, but also unlike them insofar as his approach has religious overtones and strong poetic-rhetorical values.

There is an even greater methodological distance between West and other philosophers. It seems reasonable to assume that a philosopher constructing a black tradition would refer to the texts of past black philosophers as a main source of inspiration, as well as reference. West instead turns to music and claims that the thought of Alain Locke, W.E.B. Du Bois, and Sylvia Winters is not in the same league of genius as the *intellectual* (not experiential) work of Duke Ellington, Louis Armstrong, and above all, Sarah Vaughan.[32] West has made it clear that he "ironically nurtured in the academy" his interest in literature as opposed to philosophy and there is no reason to believe that the same is not true of his interest in music.[33]

However, West understands that the timing between prophecy and what it delivers is difficult to predict. West staged an event in Riverside Church in November 2014, in dialogue with Bob Avakian, the Chairman of the Radical Communist Party, USA. The result was the 2015 film, *Religion and Revolution: A Dialogue between Cornel West and Bob Avakian*. West there says that the ruling class "won" over the past thirty years, but that progress is often interrupted by regress, so that after the breakthrough of the civil rights movement, when a small number succeeded, there has been regress.[34] In his *Black Prophetic Fire* discussion with Christa Buschendorf about Ella Baker, West distinguishes between immediate events in "market time" and "democratic time," which in Raymond Williams's terms constitutes a "long revolution."[35] We should understand that prophecy for West is not prediction of the future:

> The prophetic has little or nothing to do with prediction. Instead, it has to do with identifying, analyzing, and condemning forms of evil and forging vision, hope, and courage for selves and communities to overcome them. Radical democracy is visionary plebodicy—the grand expression of the dignity of the doxa of the suffering demos.[36]

West himself regularly performs prophecy as a certain stance toward injustice and human suffering—that is, a willingness and ability to speak the truth about what for us mortals is evil. In his 2011 address to three thousand people at Riverside Church in New York City, for an event commemorating the fortieth anniversary of the 1971 riot in Attica Prison, West said about courage at the present time:

> The condition of truth is to allow suffering to speak. If you don't talk about poverty, you're not telling the truth. If you're not talking about working people being pushed against the wall, with corporate profits high, you're not telling the truth. If you're not talking about the criminal activity on Wall Street and not one person gone to jail yet, you're not telling the truth. Don't tell me about the crime on the block with brothers and sisters and Jamal and Latisha out taken to jail, and yet gangsters who are engaged in fraudulent activity, insider trading, market manipulation, walking around having tea at night.[37]

But prophetic inspiration also comes from the past for West. He said about Ida B. Wells in his 2014 interview with Christa Buschendorf:

> She stands between Frederick Douglass and W. E. B. Du Bois and she knew both men personally. Wells was the pioneering figure in the anti-lynching campaigns of her day, and the way in which she courageously and undauntedly took up a difficult and dangerous struggle against prejudices about the "beastly nature" of the Black man, certainly renders her a worthy candidate in our series of long-distance freedom fighters in the Black prophetic tradition. . . . Ida B. Wells, in so many ways, teaches us something that we rarely want to acknowledge: that the black freedom movement has always been an anti-terrorist movement, that black people in America had a choice between creating a Black al-Qaeda or a movement like Ida B. Wells's, which was going to call into question the bestiality and barbarity and brutality of Jim Crow and American terrorism and lynching, but would do it in the name of something that provided a higher moral ground and a higher spiritual ground given her Christian

faith . . . she said: "We want a higher moral ground, but I'm going to hit this issue head-on."[38]

Not only is timing the fulfillment of black prophecy impossible, but there is no guarantee it will be fulfilled. At the close of his Attica address, West indicated that the willingness to continue the fight might be more important than winning:

> We're going to have a new wave of truth telling. We're going to have a new wave of witness bearing. And we're going to teach the younger generation that these brothers didn't struggle in vain, just like John Brown and Nat Turner and Marcus Garvey and Martin King and Myles Horton and the others didn't. And we shall see what happens. We might get crushed, too. But you know what? Then you just go down swinging, like Ella Fitzgerald and Muhammad Ali.[39]

The title of West's Riverside Church address, "Attica Is All of Us," was cashed out in this talk and subsequent talks and publications. For West, Attica is all of us after 9/11, because it was the beginning of the "niggerization" of all Americans. He has repeatedly claimed, following Malcolm X, that the oppression of a people is equal to what they will accept without resistance:

> America been niggerized since 9/11. When you're niggerized, you're unsafe, unprotected, subject to random violence, hated for who you are. You become so scared that you defer to the powers that be, and you're willing to consent to your own domination. And that's the history of black people in America.[40]

However, it is not only American black people who have been niggerized, according to West, but all post-9/11 Americans who live in fear:

> The Black prophetic tradition has never been confined to the interests and situations of Black people. It is rooted in principles and visions that embrace these interests and confront the situations, but its message is for the country and world. The Black prophetic tradition has been the leaven in the American democratic loaf. When the Black prophetic tradition is strong, poor and working people of all colors benefit. When the black prophetic tradition is weak, poor and working class people are overlooked. On the international level, when the Black prophetic tradition is vital and vibrant, anti-imperial

> critiques are intense, and the plight of the wretched of the earth is elevated. What does it profit a people for a symbolic figure to gain presidential power if we turn our backs from the suffering of poor and working people, and thereby lose our souls?[41]

The symbolic figure who has gained presidential power, to whom Cornel West repeatedly refers in such terms is, of course, President Barack Obama, "the first black president of the United States."[42] At first, West sounded hopeful about Obama, disclosing after his 2008 election: "I hope he is a progressive Lincoln, I aspire to be the Frederick Douglass to put pressure on him."[43] In other words, black prophecy might require the human agency of those inspired by it in order to activate "the material force for Afro-American freedom." If this is a correct inference, then West does not fully believe that the discourse of the black prophetic tradition can directly cause change and that would reduce this discourse to a form of secular rhetoric and persuasion.

In recent controversies with other black intellectuals, public figures, and activists, West's criticism of President Barack Obama's political, military, and economic policies has been operatic: "Ferguson signifies the end of the age of Obama," because of the injustice of the "Jim Crow US prison system that does not deliver justice to black and brown people."[44] In claiming to represent global suffering in the tradition of Frantz Fanon, West has referred to Obama's "empty neutrality, moral bankruptcy, and political cowardice."[45]

Philosophical Aspects of West's Prophecy

"My existential soulmates and intellectual sources are more life-wrestling artists than academic philosophers."[46] It is easy to understand what West rejects about academic philosophy, its cold abstraction and dryness. He works in a number of dimensions, writing and speaking for academics, college students, and general readers, and delivering public discourse for wider audiences. His thought is available on an official website and a You Tube channel with over eighty thousand entries.[47] His public prophecy and public political criticism have the same content as his writing and speech on college campuses. Therefore West's writings about the black prophetic tradition and his public political criticism can be taken together as part of a cognitive structure that is grist for abstract and dry philosophical criticism. West's basic historical insight is that black Americans have suffered unjustly, from pain and death inflicted by whites, as well as from their own nihilism, a spiritual failure to use the strength from their belief in God to face up to their ills courageously, and with dignity. Talking about black history and current battles is in itself, according to West, a valuable and worthy activity. However, his ideas and reaction to their rejection, taken together, indicate that he does not hold participation in this discourse to be morally optional, but, rather, that it is obligatory for certain people, namely black men in power. West expresses bitterness and rage when those in political office and activists such as Reverend Al Sharpton, who he thinks should join him in the black prophetic tradition, choose not to do so. Such castigation may be part of the exhortation that goes along with the preacherly aspect of West's role as a public prophet, but it is problematic for those of us who value the detachment of academic philosophy.

But what if West is right about the wrongness of the American path in moral humanistic terms? Rightness or wrongness makes no difference if others choose not to live within the black prophetic tradition, whether they do so in order to remain addicted to drugs, or to preserve their political careers, or because it does not fit into their lifestyles. The point is that in not being willing to accept disagreement or lack of interest from some people, West has turned a profound construction of an historical liberatory black tradition into an insistent ideology. West does not have the usual defense of the intellectual who claims that what he does as a person should not be used as an attack on his ideas. Because West, as a public prophet for a people, has made himself an integral part of the content of the prophecy he preaches, he has become like Midas in making black prophecy inert and lifeless in its impermeability to those who may not be with him, but are not necessarily against him.

For instance, not all advocates of black liberation within the United States or critics of the racial imbalance of the US criminal justice system agree that it is necessary to change American foreign policy or the structure of global finance in order to correct the ills of racial bias. But the globally holistic nature of West's critique does make it seem as though such fundamental institutions must be overthrown for the correction of social injustice. For a specific example already broached at the beginning of this chapter, homicide resulting from police racial profiling would be reduced if police had more cautious rules of engagement for approaching suspects.[48] This is not to say that a full understanding of contemporary racism in the United States does not require a sweeping analysis such as West's ethical Marxism, but that correction of specific conditions of suffering may not need it. It is an empirical question whether some things can be fixed without overthrowing everything, but West's insistent ideological stance blocks such questions from being asked.

However, such academic criticism of West's paradigm of the black prophetic tradition is not the end of the story. By reaching into real life public political discourse, from history, religion, and philosophy, all rolled up into one, West forces political philosophers to think about new subjects that include what thinkers who exceed the academy say. This provides a new dimension to contemporary political philosophy, as well as it reaffirms the power of spoken discourse within its own realm, and might weaken skepticism about magic words. West's written and spoken utterances remain on the verbal side of discourse, but in taking the contemporary world as a subject, he has opened a window out of the academy for cultural analysis and criticism. When West refers to historical black figures in constructing the black prophetic tradition, he brings accounts of their lives and ideas into the "magic-word" aspect of his own discourse, which is also a new approach to intellectual history.

To do philosophy or present other complex thought in public, and for the public, is not an easy task, because it calls for communication skills and nonspecialized language, which many academic philosophers have not yet developed. The degree of controversy centered on matters of race in which West has immersed himself, in a public auditorium with many reactionaries, probably carries personal risks and stresses that would be beyond the capability to sustain, of even the most highly skilled ninjas of academic politics. Time will tell whether others who identify or are claimed as philosophers successfully emulate West's kind of project.

THE DISCOURSE OF SYMBOLS

Symbols are perceptible forms of identities, beliefs, and exhortations. No one doubts that they are important. The creation, promulgation, and experience of symbols are a form of discourse that both expresses and connects speech and action. A subfield of sociology, *symbolic interactionism*, is based on the obvious premise that human beings in society process information, act, and interact, based on interpretations and meanings.[49] But symbols have complex typologies, including identifying signs, aspirational or ideological statements of belief, and expressions of humor or irony. A first order symbol might express affiliation that an individual would like others to know is part of her social identity—for example, my button that reads "Greater Eugene Municipal Bowling League" or your T-shirt emblazoned with the words "Silver Member of the National Rifle Association." However, political symbols, especially when used in liberatory movements, are more complex. The image of a clenched fist with the words "Black Power" was intended to be motivating at a time when US blacks were seeking to increase their political power, as well as identifying a bearer's aspirations. And that clenched-fist symbol seems to have retained its original meaning of divergence from Martin Luther King's nonviolent approach.

However, events external to the first publication or placement of symbols can subvert their intended meanings. Naming American streets and boulevards "Martin Luther King Jr.," or schools "Lincoln" was intended and endures as a public bestowal of honor for African Americans. But insofar as these names were often or especially adopted in poor black neighborhoods, the honor bestowed is belied by present circumstances of dilapidation, neglect, crime, and police surveillance and occupation.[50] Most Americans can understand that blacks find displays of the Confederate flag offensive, because it symbolizes a society that practiced black chattel slavery. In this case, the symbol is taken to be not only identifying in a historical sense, but aspirational for whites in present contexts. Although, for these same reasons, displays of the Confederate flag also contribute to subclimates in which many whites, as well as blacks, hold those who display that flag in contempt.

Whenever symbols are taken to be liberatory or oppressive and there are disputes surrounding their placement, meanings become difficult to explicate. If a symbol of a historical, racist oppressor remains in a context where there is still ongoing racism that activists are resisting, should that symbol be removed, or is it appropriate to retain it as a hyperbolic descriptor of present conditions? For example, as of this writing, black students and others at Cape Town University in South Africa are demanding that the school's statue of Cecil John Rhodes be removed because it does not reflect their aspirations and beliefs about future change in South African society.[51] But on the other hand, those same students and their advocates also believe that they live under conditions of severe hearts-and-minds and structural racism. Might not the Rhodes statue be a better symbol of those present conditions than an aspirational replacement would be? Of course, the answer to that question depends on whether one's leading theory of such symbols is that they are descriptive or aspirational. As a descriptive source of identity, symbols remain in the psychic realm, with their connection to action undetermined, because that depends on the psychology of individuals. But the aspirational aspect of symbols can be a rallying point for collective action.

Sometimes a symbol contributes to an atmospheric impression of who is honored and was or still is dominant (the Confederate flag as a symbol of white supremacy and black slavery) or it may remind individuals of a subject on the agenda of leaders (the black power symbol). The symbol is often visual but may also be tactile (the statues of Cecil John Rhodes and Saddam Hussein) and music may be played or evoked. Concerning the latter, it is of no little interest, perhaps in keeping with the Old Testament aural modality of prophecy, that Cornel West repeatedly refers to the music contemporary with different periods of black protest (e.g., the blues, jazz, rhythm and blues, rap, and hip-hop), as expressions of mass, collective emotional and spiritual states of their times.[52] He talks often about love in referring to the music of the 1960s and has associated a "sweetness" with that time, in contrast to harsh expressions of "getting over" in the rap music of the early twenty-first century.[53]

6

THE DISCOURSE OF POLITICAL ACTIVISM

> I do not pretend to understand the moral universe; the arc is a long one, my eye reaches but little ways; I cannot calculate the curve and complete the figure by the experience of sight, I can divine it by conscience. And from what I see I am sure it bends towards justice.—Theodore Parker[1]

> If there is no struggle there is no progress. . . . This struggle may be a moral one, or it may be a physical one, and it may be both moral and physical, but it must be a struggle.—Fredrick Douglass[2]

Active discourse is oppositional action by nongovernment individuals and groups and not all of it is political. Political active discourse or political activism has a verbal form in descriptions of existing unjust conditions and goals for justice, and descriptions of strategies and tactics for action; its nonverbal form is real life action. Speech and writing are not action, no matter how closely they may be intended to motivate action and even if they succeed in doing so. The distinction drawn in chapter 5 between discourse as speech and writing and discourse as real life action may seem like an artificial split or an attempt to return to the kind of intellectual reflection in philosophy that is irrelevant to reality. The split is artificial, because many of those who "talk the talk," also "walk the walk," and from those who "walk the walk," *organic intellectuals* may emerge.

The idea of the *organic intellectual* remains an aspiration or model for many academics who have nontraditional identities and whose presence in the academy was originally believed to automatically represent the larger minority groups they belonged to. It is now understood that such representation should be autonomous and voluntary to avoid imposing discriminatory academic service burdens and essentializing or objectifying individuals via their socially disadvantaged identities.[3] Still, the goal of changing reality through one's presence, intellectual work, and activist contact with groups outside the academic community remains a coherent value for many academics who want to make a difference.

The idea of the organic intellectual hails from Antonio Gramsci who insisted that the rule of dominant groups was mediated through the cultural work of their own distinctive intellectuals. As a means for resisting hegemonies that are held in place by consent of the subordinated, Gramsci therefore thought it was necessary for new liberatory political groups or classes to develop their own intellectuals, and he implied that they inevitably would. These emergent organic intellectuals would fulfill the specialized functions of organizing and supporting discourses of resistance and rebellion and then *represent*, or express the collective goals of the new group, to the larger society. Gramsci holds that every person has intellectual capabilities, but that the organic intellectual is defined by her role for her group.[4] Thus, what is "organic" in Gramsci's sense is a relation between the organic intellectual and the group she represents—membership in the group represented is a requirement for becoming its organic intellectual.

Gramsci's idea raises an interesting question: Is an intellectual who is granted that status by academic enrollment or employment, who identifies as a member of a group that is under-represented within the academy, writes about the problems of that group, and engages in some practical liberatory projects with other members of her group, thereby an organic intellectual? The question is not one of the importance of provenance to guarantee authenticity in the sense of genuine group identity, but of identity as an intellectual of, and for, that group. The organic intellectual of a group remains one of them in her work as their organic intellectual. She is expected to throw her lot in with them and put her well-being on the line for the group. She cannot dust herself off and walk away or go home if things do not work out as she and the group have planned. There are risks involved in being an organic intellectual if the objective is more liberty for a group—that is, if one is part of a movement. Cornel West has written that for real change to occur leaders have to be willing to act in public, to be arrested, and to be killed. It helps if they are charismatic and if members of the group they represent love them. Martin Luther King Jr. was a prime example of a charismatic organic intellectual in West's sense.[5]

West's stated conditions for becoming a successful organic intellectual are an empirical claim about what is necessary, although not sufficient, for real change. If the Left did indeed lose in the decades following the civil rights movement, as West has also claimed, then that in itself would indicate that these necessary conditions are not sufficient for lasting, sustainable change.[6] But West's conditions do give us an important distinction between political oppositional discourse as speech, and as action. In a society that protects free speech and recognizes academic freedom, speech by academics is not action. The answer to the question of whether academic enrollment and employment plus relevant group membership and liberatory discourse in speech or writing is enough to qualify a person as an organic intellectual is No. Academics are granted their status as intellectuals by the academy and not in the course of group activism. This is not to say that academic intellectuals might not also be activists. But for those who talk and write as a profession, action can be very difficult to undertake. While action added to academic intellectual status does not confer organic intellectual status, it is beyond speech and writing. So there are two distinctions worth keeping in mind, the first between organic intellectuals and academic intellectuals and the second between academic intellectuals and activists.

The main purpose of this distinction between words and action is to clear the way for an appreciation of the difficulty, uncertainty, and perplexity of real-life political activism, and how it requires dedicated (i.e., self-aware and committed) organized action over time by those who do not have official political power. The distinction thus drawn is intended to remind liberatory theorists that their words alone do not have the power to directly change the material world—people have to do things in the world if they hope to change the world, even though what they do may not have even a strong probability of getting the results they hope for. So, for example, when progressives do no more than eloquently express the shamefulness of hungry school children in a land of plenty, they remain on the side of spoken and written discourse.

But if they organize a school breakfast program in a local neighborhood, with real food going into the bellies of real kids, then their discourse has moved out of speech and writing, into real-life action. Or, today's Kantians may argue that it is wrong for individuals to give to beggars because that supports a government system that is not doing its duty to the poor.[7] But without assurance that the government cares about the poor and will pick up the slack in the absence of private charity, or efforts to change the meanness of the government, such argument is not activist in either speech or action.

Both verbal and active forms of discourse have their value and place because there has to be a certain amount of division of labor in society. Still, liberatory participants should be aware of the nature of their projects and engagements, to avoid confusing themselves and others, and for the sake of efficiency in that division of labor. To state this is not to raise skepticism about good intent motivating the speech, writing, or even activism of some academic intellectuals, but is rather a plea for self-orientation. Academics should say whatever they want to say for its own sake, or because they think what they say will support their status in the academy, but not all discourse about injustice and "what should be done" has a discernible link to reality.

This final chapter is tricky because I try to take up several things at once: present and historical facts about a contemporary situation of injustice and a critique of how those facts have been analytically presented; the distinction between what we need to know to understand specific injustices versus what the target of effective activism should be; and also issues of perspective and hope. The text proceeds by means of a discussion of revisionist history that focuses on how African American poor people are affected by the contemporary US criminal justice system that has been organized as the War on Drugs. The difficulties in deciding how broad and global a systemic view progressive theorists of race, who focus on activism, should work with, is then considered in the section, "Historical and Political Boundaries." A brief consideration of the subject of liberty and freedom then follows, because the goal of much political activism is more liberty and freedom for those who have comparatively less.

REVISIONIST HISTORY AND THE CONTEMPORARY US CRIMINAL JUSTICE SYSTEM

We saw in chapter 5 that Cornel West, the leading American public intellectual on matters of social justice in the late twentieth and early twenty-first centuries, has accepted as part of his tragic view, a certain amount of regress toward progress. West also distinguished between long-term trends and immediate, attention-grabbing events in his distinction between "democratic time" and "market time." West's perspective is consonant with well over a century of revisionist history of the progress toward correcting the injustice experienced by African Americans. The revisionist view describes both historical and contemporary events when optimistic liberation has been followed by new forms of oppression. The same white racist leaders who have experienced defeat by *progress*, design and implement new forms of institutional racism, for *regress*. Describing and analyzing such history is "revisionist" in two dimensions. First, it revises official accounts of events, which in the United States, at least, tend to leave out the reality of injustice and ignore the suffering of those affected by it. Second, this kind of history revises even realist progressive accounts of events that are based on a stepped-model of linear progress. Indeed, the Leninist "one step forward, two steps back" or, as it is more frequently translated, "two steps forward and one step back," view of American race relations has now become the received method among liberatory scholars.[8] The first formulation is tragic and pessimistic because we end up a step back; the second is aspirational and optimistic because some progress is made. Although both views are better than the milestone-timeline model discussed in chapter 5, neither one provides a coherent picture of the need for continual and sustainable struggle.

A revisionist historical approach to race relations is consonant with what West identifies as the Black Prophetic Tradition, because it reveals the need for ongoing struggle against oppression. Such struggle is called for during the times of a step back or two and its success is measured by the one step ahead or two. In *The New Jim Crow*, Michelle Alexander uses a revisionist historical approach to explain the contemporary injustice of the US criminal justice system. Alexander's account and that of some of her sources give us a comprehensive picture of a concrete political and social ill. But while there is no reason to doubt the facts they provide, their total analysis as presented blocks entrances for real life activism. So as I reprise Alexander and company's revisionist historical account in what follows, I will also show how it is somewhat ossified.

Revisionist History

The Emancipation Proclamation did not end slavery until the Thirteenth Amendment to the US Constitution was ratified by the states in 1865: "Neither slavery nor involuntary servitude, except as a punishment for crime whereof the party shall have been duly convicted, shall exist within the United States, or any place subject to their jurisdiction."[9] Reconstruction was a time of liberation, marked by black participation in southern local government, but when federal troops withdrew from former confederate states in 1877, "Redemption" followed. Racist "racial order" was restored through widespread imprisonment of black men for being unemployed (when and where few jobs for them were available), which allowed for convict leasing under conditions often more harsh than slavery. When convict leasing was struck down by the courts, explicit segregation, backed up by lynching and other forms of antiblack terrorism, was instituted under Jim Crow. As soon as Jim Crow segregation was legally abolished, a new rhetoric of law and order fed an increase in the black male prison population.[10] President Richard Nixon's emphasis on law and order appealed to the fears of economically insecure white voters by deliberately manipulating their racism, but without mentioning race. Nixon's program was accelerated by President Ronald Reagan's War on Drugs. As traditional male jobs were outsourced from the inner cities to countries with cheaper labor, during the early 1980s, the prison population began a ten-fold increase, with commensurate growth in government funding.[11]

The Post–Civil Rights US Criminal Justice System

Vesla Weaver identifies the projects of "issue entrepreneurs" as "frontlash." Representatives of conservative groups, whose interests had been obstructed by the 1964 Civil Rights Act and 1965 Voting Rights Act, designed and put into effect new programs to block the civil rights gains of African Americans, which also provided economic incentives to a broad base. President Johnson's Law Enforcement Assistance Administration (LEAA), known as the Office of Justice Programs after 1984, provided federal aid to local law enforcement departments, so that they could increase arrests. Over the same time period, mandatory minimum sentences instituted for possession of small amounts of drugs disproportionately affected racial minorities.[12] We can add to Weaver's account, the current "Broken Windows Policy," through which local police disproportionately target nonwhite minorities for minor offenses and have responded to collective protests against innocent deaths resulting from racial profiling with the full force of surplus military weaponry and armament.[13]

Alexander notes that Loïc Wacquant has offered the somewhat optimistic interpretation that each situation of regress "is less total, less capable of encompassing and controlling the entire race."[14] Wacquant emphasizes that mainly poor African American men have been easy candidates for War on Drugs incarceration, but not all African American men and not poor African American women who have been managed by welfare and workfare programs that are steadily reduced.[15] Moreover, the emphasis on "workfare" channels women previously on welfare into jobs that are least desirable, lowest paid, and most vulnerable to economic recession.[16]

Wacquant argues that the use of the carceral system to manage the black urban poor cannot be fully understood solely in terms of domestic American hearts-and-minds racism or bias against blacks, with institutional racism taken into account, but requires a broader understanding of the nonpenal functions of the prison system. Wacquant convincingly suggests that the prison system is no longer simply an institution that punishes crime, but a mechanism of social control that bears little relation to crime as actual harm to individuals or society. Although government safety-net state services have been reserved for women and children who are not themselves "in" the criminal justice system, many aspects of their lives are affected by it. Wacquant concludes that the ghetto of the black urban poor has become part of the same social control structure as the contemporary prison system.[17] And the results of that reorganization are partly why the United States has proportionately more people and more minority group members in prison than any other country.[18]

The idea of the prison-ghetto system also explains the persistence of hard-core intergenerational poverty, because the same mechanisms of surveillance, government intrusion into family life, and imprisonment, which keep some people poor, provide economic rewards for other middle class and rich people. Thus, added to otherwise racist or fear-driven motives for use of the prison system to control poor blacks are the economic factors of jobs made possible by the construction of prisons, jobs for prison employees, jobs for law enforcement officers who police the ghettos, as well as profits earned by government contractors who build and run prisons. Because the nonwhite prison population and their families (both of origin and the ones they create) are undereducated, their unskilled or semi-skilled labor is more profitably replaced by outsourced workers in poorer countries.[19] The net effect is that instead of directly contributing to the economy through their work, the incarcerated population indirectly contributes to the economy through the wages paid to those who build prisons, send people into them, guard and care for prisoners, and manage incarceration, as well as the profits of prison construction and administration companies.

GLOBAL CRITIQUE

What is the relevance of a global critique or international economic analysis for relating the contemporary US prison system to the progress/regress model? More to the present point, how does this analysis relate to contemporary activist progress? On its own, the progress/regress method seems to evoke the vagaries and moral ambivalence of human nature. In terms of recalcitrant hearts-and-minds racism, recent racial changes in the US prison system are regress. It can be hoped that eventually whites will come around to addressing the injustice of this system—that is, shocked, shamed, and persuaded to change it. However, the global critique introduces much broader causal factors. Large-scale economic changes are implicated in the new ghetto-prison system, which are directly related to the profit motive of now-international corporations that seek to keep their labor costs as low as possible. In addition, and more ominously, the recent acquisition of military weapons and vehicles by local police departments in the United States and the discretionary power of the police to execute suspects with impunity in failed stops and frisks could be viewed as a use of military methods previously reserved for foreign combat, in preparation for a color-blind police state.[20]

It is understandable that some theorists consider this much larger American global economic and military system to be the overriding obstacle that must be changed in order for race relations in the United States to be alleviated. However, this global view makes the task of change, or even a reiteration of the 1960s civil rights movement, a hugely challenging international project. Still, critical examination of such global economic and political factors is crucial for understanding ourselves at this time. This is especially important for academic intellectuals. The current picture in terms of race, class, gender, and military power, inflected by concerns about environmental destruction and climate change, is an approach to history and current conditions that is the product of changes in humanistic scholarship that were a lasting and thus far sustainable effect of the 1960s civil rights movement. But if all we do is contemplate the Evil Empire that has emerged and in which we comparatively affluent American academics are complicit, the net effect is paralysis in terms of real-life action for change, not only for ourselves, but for others we might attend to and encourage.

The problem that dogs broad, liberatory global critique is that the complex and enormous monstrosity addressed is beyond the abilities to effectively intervene of all benevolent observers. Only a fabled society of Doctors Frankenstein, such as the Bilderberg group, could stop the monster they have created.[21] This is not to say that theoretical reflection on a global system is even akin to conspiracy theorizing, but that it is very difficult to move from a global level of theorizing to practical points of access for change. The global liberatory critique is more likely to motivate more academic theorizing about what a just global system would look like. But even if a model of global justice that represented a consensus of the enlightened could be constructed, the question of how to apply that model in reality, would persist unanswered. We already know that the 1948 United Nations Universal Declaration of Human Rights, which starts with the problem of correcting existing global injustices, has not had impressive, widespread practical effects. (Perhaps the rebellions predicted if the common people are deprived of their rights have been successfully nipped in the bud?)

Fortunately, to the extent that the present global capitalistic system is the ultimate structure supporting regress in internal US progress toward social justice for African Americans, resignation is not the only realistic or prudent response. A global system works on many institutional levels of governmental and economic structure, including its injustice as experienced by real people who suffer from it in their concrete daily existence. And it is that kind of individually experienced injustice, which can be addressed, on the ground. It may not be (as Alexander and West have, respectively, called for and proclaimed to have begun) that even a movement is necessary or sufficient in order to address specific contemporary experiences of injustice. It may be that tangible practical first steps can be taken on the level of local activism and it may be that in societies with democratic structures, such activism is more effective than the promulgation of liberatory global system theory. If local problems are corrected without at the same time calling for a new national or global movement, there may be less political opposition on local levels. We will return to this question of "scope of activism" in the next section, after more theoretical ground has been reclaimed for "what to do."

NEW CONSTRUCTIONS OF RACE

Global understanding is important—we are all required to be informed about the world—but it is not the only worthwhile theoretical goal. Theory and analysis are also important for developing ideas for how to correct injustice on concrete, specific levels. Under-examined in the construction of revisionist history, as well as in the idea of regress, is a circular theory of human history. We seem to go ahead, and then we go back. But what could it mean to "go back"? No one has claimed that the present or recent past duplicates the more distant past or literally replays it. Although, some scholars have claimed that some structures of status are remarkably resilient, even though the principles defending them have been rejected. For example, the idea that nonwhites are inferior to whites and need to be kept separate from them for the benefit of both groups has been abandoned as an explicit, official justification for racial segregation, but racial segregation—in US housing, education, and social life—has not been abandoned. (Residential segregation continues without legal requirement as the result of real estate prices, sedimented social practices, poverty, and mortgage lenders who redline.)

Rival Siegel argues that status arrangements may persist with complete legality after their original justificatory principles are struck down, so long as different justifications are concocted:

> The ways in which the legal system enforces social stratification are various and evolve over time. Efforts to reform a status regime bring about changes in its rule structure and justificatory rhetoric—a dynamic I have elsewhere called "preservation-through-transformation." In short, status-enforcing state action evolves in form as it is contested.[22]

Siegel's thesis raises the question of what kind of thing or relation the original social stratification is, so that it can persist from generation to generation under different names, with different justifications. The social metaphysics could involve "memes," or intergenerational habits, or outright lies and conspiracies. Perhaps there are power relationships between blacks and whites that members of each group inherit and whites are loathe to give up, because they have more power. To relate the present to the past in such ways is a complex interdisciplinary work consisting at least of sociology, history, and legal and political history, before philosophers and other theorists could formulate their own disciplinary interpretations. It may be simpler and more conclusive to approach this issue of permanent-status-through-change by starting fresh with present power and status differences.

When Alexander calls the present racially biased prison system "the new Jim Crow," she adds that she does not mean to draw a literal comparison, but to write metaphorically.[23] This raises the question of why we need a metaphor that invokes the past to describe present conditions that are well studied by contemporary social scientists, with events reported by journalists and recorded on video, as they occur. What would happen if we simply stayed with our current best descriptions and attempted to theorize them? One result might be to shift the discourse from a somewhat rigid idea of types of events, a kind of essentializing of history, to the use of more recent tools involving the idea of social construction.

It's already well accepted within the academy that biological human racial divisions, as well as their social meanings, were constructed in the past.[24] We also know that biological foundations for human races are now repudiated in the same scientific fields that invented them. That knowledge supports recognition of racial construction within society, which was explicitly based on assumed biological determinism in the past. Indeed, one indication of a lack of biological foundation for racial taxonomies in society is the historical and geographic variation of the epistemology of social race. Thus, for example, before they were assimilated into the middle class, Europeans who were Irish, Italian, Jewish, Finnish, Polish, and even German, were not considered white; the ethnic category of Hispanic/Latino was created by the US census and has since been regarded as a race or at least an object of racism; Middle Eastern Americans came to be identified as a nonwhite racial group after 9/11; mixed black and white people are conventionally identified as black. Such social construction of race has always been closely associated with citizenship rights and social status and it has been maintained and changed for changing political and economic purposes.[25]

Race and racial divisions should be viewed as constantly "under construction." Dominant groups may reiterate some general ideas based on their knowledge of history, but their present focus is always on their present goals for dominance. Race as it has been known, and as we continue to know it, is a dynamic process. Consider, for example, Richard Nixon's reported intentions to appeal to white racists, with language that would not explicitly mention blacks or other nonwhites. The social construction of black men as criminals that has accompanied broad public acceptance of police racial profiling, as well as the racial imbalance in incarceration, has its origins in this early 1970s political rhetoric and policy. That is, our present form of the social construction of black men started as a relatively new, post–civil rights movement strategy for getting votes. This is not to say that the strategy had not been successfully used before then, for instance, as Alexander notes, in extinguishing the late nineteenth-century populist movement.[26] But it was a new political strategy for the 1970s. And all that was required to sustain it from then on was a steady increase in the funding and construction of the infrastructure supporting it, and occasional ideological revitalization. For example, in the 1988 presidential campaign, George H. W. Bush used against Michael Dukakis, his Democratic opponent, the example of William "Willie" Horton, a convicted first-degree murderer. Horton committed rape and assault when released on furlough during Dukakis's second term as governor of Massachusetts. In his first term as governor, Dukakis had vetoed a bill that would have stopped furloughs for first-degree murderers. Ergo, Dukakis was portrayed as "soft on crime," and Bush won the election. [27]

If we view the social construction of race as an ongoing dynamic process, we need to understand that Nixon and H. W. Bush were not merely manipulating existing public fears about black men, but fanning them, exacerbating them, and giving them new faces—faces from their time, not faces from the late nineteenth century—and in that process *reconstructing* race. They were not turning the clock back to the beginning of a new era of Jim Crow (no matter how metaphorically that may be understood) but moving forward with new ideas about black male identity. Of course, these ideas were not difficult to "sell" because the paradigm case of black manhood they held up was genuinely scary and the mass of economically insecure white voters was already predisposed to accept a racist ideology. But "predisposed" does not mean "predetermined."

The construction of the idea of the late twentieth-century black male ghetto dweller as an inherently dangerous and later crack-crazed maniac was a newly constructed stereotype. It prompted a whole new generation of nonblack women to clutch their purses when a black man stepped onto elevators with them, and signaled everyone else to click their car doors into "locked" when they saw a black man advancing down the street.[28] In turn, these attitudes can be viewed as antecedents to acceptance of the legality of recent high profile cases of police homicide following attempted stops and frisks of unarmed young African American men. Overall, such stereotypes support the criminalization of black male bodies in the public imaginary because those bodies have become *icons*—they both symbolize criminals and are perceived as physically dangerous.

That Willie Horton, who was a violent black male criminal, became the face of black male crime and not any one of hundreds of thousands other black men, who had already been incarcerated for possession of small amounts of marijuana or cocaine, meant and continues to mean, that the preoccupation with crime in America is a focus on physical crime. There is now a prevailing impression that "crime" means "physical violence," so that "white-collar crime" (a term now out of date sartorially) is not viewed as truly dangerous. And physical crime is imagined to be mainly perpetrated by black men, an association so strong that being a criminal has become part of the casual identity of being a black male. The quotidian phenomenology of that new construction of race for all black men, especially poor black youth, is nothing less than the phenomenology of traumatic encounters with bullies against whom the victim cannot win—if the victim tries to win, he can be killed by police officers, with impunity.[29]

I suggest that we view the post–civil rights movement association of crime with African American men and boys as a new construction of race. Alexander names this construction "criminalblackman,"[30] but does not sufficiently treat it as a new racial construction. She is aware that something new has occurred, but she views it as an attribute of crime, rather than a reconstruction of black maleness: "For black men, the stigma of being a 'criminal' in the era of mass incarceration is fundamentally a *racial* stigma. . . . Whiteness mitigates crime, whereas blackness defines the criminal."[31] Alexander does not tell us what she means by the preexisting "blackness" that defines the criminal. There is no preexisting blackness, except for dark skin and poverty. In this case, "criminal" defines and constructs blackness. And that is why the almost 70 percent of African Americans who are black, but not poor, also suffer from this new construction of "criminalblackman."

Such slanderous characterizations of an entire group as dangerously criminal do not directly result from the financial and economic structures of a system of global capitalism, descending like the forefinger of God to shape the minds of the white populace. They are opportunistically discovered by politicians seeking votes, based on their assumptions that their highest good is getting elected, instead of getting elected for the right reasons. (It should go without saying that such politicians cannot be presumed to believe what they say in order to get people to vote for them.) If the politicians get elected, they try out a few new programs. If those on whom the programs are inflicted (e.g., the victims of Reagan's War on Drugs that followed a general valorization of "law and order") are already vulnerable to government power and the rest of the population is not vigilant about everyone's rights, the programs succeed and their growth accelerates in new times of crisis. Such programs will only work if they are able to intersect with existing or burgeoning corporate interests, in this case, private prison contractors. If the intersection "takes," then soon enough, a criminal justice system such as the one in place is the historical result. It is a historical result because it developed over time and at many different stages its present state could not have been predicted with a high degree of probability. It may therefore be an unduly Manichean use of history to view such a system as a deliberate design by the ultimate architects of global corporate capitalism.

That is not to say that individuals, especially poor and nonwhite people, do not encounter the present criminal justice system as both real and unyielding. And it is not to overlook the jobs provided to law enforcement officers, prison personnel, and civilians who prosper from the economic stimulus of prisons in their locales.[32] In addition, we should be concerned about Alexander's account of the dire consequences for eligibility for government aid and prospective employment, as well as loss of personal and familial regard, suffered by contemporary felons. Once convicted, or sometimes, even only arrested for minor drug offenses, the poor and especially black victims of this system become branded as lifelong criminals. They are usually barred from both jury duty and voting and are precluded from ever fully rejoining respectable society. Their inability to vote in geographical areas with large poor black populations can tip the results of key elections. Most of the victims and fearful observers are now accustomed to this system, their habits settled within and outside it, as though it were completely natural, "just the way things are."[33] These are terrible conditions of existence for millions of poor black people. However, the question is not whether or not they are related to larger historical trends, which they without question are, but whether the most effective way to address them via activist discourse is to take on the big global picture or focus on comparative ways in which American blacks and whites, poor and middle class, are treated by their—everyone's—government.

The prison-poverty system became an entrenched institution by the mid-1990s. Alexander notes that during the Clinton administration, the prison budget, after increasing by 171 percent, became twice what was allocated to Aid to Families with Dependent Children (AFDC) and that funding for public housing was reduced by 61 percent. At the same time, those who had been convicted for drug offenses were barred from public housing and faced homelessness.[34] Described in these terms, the prison-poverty system exceeds the institution of Jim Crow because of its dedicated federal funding. In studying this structure, everything that happens can be described as though it were designed to oppress poor black people, for the benefit of others. But even that description, in addition to its transcendental excess, may rely too much on the net results of contingent, uncertain, incremental components. Moreover, although poor black ghetto dwellers are the main human resources for this system and the rate of poverty among American blacks is twice that among whites, most American blacks, about 75 percent, are not at this time poor ghetto dwellers.[35] The majority of American blacks, who are neither poor nor incarcerated are stigmatized and thereby endangered by stereotypes that connect the prison to the ghetto, but they are not directly part of that connection. This does not mean life is not unjust for all African Americans, but it does mean that the majority retains its civic ability to educate the next generation, vote, protest, and cultivate optimism about the future. (A visitor from another planet might wonder if that majority is doing enough to fulfill its civic obligations in the early twenty-first century.)

HISTORICAL AND POLITICAL BOUNDARIES

Unlike Jim Crow, which had mainly excluded blacks from mainstream economic and social life, the post–civil rights criminal justice system initiated positive federal programs that were intended to directly and punitively address African Americans, partly because key people in government believed that was what white Americans wanted. While it seemed at first that affirmative action for middle-class African Americans was a helpful positive program—and it did in fact help many—white backlash attacking it as "reverse discrimination" has curtailed explicit affirmative action policies, under the direction of the US Supreme Court. Antidiscrimination laws remain on the books, but there is little evidence that antidiscrimination lawsuits, since 1980, have been effective. In place of affirmative action there has been a perceived need for racial diversity in organizations and some observers conclude that compliance reviews are more effective than lawsuits for organizational change, especially in the diversification of management positions.[36] Overall, the twenty years following the success of the civil rights movement was a period of regress, which many observers in 2015 consider to remain in full swing. But, what is happening during this period is exactly a competition among interest groups, and as Bentley might have predicted, with no clear-cut resolution yet. It therefore makes sense to consider appropriate time frames with which to think about the current situation of racial injustice.

Raymond Williams was a twentieth-century English cultural critic who seems to be largely unknown to US philosophers of race who write about social justice. He was one of the founders of the British *New Left Review*, but his ideas were a site of contention for more orthodox Marxists, because he was skeptical of economic analyses that did not take lived cultural experience into account. Williams believed that masses, and also perhaps classes, did not literally exist, except for how theorists defined and viewed them. He also anticipated later feminist emphases on "nutritive and generative" aspects of lived experience as a major social institution on a par with the economy and politics. Williams has been considered most influential for his ideas that all members and groups in society contribute to its *structured feelings* at any given time and for his idea of the long revolution that recurred throughout his writing, after he introduced it in a 1961 book of the same title.[37]

The Long Revolution named by Williams was a process of social change toward democracy, which began in modernity in the late eighteenth century with the French Revolution, "the mould in which experience was cast."[38] By "experience" in this context, Williams meant the experience of writers and poets, and he believed that what was expressed in literature both reflected feelings in society and influenced them. The structured feeling of the Long Revolution is centered on goals of universal human recognition, for all members of society, as whole human beings. Everyone is to be accepted for what they are in the system to come after capitalism: "There can be no acceptable human order while the full humanity of any class of men is in practice denied."[39]

In disagreement with contemporary Marxists, Williams was skeptical of the ability of socialism or state control that would entail complex bureaucracy to realize the goal of universal humanity: "We seem reduced to a choice between speculator and bureaucrat and while we do not like the speculator, the bureaucrat is not exactly inviting either."[40] His proposed solution was a form of self-rule based on open discussion and voting, with representatives to larger governing bodies responsible to their constituents. Williams has been interpreted as advocating that "the people" rule themselves, but he is not usually associated with anarchism.[41]

It is very difficult for a theorist to decide how big a picture to consider, how long a period of history to take as a unit for long-term trends. Since we cannot successfully intervene in a global system, and the same facts can usually be explained by more than one theory, there is little that can or should interfere with a long-term view that is tilted toward optimism. The temporal perspective introduced by Williams, although he probably would not have described it in these terms, permits us to think about history as extending into the future, as well as the past.[42] Suppose that there is a Long Revolution and there are Wide Humanistic Values to match it, which preclude racism, because the full humanity of all human beings will be recognized, eventually. It might be useful, as a matter of sanity, as well as hope, to see the present conditions of American antiblack punitive racism as a relatively short span of events within those lengths. Such events need to be endured and the hope is that they will pass into the past at some stage in the future of the Long Revolution. About hope, Williams wrote the following at the end of *Towards 2000:*

> It is only in a shared belief and insistence that there are practical alternatives that the balance of forces and chances begins to alter. . . . Once the inevitabilities are challenged, we begin gathering our resources for a journey of hope. If there are no easy answers there are still available and discoverable hard answers and it is these that we can now learn to make and share. This has been, from the beginning, the sense and impulse of the Long Revolution.[43]

The Elasticity and Inclusiveness of Identities

Since the US civil rights movement, African American theorists, academics especially, have emphasized the importance of black identity, in the tradition of W. E. B. Du Bois and Frantz Fanon. There has been a shift toward prophecy in Cornel West's sense of speaking the truth about oppression in the present, but overall, the methodological consensus is that improvement in the conditions of African Americans needs to be demanded by and for African Americans, as a racial group.

This discourse displays little confidence in human rights or a humanitarianism such as Williams emphasized, because there is a longstanding belief that many whites have in the Long Oppression failed to recognize the humanity of blacks. Moreover, the language of "color blindness," which does not mention race, is strongly associated with the regress of post–civil rights movement black poverty and deep experience of injustice in the criminal justice system. However, this view may be too concrete, too focused on short-term historical contingencies, to get us from here to where and how we want the future to be.

American politicians have been able for a while to manipulate and implement racism in racially neutral language, which leaves little opportunity for either nonwhite racial affirmation or successful race-based litigation—that is, judges do not accept wholly race-based affirmative action or complaints about antiblack racism in situations that have been already described in race-neutral language, such as the War on Drugs. Nevertheless, it does not follow from any of this that neutrality about race is not a humanistic ideal or that humanistic ideals are not valid general ideals. It may be a self-defeating long-term error, albeit expedient in the short term, to insist that all efforts toward improving the present conditions of poor African Americans be described in terms of their racial identities, rather than their human identities.

There are more poor whites than poor blacks or Hispanics in the United States, even though black poverty is twice as common as white poverty and the residential segregation of the black poor creates additional race-associated vulnerabilities.[44] African American poor people are more vulnerable to the exploitation of being inducted into the US criminal justice system, as well as more vulnerable in lacking adequate housing, food, a living wage, and public education that provides real opportunities for their children. All of these ills and comparative disadvantages create distinct circumstances of the "blackpoor." But the condition of poverty itself, where the poor have less income and wealth than those who are not poor, is a measurable condition that includes people of all races, including whites and especially whites who are homeless or unemployed. There has been much debate about whether race or class is more important to consider for understanding the situation of poor African Americans: Does black racial identity in an antiblack racist society predetermine a high likelihood of poverty, which persists over generations as antiblack racism continues? Or, is poverty sufficiently oppressive to account for its own persistence, regardless of race? Does race and racism change the nature of poverty? Or, is poverty, like criminality, part of a new black identity? Much can be said in answer to such questions about the theoretical aspects of race or class as a lens for studying the oppression of the *blackpoor*.

Lucius Outlaw has developed a now paradigmatic perspective that historical and contemporary studies of race support a critical theory of race that is more relevant to African American experience than traditional critical theories based on class.[45] Still, the question in terms of activism and the correction of concrete social injustice is not how poverty has been caused, but how it can be corrected. (It may have causes mainly in racism but mainly economic corrections.) To correct poverty and attendant issues such as food insecurity and homelessness among children, it neither makes sense, nor is it morally principled, to focus on the poverty of only African Americans. The discourse of social class may not be adequate to account for institutional racism and specifically racist institutions, because there is usually an added element of ignorance, neglect, or malice, concerning blacks. But addressing poverty needs to be an inclusive project. It would not only become another contentious form of "affirmative action" if only the blackpoor were considered, but it would be cruel insofar as the poor of all racial groups suffer.

In 1961, at the age of ninety-three, W. E. B. Du Bois joined the Communist Party and then said the following to the *New York Times*: "Capitalism cannot reform itself; it is doomed to self-destruction. No universal selfishness can bring social good to all. . . . Communism—the effort to give all men what they need and to ask of each the best they can contribute—this is the only way of human life."[46] Black spokespeople have for many decades emphasized poverty as a primary human problem and not a problem for only black Americans. Martin Luther King Jr. expressed that humanitarian emphasis, as has Cornel West, in our own era. Following his award of the Nobel Peace Prize in 1964, King announced a shift from civil rights to human rights, through his organization of the multiracial Poor People's Campaign. Before he was assassinated in 1968, King envisioned a Poor People's March on Washington, D.C.[47] West and Tavis Smiley, in their Poverty Tours, have emphasized the importance of "jobs with a living wage," as a goal for millions of Americans of all races.[48] Poverty is also a world concern.

In a way similar to this racially inclusive view of poverty, US government action toward peoples of nonwhite races outside of our borders has been an African American concern, in black liberatory discourse. As early as 1919, nine years after he founded the NAACP, Du Bois organized a second Pan-African Congress in Paris, presenting a petition to the Versailles Peace Conference for recognition of worldwide peoples' rights to anticolonialist self-determination. The petition was rejected. Du Bois continued to connect the situation of American blacks with that of global people of color, until the NAACP expelled him in 1948, for reasons of political prudence involving the Cold War.[49] King carried on Du Bois's insights that the treatment of African Americans was related to America's international policies, especially after he was awarded the 1964 Nobel Peace Prize. His protests of the Vietnam War and beyond that his call for land reform (in his 1967 Riverside Church speech), against US policy in Latin America, resulted in harsh assessments and dissention within the civil rights movement he had come to symbolize. He was also disinvited from the Johnson White House.[50] We have already noted, in chapter 5, West's emphasis on US foreign policy, as part of the black prophetic tradition, as well as his harsh remarks about President Obama. West is also not welcome in Obama's White House.[51]

These projects of making African American concerns more broad by extending the area of complaint and protest to nonblack American poor people and non-American people of color have not met with great success. They have neither strengthened the movements of their time, nor reduced or ended poverty (and American foreign policy has been impervious to their demands). Bitter reactions from the African American community to the US presidency reverberate when black liberatory spokespeople voice strong opinions on foreign policy. It is unimaginable at this time that such issues can be related to African American activism in official or public understandings, but it is also unimaginable that the issues are not related in reality. This is a situation of stasis.

However, there is now another dimension to global aspects of US social justice activism—media. The pleas in a number of local demonstrations and protests about police homicide of unarmed African Americans, such as "Hands Up, Don't Shoot," "I Can't Breathe," "Black Lives Matter" and "No Justice, No Peace," have been highly publicized by the mainstream media, as have successive police homicides after the death of Trayvon Martin in 2012.[52] The *New York Times* brought all of this to a head on April 6, 2015, by posting a video of Walter Scott being shot in the back while fleeing a police officer in South Carolina.[53] With prose befitting the cool temperature of *The New Yorker* magazine, Philip Gourivitch posted the following about that video:

> There it was, front and center, on the home page of my local paper, the *Times*, and on the BBC, and the *Guardian*, and the *Wall Street Journal*, and thousands of other news sites, as well as hundreds of thousands of Facebook pages and Twitter feeds: a freeze-frame showing a white policeman in the process of shooting a black man to death, with a play button you could click to watch the whole killing from start to finish.[54]

Gourevitch went on to discuss the ethics of journalistic displays of people getting killed and raised a question of respect for death on the part of viewers. What Gourevitch neglected to point out was the power of this video to provide conclusive evidence of contemporary injustice concerning the contemporary issue of police officer killings of unarmed black men, for which there have customarily been acquittals or failures to indict. The usual justification that an officer has acted out of fear for his own life is not supported by this video. What Gourevitch does succeed in pointing out is the global publicity that now attends such incidents. This international dimension of US race relations is different from the connection between US domestic and foreign policy on a theoretical level because it has the potential to spark vast external moral pressure on American government entities, perhaps similar to the Cold War pressures that were influential in *Brown v. Board of Education* and the 1964 Civil Rights Act, as discussed in chapter 4.

Issues of poverty, including global poverty, expand theoretical concerns about the carceral and other existential vulnerabilities of poor African Americans, to include people of other races, notably whites domestically and other peoples of color abroad. By the same token, US foreign policy raises issues of global white–nonwhite racial divides. Still, in terms of activism, these have largely remained theoretical issues that support broader understanding. They may describe issues for movements lost, past, or yet to be developed, but in terms of contemporary social justice activism, concrete change is a matter of US domestic issues concerning race relations and the practical tradition of the undramatic, obscure aspects of the Long Revolution is very important.

The vagueness of Williams's idea of the Long Revolution promises an ordinary, day-to-day methodology for addressing racial injustice. Ordinariness is required given the time span of the Long Revolution that according to Williams began in 1789. The ability to sustain continual low key and undramatic liberatory efforts may require the kind of faith found in activists within the black prophetic tradition, who were not as charismatic as Martin Luther King Jr., but attended to specific issues over decades. For instance, West contrasts the contributions of Ella Baker to those of King, describing her as "an unassuming person who helps the suppressed to help themselves." Baker's organizing work included her service as secretary of the NAACP, executive director of the Southern Christian Leadership Council, and cofounder of the Student Non-violent Coordinating Committee. Baker knew both Du Bois and King and was skilled at grassroots organizing, but she did not write essays or books or produce mesmerizing speeches. She talked about humility and service alongside everyday people and insisted that members of a movement motivate themselves.[55]

"Think Globally, Act Locally"

In light of the insight that amounts to "Think globally, act locally," borrowed from environmentalist planning discourse,[56] let's return now to Wacquant's general model of the contemporary carceral system as a form of social control that extends beyond punishment for crimes. Wacquant's analysis suggests that at least three different social situations would be more accessible to activist-sparked change than the overall global capitalist system: race-based residential segregation; impoverishment of the educational system as it serves the poor; assumptions about the traditional family that have had a slanderous effect on black family images. Residential segregation enables the architectural and geographic formation of ghettos as areas targeted for intrusive law enforcement surveillance, because poor and powerless blacks are physically clustered in one place.[57] Also, insofar as schools are financed by taxes based on property values, residential segregation results in impoverished resources for K–12 education.[58] Both segregated substandard housing and inadequate schools are issues that can be addressed through local activism and support for the development of employable skills and jobs.

While the "feminization of poverty" has been well-documented, additional attention could be paid to the assumption that women will be the primary caretakers for children, which explains why welfare and workfare programs have been concentrated on them, with the state replacing the function of a male provider in a nuclear family. However, ever since reactions to the 1965 Moynihan Report, and earlier in the work of E. Franklin Frazier, it has been known that many African Americans do not grow up in, or themselves form, traditional nuclear families with stay-at-home mothers and male breadwinner fathers. Positing poverty as the cause of this unconventional family structure had been the standing practice in sociology until Patrick Moynihan, writing for the US Department of Labor, claimed that the cause of black single mothers, illegitimacy, and extended family structures, was cultural pathology with roots in social arrangements that had been necessary under slavery and Jim Crow.[59] Despite the obsessive morbid interest in Moynihan's characterization of family organization among the black poor, it has been outpaced by more broad historical changes.

Not only have women of color, especially African American women, always worked outside of their homes, but most white women and women in other racial and ethnic groups, on all socioeconomic levels, now work outside of their homes. For poor women, their employment hinges both on skills and available and accessible jobs. The surrogate traditional-family aspects of welfare and workfare can therefore be viewed as so outdated as not to be worth theoretical consideration. This means that the need for welfare and workfare programs reduces to a need for more jobs for poor black women—and a need for transportation to and from those jobs, as well as affordable childcare.[60] As of April 2015, adult African American women had the highest rate of unemployment at 9.2 percent, compared to 6.5 for Latinas and 4.2 for white women.[61] (The website of the National Women's Law Center has portals for instructions on how those concerned about this issue can email their congressmen and senators.[62])

Finally, a contemporary example of spoken and active discourse about an immediate problem has been provided by activists in Ferguson, Missouri, who met with President Obama in December 2014 to discuss their attempts to influences changes in local police practices.

Said Ashley Yates, cofounder of the group Millennial Activists United, "We're definitely going to keep doing the work on the ground, but meeting with the president, for me—well, I'll say for everybody—is just an affirmation that this movement is working."[63] In February 2015, Ferguson activist groups called for 250 students to join them during spring break to provide community service such as clearing wreckage from earlier demonstrations and helping plant gardens. Said Patricia Barnes, a Democratic committeewoman for Ferguson, "The protests have got us here. The next step is to target the ballot box, to get people elected and to change policy. Students should take that back to their college campuses and build an infrastructure. . . . There is plenty to do."[64] Yes, there is plenty to do, but what needs to be done are fairly straightforward, day-to-day, community-based actions. Global systems are overreaching causal factors of local vulnerabilities, but there is no reason to believe that their local effects cannot be addressed on their local levels.

LIBERTY, FREEDOM, AND INJUSTICE

From a more abstract philosophical perspective, the foregoing discussion of revisionist history and active discourse, proceeding as they have from the concrete contemporary issue of racial injustice in the US criminal justice system, is a matter of liberty and freedom. Imprisonment is, after all, the classic, concrete example of not having liberty. And if we follow John Locke in saying that it is the whole person, and not the will, that can be free,[65] then a person in prison is not free. But philosophically, being in prison or not does not capture the abstract nature of liberty and freedom as political ideas and ideals.

The terms "liberty" and "freedom" have been used interchangeably by influential political philosophers, for instance Isiah Berlin in his canonical 1958 lecture, "Two Concepts of Liberty."[66] Berlin distinguished between negative liberty, or what others including government officials are not permitted to do to a person, and positive liberty, an area of personal autonomy allowing for individual choice and development. He was wary of the abuses by paternalism or quietism to which the idea of positive liberty could be subject. On the one hand, paternalistic or despotic leaders could take it upon themselves to determine what was good for others (for the good of a harmonious social whole, as well as the individual freedom of rational beings). And, on the other hand, stoic quietists might seek to shrink individual choice to what was not prohibited by law or punishable by government force:

> For this doctrine, as it applies to individuals, it is no very great distance to the conceptions of those who, like Kant, identify freedom not indeed with the elimination of desires, but with resistance to them and control over them . . . a sublime but, it seems to me, unmistakable, form of the doctrine of sour grapes.[67]

Insofar as Berlin championed the idea of negative liberty, in the tradition of J. S. Mill, three important qualifications tempered his libertarianism in ways that make it still relevant for active oppositional discourse. First, following Mill in equating incursions on core or essential negative liberty with coercion or slavery, Berlin acknowledged that freedom is only of value to those who can make use of it: "It is only because I believe that my inability to get a given thing is due to the fact that other human beings have made arrangements whereby I am, whereas others are not, prevented from having enough money with which to pay for it, that I think myself a victim of coercion or slavery."[68] Second, Berlin understood that people who are not free may take action against those who are limiting their freedom(s): "Those who are wedded to the 'negative' concept of freedom may perhaps be forgiven if they think that self-abnegation is not the only method of overcoming obstacles; that it is also possible to do so by removing them . . . in the case of human resistance, by force or persuasion." Third, Berlin recognized the importance of status or recognition, which in some cases might outweigh the value of negative liberty, to members of groups with a history of oppressive rule by others.[69]

However, in rethinking Berlin (as well as Locke), a focus on active discourse against injustice may require a distinction between liberty and freedom. What that distinction amounts to is that freedom can be used to expand the possibilities for resistance against unjust curtailments of liberty. The term "liberty" (or negative liberty in Berlin's sense) can be used to refer to lack of external constraint and "freedom" to refer to decisions, choices, and interests of a subject, apart from their expression. For example, racially biased stops and frisks infringe on the US constitutional liberty of black subjects to be free from arbitrary searches and seizures, according to the Fourth Amendment. Poverty, viewed as a cross-racial or multiracial condition, may also be a limitation on freedom.

Liberty is an external political matter, usually pertaining to rights under positive law and compliance or noncompliance with such rights. Freedom is a contested, psychic issue. If constraints on liberty are persistent and systematic, they may limit a people's freedom, because individual decisions, choices, and interests are influenced and inspired by what individuals are practically able to do—that is, by their liberties. We can say that a people with a history of poverty accompanied by restrictions in economic liberty will not be as economically advantaged as a people whose history did not contain such restrictions because the accumulation of wealth is passed on from generation to generation. The disparity in family wealth between American blacks and whites is a strong example of this kind of ongoing constraint.[70] However, when economic disadvantage is combined with racist attitudes and undereducation, the distinction between liberty and freedom may be eroded. Children growing up in constrained circumstances may not develop freedom in the psychic sense, in addition to restrictions on their liberty. An important part of the choices enabled by psychic freedom requires imagination, as well as self-esteem and knowledge of the broader world beyond one's immediate family and neighborhood.

Jean-Paul Sartre emphasized that the ability to realistically project oneself into a future set of circumstances that are different from undesirable present ones requires some knowledge of those future circumstances to cultivate a motivational dissatisfaction with present conditions. Progressive activists have shown how Sartre's hypothesis can become a politicizing method: Organizers during early stages of Second Wave feminism conducted "consciousness raising" exercises to make women aware of their oppression;[71] practical leaders of ethnic and racial liberatory movements from Ella Baker to Paolo Friere have proceeded with education of members of oppressed groups,[72] exactly to activate their freedom, so that they can choose greater liberty as a goal.

The Distribution of Liberty

To speak of rights violations is to speak of unjust curtailments of liberty. It is presumed here that liberty consists of all the things that people are able to do, that they are in some sense entitled to do, as human beings, and which government is not supposed to obstruct them from doing. The reduction of procedural justice to distributive justice in chapter 4 is now useful for considering liberty and freedom as relevant to oppositional active discourse. The view of liberty and freedom, but especially liberty, as a matter of procedural justice is more nebulous than a view of liberty as a good that is distributed. Procedures tend to be imagined as methods that need only be justified by those who administer them and their superiors. But distributions give goods out and they have end recipients. If procedures are not always followed in the same way for blacks and whites, this can be defended by saying that something unusual happened in a particular case or that there was an innocent error. It may be claimed as an excuse that the client/citizen/resident/plaintiff/defendant did not correctly perform her role in the procedure, interfered with the procedure delivered by officials, or failed to act in a way that expressed reasonable understanding of the procedure, for example, there was a "language barrier."

Procedures can be legally designed in ways that have different effects on members of different groups. Police racial profiling as part of a general procedure for maintaining law and order, photo ID requirements for voter registration, and English instructions to residents who do not speak English are all examples of legal procedures that have been justified without mention of race or ethnicity, but have different effects on members of different populations. However, if justice is viewed as a matter of distribution, the relevant test that it has been carried out, given all other things equal, is whether the social good that the procedure is supposed to be a fair or neutral means for distributing, does get fairly and neutrally distributed. The view of just procedures as distributed goods, bypasses color-blind policies that do not have race-neutral effects.

When the distribution of negative liberty or procedural justice is unfair, the result is distributional injustice. Judith Shklar, known mainly for her claim that cruelty should be a primary or foundational concern of secular, liberal political philosophy,[73] addresses injustice as a subject in its own right. Although Shklar does not refer to Berlin, her focus on the distinction between an external judgment that another who is disadvantaged is suffering from misfortune and the sufferer's perception that she has been treated unjustly does echo Berlin's qualification that there may be minimal material and cultural requirements for a person's negative liberty to be of value to her. A poor, uneducated person, who does not understand the broader institutional causes of her poverty, may not be able to use the negative liberty legally afforded her to do anything she chooses with her life. She might not have the freedom to take advantage of her liberty. It may not occur to her to resist micro-oppressions or try to move into a better neighborhood because she has not been educated in ways that stimulate imagination. Externally, she may be viewed as having made poor choices or lacking the virtue of a work ethic, but subjectively she may experience her situation as unjust. And if her freedom has been impaired by restrictions on her liberty, her situation is objectively unjust.

In *The Faces of Injustice*, Shklar expresses an overall dissatisfaction with philosophical theories of justice, which is parallel to the project undertaken in this book. However, although she begins by defining injustice as "an act that goes against some known legal or ethical rule,"[74] her approach to defining injustice in this short text continually wrestles with the distinction between injustice and misfortune. On the way, Shklar is very mindful of the overwhelming odds against victims of injustice in societies considered just: they are not heard; their resignation is taken for granted; they do not have remedies for redress or timely access to rectification in the form of punishment against those who have been unjust to them; they lack the means to change social practices that cause their injustice. Shklar is particularly sensitive to the plight of those who suffer injustice in concrete ways on account of their "ascriptive" identities, such as women until very recently and US racial minorities more or less permanently.[75] Nevertheless, and this is where Shklar's otherwise pessimistic combination of history and political philosophy makes an invigorating contribution to the subject of activist political discourse, she posits the recognition of injustice as both an eons-long and fundamental human moral intuition and a general civic right and obligation in democratic societies. Shklar writes:

> A black American may well expect that she will not get a fair hearing from certain public agencies, but as a citizen she knows this is not what is expected *of* our public servants, and she can certainly feel and communicate her sense of injustice when her claims are ignored. There is, however, a bond between these two kinds of expectation. Unpredicted, sudden injustices are resented far more intensely than

> those one has learned to endure as a member of a group. They tear away the emotional protection created by resignation and allow distress to burst from its confines.[76]

Furthermore, in a way that just happens to capture the spirit of this chapter and complete the book, Shklar provides this statement of legitimation for political activism:

> Democratic principles oblige us to treat each expression of a sense of injustice not just fairly according to the actual rules but also with a view to better and potentially more equal ones. To be sure, democracy does not fulfill its immanent promises quickly, but at least it does not silence the voice of protest, which it knows to be the herald of change.[77]

Shklar here proclaims the democratic legitimacy of expression of a sense of injustice. When we add that idea to the known existence of injustice as part of a Bentleyan process of government, active political discourse in the form of real life action can be recognized as part of the whole process of government. There is sound reason to undertake it and support its undertaking with confidence, both for change now and in view of the Long Revolution.

7

POSTSCRIPT: AN INVITATION TO THE READER

I have tried throughout this book to be only as abstract and idealistic as absolutely necessary. I have followed Bentley's idea that political action in reality should be considered along with words, as part of political life. I have insisted that not only is an ideal of justice unnecessary but that it distracts us from what we really care about in real life, which is injustice in a comparative sense: Compared to how whites are treated, blacks in America are not treated justly and the main problem is that they are treated in ways that whites are not treated.

I have tried to show how just political procedure in an unjust society is in principle no different from other things that are distributed. I have treated academic liberatory discourse as a valid political activity in a democratic society where about half who can vote do not vote or otherwise take an interest in politics beyond news-entertainment. I have insisted that words are not action and also drawn a distinction between Big Picture theoretical understanding and small picture sites for action. And, as my descriptions of our current era of white-black race relations perforce became more grim, I have tried to create an optimistic perspective, for the long term. With help from Judith Shklar, I found a way to include oppositional political discourse as a legitimate component of a Bentlyan view of political life in a democracy. But this is just a book, so it's not action and it has no sure path to action. Worse than that, I have not spent a lot of time and effort on What Is to Be Done?

The most important thing that could be done at this time to ease, provide liberatory progress in, and reconcile differences in US race relations, the one thing that we have never had and never had a greater need for is a "common narrative." A common narrative is not a debate or one side in a debate, not even the side that sees more deeply or is morally right. A common narrative is not a history lesson or a critique of national foreign policy, capitalism, war, commercialism, materialism. It does not criticize any religion or proselytize for any religion and neither does it proceed from special religious authority or anointment. It is neither a jeremiad nor a picture of utopia for our time. It is neither bitter nor saccharine. It does not blame or valorize any racial group in the present or dramatize or minimize the suffering of any racial group in the past. A common narrative about race in our time would be an account of the present situation that contending factions could agree upon, which made it possible to move forward to better relations between American whites and American nonwhites, especially blacks.

The first problem in constructing a common narrative about race, on the basis of which members of all groups, both oppressive and oppressed, could experience a sense of belonging to one larger whole is an epistemological issue. Any common narrative or account or story must be based on background knowledge that is shared by all. That is, people who can appreciate the same narrative share some implicit or explicit background information. In this regard, the problem or issue of *ignorance* becomes intensely relevant.

The term "ignorance" refers to what is not known. Present writings about epistemological ignorance with regard to race reemphasize that whites do not know certain things about nonwhites, because it doesn't serve them to have that knowledge. To this extent, white ignorance is willed. A large part of what whites do not know concerns the history and present circumstances of unjust suffering and realities of the equal or random distribution of human capabilities, yearnings, strivings, virtues, and aptitudes, among all racial groups. Some of this particularly white ignorance is mirrored by ignorance among nonwhites about their own group histories, oppression, and individual capacities.[1] Analysts of such ignorance in effect describe conceptual schemas that are difficult to change, because they are rooted in individual emotional responses and identities. It is important to relate relevant ignorance to such noncognitive schemas, in order to appreciate the automatic nature of this ignorance, because once a whole ignorant schema is in place, it can be activated without conscious deliberation. This activation brings with it certain kinds of blinders or blocks to originally unwanted information that has no place in the schema and which therefore cannot be processed. However, this is only part of the epistemological racial situation concerning ignorance and only part of the epistemological human situation concerning immorality and injustice.

Another part of what members of oppressive or dominant groups fail to know about members of oppressed or subordinate groups is the moral belief that members of those groups share with them. That moral belief counts as shared background knowledge, because it is a guideline for the most basic assessment and action, even though it tends to become most obvious in times of crisis, tragedy, and grief. It has been repeatedly claimed that nonwhites have lesser degrees of humanity or have been viewed and treated as subhuman, by whites, and to some extent by other nonwhites and in the form of self-contempt. This assessment of subhumanity could not be made or put forth with any expected influence if there were not a shared presumption that all human beings share the same humanity. (The assessment of subhumanity has a history of argument for it as an exception, for example, "All humans share humanity, except for humans X, for reasons Y and Z.") It is this shared belief in shared humanity that needs to be nourished and emphasized for there to be common narratives about race. Of course, more than species membership is at stake here, because the gene-spliced cyborgs, who will likely be our descendants, will also need the belief. What is shared is a vague but deep and disturbing recognition that others suffer, the capacity to be moved by their high achievements, and the ability to be touched by their immersion in the humbleness of daily details.

The subject is not empty platitudes of color blindness, such as "I don't see race," but a full perceptual, intellectual, moral, emotional, and spiritual ability to perceive and recognize the humanity of another human being and a moral or spiritual capacity to respond to that. If we think about Tamir Rice, the wrongness of his killing is that he was a twelve-year-old human being—a child with the vulnerability and potential of every human child—who was instantaneously executed without due process or probable cause.[2] If a common narrative cannot be generated by that case, because he was brandishing a toy gun that may have looked real, or because some may know that some twelve-year-olds are already rotten, then there is a common narrative in the case of Walter Scott: We already all know that it is wrong to shoot an unarmed person in the back when he is running away from you and presents no immediate danger.[3]

One could propose, as was implied in the 1996 movie *A Time to Kill*, that racial difference blocks the recognition of shared humanity.[4] On that view, for whites to recognize the shared humanity of blacks, they have to imagine that those blacks are white. However, the same inability to perceive and respond to shared humanity across racial difference also occurs within racial groups. For example, many academics, as well as other career-focused professionals, get so caught up in their game that they fail to attend to injuries to their opponents and subordinates on a human level. They may seize opportunities at the expense of someone who is already vulnerable in some way, if only in having less power in the organization. In academic life at this time, within institutions both externally pressured and internally hell-bent on success, cronyism, retaliation, and preemption is practiced with impunity against perceived opponents. This moral barbarism in higher education is indeed color blind, although it also manages to specially blindside and mangle people of color, who always have preexisting disadvantages due to their racial identities.

Still, here in the academy, where most readers now live and work, there is plenty of rhetoric about humanity and even universal or common humanity, so the positive side of ignorance, namely what is universally believed—and presumably for all practical purposes, known—should not be difficult to tap into, as a foundation for resistance and a background for a common narrative. One objection to a common narrative, thus broadly drawn, might be that it fails to specifically address injustice in its focus on what enables oppressors, as well as the oppressed, to move ahead.[5] But what is understood as shared can be the basis for demands that some human beings should not be treated as others are already not treated, not always on the grounds of race, but always on the grounds of humanity. And it would be a lack of grace to begrudge oppressors recognition of their shared humanity, especially when their cooperation is required in order to move on.

Shakespeare understood the reciprocal nature of shared humanity (sometime between 1596 and 1598 in *The Merchant of Venice*), with its inherent dangers for oppressors:

> Shylocke: I am a Jew. Hath not a Jew eyes? hath not a Jew hands, organs, dimensions, senses, affections, passions? fed with the same food, hurt with the same weapons, subject to the same diseases, healed by the same means, warmed and cooled by the same winter and summer, as a Christian is? If you prick us, do we not bleed? if you tickle us, do we not laugh? if you poison us, do we not die? and if you wrong us, shall we not revenge? If we are like you in the rest, we will resemble you in that. If a Jew wrong a Christian, what is his humility? Revenge. If a Christian wrong a Jew, what should his sufferance be by Christian example? Why, revenge. The villany you teach me, I will execute, and it shall go hard but I will better the instruction.

Some of the fear that US whites express about US blacks is of the villainy they have taught turning back on them in revenge. There has never been such substantial revenge, but fear of it does stem from an implicit recognition of shared humanity. However, if such recognition can cause fear, it could also lead to humility. Indeed, recognition of shared humanity works best with the gentler emotions, which is why religious affiliation in black communities often gives rise to a call for love—or grace.

When President Obama delivered the eulogy for Reverend Clementa C. Pinckney, who was among nine killed by a twenty-one-year-old white supremacist at Emanuel A.M.E. Church in Charleston, South Carolina, his theme was grace. As American presidents do in times of national stress, Obama evoked God. He spoke of God's grace as unearned benevolence and favor. He also spoke of the grace of those killed in their dedicated struggles for racial justice and the grace of their family members in expressing forgiveness of the killer.[6]

Obama used two different meanings of grace. The first flows from a deity to whom not all who have something at stake in American race relations give credence. The second meaning of grace is secular. It is what Shylock admonishes that he lacks. Not to seek the revenge that one's oppressors have taught one that it is natural to seek is the form of grace as forbearance. In a secular sense, grace as forbearance does not involve turning the other cheek, but of having enough reserve strength to experience great loss without lusting after the revenge taught by oppressors. There are two reasons a person might have grace as forbearance: to respect one's own value despite loss and diminishment, and, to recognize the humanity of another despite his or her being an oppressor. The first bestows grace on oneself, the second on someone who more clearly does not deserve it. Bestowing grace on oneself requires intangible privilege or quite simply, enough strength to keep alive the future, as well as hope. Any human being can do both of these things, but neither one is easy and there are few opportunities to build habitual behavior, when such grace may be a response to events that happen but once in a person's lifetime.

Beyond a call to fundamental principles of our shared humanity, which would include recognition of, with grace as forbearance, the badness of pain, humiliation, and undeserved death, I do not know what such a common narrative would be in its positive content. However, I am sure it can be built if we assume neither a benevolent nor a malevolent universe, but merely an indifferent one. If we think we cannot build it, then we have to agree with Martin Heidegger's 1966 remark that "only a god can save us."[7] In anticipation of divine salvation, politics becomes religion. But there are too many religions in the United States and the rest of the world to justify a state privileging one. Moreover, theocracy is an arbitrary form of rule, depending on the interpretations of the self-proclaimed anointed. It endangers everyone if the Supreme Leader of the United States suggests that an administration and its supporters have a special dispensation from God or are merely doing God's work or carrying out God's will. President Bush identified his administration with the presence of God and President Obama identified the congregation to whom he delivered the eulogy with moral goodness blessed by God. A religious idea of grace, especially only Christian grace, excludes too many human beings.

The common narrative would need to be very general so that it could be compatible with specific local narratives formed for concrete objectives.[8] Presidents Bush and Obama each drew from too-narrow local religious narratives in speaking to Americans as a whole. In a common narrative, shared spirituality could be evoked, but in terms general enough to include all human religions (not just Christianity).

A common narrative would tell us, like the promise in the title of Paul Gauguin's painting, "Where Do We Come From? What Are We? Where Are We Going?"[9] I invite the reader to create such a narrative, either collaboratively or individually, and email it to me as an attachment in a Word document (nzack@uoregon.edu).

NOTES

PREFACE

1. For example, of course: Richard Overton's *An arrow against all tyrants and tyranny, shot from the prison of Newgate into the prerogative bowels of the arbitrary House of Lords and all other usurpers and tyrants whatsoever. Wherein the original, rise, extent, and end of magisterial power, the natural and national rights, freedoms and properties of mankind are discovered and undeniably maintained; the late oppressions and encroachments of the Lords over the commons legally (by the fundamental laws and statutes of this realm, as also by a memorable extract out of the records of the Tower of London) condemned; the late Presbyterian ordinance (invented and contrived by the diviners, and by the motion of Mr Bacon and Mr Tate read in the House of Commons) examined, refuted, and exploded, as most inhumane, tyrannical and barbarous. Printed at the backside of the Cyclopian Mountains, by Martin Claw-Clergy, printer to the reverend Assembly of Divines, and are to be sold at the sign of the Subject's Liberty, right opposite to Persecuting Court. 12 October 1646*. Available at http://theindependentpatriot.com/.

2. Naomi Zack, "Racial Inequality and a Theory of Applicative Justice," *Philosophy and the Black Experience*, American Philosophical Association Newsletter, vol. 13, no. 1 (Fall 2013), 6–11.

3. Naomi Zack, "Philosophical Theories of Justice, Inequality, and Racial Inequality," *Graduate Faculty Philosophy Journal*, Special Issue on Race in the History of Philosophy, New School University, 2014, 353–68.

4. Naomi Zack, *White Privilege and Black Rights: The Injustice of US Police Racial Profiling and Homicide* (Lanham, MD: Rowman and Littlefield, 2015).

1. IDEAL THEORY, NONIDEAL THEORY, AND EMPIRICAL POLITICAL THEORY

1. Harry S. Truman, *Off the Record: The Private Papers of Harry Truman*, Robert H. Ferrell, ed. (Columbia: University of Missouri Press, 1980), 119.

2. Literature on such training, and the need for it, abounds. See, for instance, L. Robert Kohls and John L. Knight, *Developing Intercultural Awareness: A Cross-Cultural Training Handbook* (Yarmouth, ME: Intercultural Press, 1982).

3. For the civil rights movement and Vietnam War images, see Michelle Miller, "The Children Who Marched into Civil Rights History," CBS News, May 3, 2013, http://www.cbsnews.com/news/the-children-who-marched-into-civil-rights-history/; Daily Mail Reporter, "I've Never Escaped from That Moment: Girl in Napalm Photograph That Defined the Vietnam War 40 Years On," *Daily Mail*, UK News, June 1, 2012, http://www.dailymail.co.uk/news/article-2153091/Napalm-girl-photo-Vietnam-War-turns-40.html; concerning implementation of the 1990 Americans with Disabilities Act, see: "Disability," *National Campaign to Restore Civil Rights*, http://www.rollbackcampaign.org/issues/item.disabilityrights2143 (1999–2014); Arlene Mayerson, "The History of the Americans with Disabilities Act," Disability Rights Education And Defense Fund, 1992. http://dredf.org/news/publications/the-history-of-the-ada/; concerning Walter Scott, see Michael S. Schmidt and Matt Apuzzo, "South Carolina Officer Is Charged with Murder of Walter Scott," April 7, 2015, http://www.nytimes.com/2015/04/08/us/south-carolina-officer-is-charged-with-murder-in-black-mans-death.html.

4. There are many varieties of such ignorance about oppression. On the psychological aspects of denial as understood by counselors at this time, see, for instance, George Simon, "Understanding Denial as a Defense Mechanism," *Counseling Resource*, http://counsellingresource.com/features/2008/10/08/denial-as-defense-mechanism/.

5. For discussions of the deliberate nature of such ignorance, see the articles in Shannon Sullivan and Nancy Tuana, eds., *Race and Epistemologies of Ignorance* (Albany: State University of New York Press, 2007). On contemporary denial of oppression, see Barbara Perry, "'No Biggie': The Denial of Oppression on Campus," *Education, Citizenship and Social Justice* 5, no. 3 (November 2010): 265–79 , doi: 10.1177/1746197910387543. See also, Kimberly D. Brostrom, " Teaching Inequality: Denial, Defensiveness, and the Diminishing of Oppression," *Faculty Focus*, June 17, 2013. Brostrom quotes "members of privileged groups are culturally authorized to interpret other people's experiences for them, to deny the validity of their own reports, and to impose their views of reality," from Allan G. Johnson, *Privilege, Power, and Difference*, 2nd

ed. (Boston: McGraw-Hill, 2006), 109, http://www.facultyfocus.com/articles/teaching-and-learning/teaching-inequality-denial-defensiveness-and-the-diminishing-of-oppression/.

6. This interpretation of what Rawls really meant is a composite of criticism and suggestions offered by Cheyney Ryan, Colin Koopman, Alan Reynolds, and one of the press's anonymous external reviewers.

7. A. J. Simmons, "Ideal and Nonideal Theory," *Philosophy & Public Affairs* 38 (2010): 5–36. doi: 10.1111/j.1088-4963.2009.01172.x, p. 7. Simmons's quotations are from: John Rawls, *A Theory of Justice* (Cambridge, MA: Harvard University Press, 1971); John Rawls, *The Law of Peoples* (Cambridge, MA: Harvard University Press, 1999).

8. Simmons, "Ideal and Nonideal Theory," 8, n. 9. Referring to Rawls, *Law of Peoples*, 90.

9. Congress of the United States, "The Preamble to the Bill of Rights," http://www.archives.gov/exhibits/charters/bill_of_rights_transcript.html.

10. See Peter Laslett, "*Two Treatises of Government* and the Revolution of 1688," Introduction, Part III, in Laslett, ed. *Locke: Two Treatises of Government* (Cambridge: Cambridge University Press, 1967), 45–66; Locke's justification of private property rights is somewhat beside the point here, but in terms of its relationship to political theory and models for democratic government, see C. B. MacPherson, *The Political Theory of Possessive Individualism* (Oxford: Oxford University Press, 1962). In moral philosophy, Locke offered a justification for private property based on workers deserving to own that upon which they have labored and the assumption that labor is necessary for human life, both practically, and because God decrees it. For a discussion of the metaphysics of Locke's theory of ownership and a critique, see Naomi Zack, *Bachelors of Science: Seventeenth Century Identity, Then and Now* (Philadelphia: Temple University Press, 1996), chap. 6, "Propriety and Civic Identity." On the enclosure movement, see Ellen Meiksins Wood, "The Agrarian Origins of Capitalism," *Monthly Review*, 1998, http://www.monthlyreview.org/798wood.htm.

11. See Stanley N. Katz, "Thomas Jefferson and the Right to Property in Revolutionary America," *Journal of Law and Economics* 19, no. 3 (1976): 467–88.

12. Economic benefit and racism have been well examined as causes of slavery, but often neglected is the overvaunting idea of ownership that was allowed to extend to human beings themselves. While the distinction between slaves and freemen as a fundamental division in society appears as a matter of fact at the beginning of the Code of Justinian, modern slavery during the Age of Enlightenment required special justification and property rights were part of that. See Naomi Zack, *The Ethics and Mores of Race: Equality after the*

History of Philosophy (Lanham, MD: Rowman and Littlefield, 2011), chap. 4, "Moral Law and Slavery."

13. The Bush administration had a policy of increasing the number of racial and ethnic minorities who owned their own home. Lenders obliged by financing mortgages that were beyond the financial capacity of many borrowers. Housing prices were going up during this process. When the housing price bubble burst, many new homeowners, minorities especially, lost their jobs and then their homes. The ownership society thereby became a new mechanism of dispossession for many who were disadvantaged to begin with. Criticism of Bush for contributing to the housing bubble of 2007 occurred on both the left and the right. See Jo Becker, Sheryl Gay Stolberg, and Stephen Labaton, "Bush Drive for Home Ownership Fueled Housing Bubble," *New York Times*, December 21, 2008, http://www.nytimes.com/; Steve Sailer, "2002: Bush's Speech to the White House Conference on Increasing Minority Homeownership," VDare.com, September 24, 2008, http://www.vdare.com/. Accessed July 3, 2013.

14. Matthew R. Durose and Patrick A. Langan, "Felony Sentences in State Courts," *Bureau of Justice Statistics Bulletin*, U.S. Department of Justice, Office of Justice Programs, 2002, http://www.bjs.gov/content/pub/pdf/fssc02.pdf. Accessed June 3, 2013.

15. Gretchen Morgenson and Louise Story, "In Financial Crisis, No Prosecutions of Top Figures," *New York Times*, April 14, 2011, http://www.nytimes.com/.

16. For instance, Johanna Luttrell, in examining the plight of women in contemporary third-world slums, argues against their exploitation for the national aims of increased productivity, on the grounds of their human dignity (PhD dissertation from the Philosophy Department of the University of Oregon, 2013).

17. See n. 12, supra.

18. See *Original Letters of John Locke, Algernon Sidney and Lord Shaftesbury: With an Analytical Sketch of the Writings and Opinions of Locke and Other Metaphysicians:1847*, ed. T. Forster, https://play.google.com/.

19. John Rawls, *A Theory of Justice* (Cambridge, MA: Belknap Press, Harvard University Press, 1999), 117–18.

20. Rawls, *A Theory of Justice*, 307–8.

21. See Charles Mills in Carole Pateman, and Charles W. Mills, *Contract and Domination* (Malden, MA: Polity Press, 2007), chaps. 3 and 4.

22. Charles W. Mills, "Rawls on Race/Race in Rawls," *The Southern Journal of Philosophy* 47 (2009): 160–85, quote from page 161, http://www.havenscenter.wisc.edu/files/Mills-Rawls%20on%20Race.pdf. Accessed June 3, 2013.

23. It is possible to neglect racial oppression in political philosophy, while doing nonideal theory. This is evident throughout political philosophy and Hume, Kant, Rousseau, and John Stuart Mill are only a few examples. See Zack, *The Ethics and Mores of Race*, chaps. 3–7.

24. Amartya Sen, *The Idea of Justice* (Cambridge, MA: Harvard University Press, 2009), 5.

25. See ibid., 4–10, 10–11, 12, 21–22, 24–27, 45–46, 80–81.

26. Ibid., 15–16.

27. Ibid., 9.

28. Ibid., 20.

29. Ibid., 20–22, quote from page 21.

30. For overviews of Bentley's main ideas and reception in academia over the first half of the twentieth century, see Bertram M. Gross, "*The Process of Government; A Study of Social Pressures* by Arthur F. Bentley, *The American Political Science Review* 44, no. 3 (September 1950): 742–48; and Sidney Ratner, "Arthur F. Bentley, 1870-1957," *Journal of Philosophy* 55, no. 14 (July 3, 1958): 573–78. For a more recent account, see Nicholas Lemann, "Conflict of Interests," *The New Yorker*, August 11, 2008, http://www.newyorker.com/.

31. John Dewey and Arthur Fisher Bentley, *Knowing and the Known* (Boston: Beacon Press, 1949).

32. Arthur F. Bentley, *The Process of Government* (Chicago: University of Chicago Press, 1908), 22.

33. Ibid., 30.

34. Ibid., 45.

35. Ibid., 91.

36. Ibid., 92.

37. Ibid., 55.

38. Ibid., 56.

39. Ibid., 107.

40. Ibid., 109.

41. Ibid., 246.

42. Ibid., 249.

43. Ibid., 110–36.

44. Ibid., 154–55.

45. Ibid., 171.

46. See, for instance, John C. Moskop and Kenneth V. Iserson, "Triage in Medicine, Part II: Underlying Values and Principles," *Annals of Emergency Medicine* 49, no. 3 (2007): 282–87; Gerald R. Winslow, *Triage and Justice* (Berkeley: University of California Press, 1982), 143–55. For discussion of this kind of usage or application of Rawls's ideal theory, see Naomi Zack, *Ethics for Disaster* (Lanham, MD: Rowman and Littlefield, 2009, 2011), 24–25.

47. See Paul F. Kress, *Social Science and the Idea of Process: The Ambiguous Legacy of Arthur F. Bentley* (Urbana: University of Illinois Press, 1970). Kress writes:

> [Morton] White's study of American social thought extends to history, law, philosophy, and economics and includes such individual scholars as Charles Beard, James Robinson, Oliver Wendell Holmes, John Dewey, and Thorstein Veblen. Although White does not discuss Bentley, his conception of what these insurgents were trying to do has undeniable parallels with the program of *The Process of Government*. All of them insist upon coming to grips with life, experience, process, growth, context function. They are all products of the historical and cultural emphases of the nineteenth century, following, being influenced by, reacting from its great philosophers of change and process. (page 22) (Referring to Morton White, *Social Thought in America: The Revolt against Formalism* [Boston: Beacon Press, 1957], 13.

2. LIMITS OF LAW AND GOVERNMENT

1. Frédéric Bastiat, "The State," in *Journal des débats* (1848) par. 5.20. http://www.econlib.org/library/Bastiat/basEss5.
2. Arthur Bentley, *The Process of Government: A Study of Social Pressures* (Chicago: University of Chicago Press, 1908), 272.
3. Ibid., 175.
4. Ibid., 260–61.
5. Ibid., 274.
6. Dean Mathiowetz, "'Interest' Is a Verb: Arthur Bentley and the Language of Interest," *Political Research Quarterly* 61, no. 4 (December 2008): 622–35.
7. Bentley, *The Process of Government*, 211.
8. Ibid., 210–22.
9. Ibid., 225.
10. Ibid., 236.
11. Ibid., 279. Bentley also refers to lynching in neutral terms on pages 259 and 400.
12. Of course, this complicity was not limited to government officials but included many white citizens and local residents. For a comprehensive history, see Sherrilyn A. Ifill, "Creating a Truth and Reconciliation Commission for Lynching," *Law & Inequality* 21 (2003): 263–311, http://digitalcom-

mons.law.umaryland.edu/. On black leadership silence about lynching in the late nineteenth century and Ida B. Wells's courageous exception, see Cornel West with Christa Buschendorf, *Black Prophetic Fire* (Boston: Beacon Press, 2014), 139–60.

13. For YouTube postings of President George W. Bush saying he was "the decider," see "I'm the decider and I decide what is best," from http://www.crooksandliars.com/, April 19, 2006, and https://www.youtube.com/watch?v=irMeHmlxE9s.

14. John Cottingham, Robert Stoothuff, and Dugald Murdoch, trans. *The Philosophical Writings of Descartes* (Cambridge, UK: Cambridge University Press, 1991), 358–59.

15. Natural law was used both to prove God's existence and attest to his goodness, as well as it could suggest a standard of reason and order apart from God. These themes have been identified in philosophical writings spanning from Plato (*Euthyphro*), to Aquinas, Leibniz, the Cambridge Platonists, and more recently, Richard Swinburne. See Jonathan Bennett, "Descartes's Theory of Modality" (from *The Philosophical Review* 103, no. 4 [1994]) *Early Modern Texts*, http://www.earlymoderntexts.com/jfb/descmod.pdf, and Richard Swinburne, "The Existence of God," at http://users.ox.ac.uk/. Accessed November 2014.

16. On the issues involved in Agamben's differences from other state-of-exception theorists, see Stephen Humphreys, "Legalizing Lawlessness: On Giorgio Agamben's *State of Exception*," *The European Journal of International Law* 17, no. 3 (2006): 677–87, at http://www.ejil.org/pdfs/17/3/208.pdf.

17. Giorgio Agamben, *The State of Exception*, Kevin Attell, trans. (Chicago: University of Chicago Press, 2005), 86.

18. See Humphreys, "Legalizing Lawlessness," 679–80.

19. Humphreys in "Legalizing Lawlessness" (684–87) refers to U.S. Supreme Court and Britain's Law Lords cases decided against those governments on the basis of human rights obligations.

20. Slavoj Žižek, "Biopolitics: Between Terry Shiavo and Guantanamo," *ArtForum*, December 2005, http://www.lacan.com/zizartforum1205.htm.

21. See Humphreys, "Legalizing Lawlessness," 680; Agamben, *The State of Exception*, 58–59.

22. Agamben, *The State of Exception*, 88.

23. Locke's interest derived from the interest of his wealthy patron, Lord Shaftesbury. Peter Laslett presents an interesting case that Locke wrote in the *Second Treatise* years before the 1689 regime change and not just following it, as its 1689 date of publication by an anonymous author indicates. See John Locke, *Two Treatises of Government*, Peter Laslett, ed. (Cambridge: Cambridge University Press, 1965), 30–66. For Locke's representation of the inter-

ests of the new class of wealthy landowners, see C. B. Macpherson, *The Political Theory of Possessive Individualism* (Oxford: Oxford University Press, 1962), esp. chap. 5, 197–220.

24. On the history of British parliament, see "Birth of the English Parliament," *Living History*, http://www.parliament.uk/about/living-heritage/evolutionofparliament/originsofparliament/birthofparliament/overview/origins/.

25. Locke, *Second Treatise*, in Laslett, *Two Treatises*, II, vii, secs. 87–89, 323–25.

26. Locke, *Second Treatise*, in Laslett, *Two Treatises*, II, vii, sec. 12, 274–75.

27. Locke, *Second Treatise*, in Laslett, *Two Treatises*, II, ix, sec. 211, 406–7.

28. Locke, *Second Treatise*, in Laslett, *Two Treatises*,II, vii, secs. 77–82, and sec. 119, 318–21 and 347–48.

29. Locke, *Second Treatise*, in Laslett, *Two Treatises*, II, v, secs. 32 and 35, 290–91 and 292.

30. Locke, *Second Treatise*, in Laslett, *Two Treatises*, II, v, sec. 91, 296–97; II, viii, sec. 104, 336.

31. Locke, *Second Treatise*, in Laslett, *Two Treatises*, II, iv, sec. 22, 284.

32. Locke, *Second Treatise*, in Laslett, *Two Treatises*, II, iv, sec. 22, 328; II, x, sec. 135, 357–58.

33. Locke, *Second Treatise*, in Laslett, *Two Treatises*, II, v, secs. 32 and 35, 290–91 and 292.

34. Michel Foucault, *The History of Sexuality*, vol. 1, Robert Hurley, trans. (Paris: Éditions Gallimard, 1976), 138.

35. On Kropotkin's views, see his own entry, s.v. anarchism, *Encyclopedia Britannica*, 11th ed. (Cambridge: At the University Press, 1910), 914–19; also, Peter Kropotkin, *Kropotkin, Selected Writings*, Hubert Read, ed. (London: Freedom Press, 1992).

36. Friedrich Engels, *Anti-Dühring* , Emile Burns, trans. 3rd ed. Part III, sec. 2. 1894, 290.

37. Agamben, *The State of Exception*, 88.

38. Hannah Arendt, "Philosophy and Politics," *Social Research* 57, no. 1, Philosophy and Politics II (Spring 1990): 73–103, quotation page 90. Arendt's thoughts here were further developed in her reflections on Eichmann, as she covered and reported on his trial for the *New Yorker Magazine* in 1961. See Hannah Arendt, *Eichmann in Jerusalem* (New York: Viking Press, 1963).

39. Arendt, "Philosophy and Politics," 101.

40. See United Nations, "Universal Declaration of Human Rights," http://www.un.org/en/documents/udhr/index.shtml#ap; "The United Nations Universal Declaration of Human Rights—An Historical Record of the Drafting Process," http://www.un.org/depts/dhl/udhr/members_cduke.shtml. The eight

members of the drafting committee were chaired by Eleanor Roosevelt. Two of the members were philosophers and the remaining members had distinguished careers in law and government.

41. See Eric S. Hall and Zorka Karanxha, "School Today, Jail Tomorrow: The Impact of Zero Tolerance on the Over-Representation of Minority Youth in the Juvenile System," *PowerPlay* 4, no. 1 (2012): 1–30.

42. Agamben, *The State of Exception*, 88.

43. Agamben, *The State of Exception*, 88.

44. Jean Baudrillard, *In the Shadow of the Silent Majorities or, the End of the Social and Other Essays*, Paul Foss, John Shonston, and Paul Patton, trans. (New York: Semiotext(e), 1978), 21.

45. Ibid., 22.

46. Fair Vote, "Voter Turnout," *The Center for Voting and Democracy*, 2000–2014, http://www.fairvote.org/research-and-analysis/voter-turnout/.

47. Ibid. "What Effects Voter Turnout Rates in the U.S.?"

48. Baudrillard referred to similarities in style of presentation between news and entertainment but more recent combinations of comedy with news take the merger of these genres to another level, moving from distraction (from the news) to absurdity (of the news), perhaps. See ibid., 37–38. On terrorism and hyper-reality, see ibid, 48–58.

49. Ibid., 20.

50. See note 9. Supra.

51. Thanks to Sarah Hamid for insisting on the political potential of new electronic media in our discussion of the penultimate copy of the book manuscript.

52. Arendt, "Philosophy and Politics," 92.

53. Nicholas Lemann, "Conflict of Interests," *New Yorker*, August 11, 2008, http://www.newyorker.com/arts/critics/atlarge/2008/08/11/080811crat_atlarge_lemann?currentPage=all.

3. IDEAL EQUALITY AND REAL INEQUALITY

1. George Orwell, *Animal Farm* (New York: Penguin Press, 1956), 133.

2. This is the epigraph to Clive Barker's *Books of Blood* (New York: Berkeley Publishing, 1984), vols. 1–3.

3. Mill's claim that there is and ought to be more freedom of speech than action seems intuitively obvious, because speech requires less effort than action and does not have immediate physical effect. Mill's reason was that unrestrained action could be harmful: "All that makes existence valuable to any one, depends on the enforcement of restraints upon the actions of other people."

John Stuart Mill, *On Liberty* (Kitchner, Ontario: Batouche Books, 1859, 2001), 9. Still, unrestrained speech, for example, insults, devaluation, slander, can also be very harmful.

4. Immanuel Kant, *Groundwork of the Metaphysics of Morals*, trans. and ed. Mary Gregor (Cambridge: Cambridge University Press, 1998), 42.

5. Ibid., 25.

6. United Nations, preamble to "The Universal Declaration of Human Rights," http://www.un.org/en/documents/udhr/; henceforth, references to the preamble appear as UDHR.

7. See Jacques Maritain, "The Grounds for an International Declaration of Human Rights," in *The Human Rights Reader: Major Political Essays Speeches, and Documents from Ancient Times to the Present*, ed. Micheline R. Ishay (New York: Routledge, 2007), 2–6.

8. Part of the efforts of Du Bois and others to get the United Nations to focus on the 150 million inhabitants of Africa was connected to their concomitant effort to get the UN to consider the plight of African Americans, the consideration of which never got out of committee. For contextual information, see W. E. B. Du Bois, *Selections, 1944–1963*, vol. 3 of *The Correspondence of W. E. B. Du Bois*, ed. Herbert Aptheker (Amherst: University of Massachusetts Press, 1978), 153–55, 492.

9. See Charles Mills, "Contract of Breach: Repairing the Racial Contract," chap. 4 in Carole Pateman and Charles Mills, *Contract and Domination* (Malden, MA: Polity Press, 2007), 106–33.

10. Overall, this chapter, like the paper on which it is based (see note 3 supra) is a rethinking of the main themes of several chapters from my *Ethics and Mores of Race* (Lanham, MD: Rowman and Littlefield, 2011). In this book my focus was on the narrowness of philosophical theories of justice, which I described as an expression of historical and contextual mores or the ethnocentrism of privileged white writers. Here, I am proceeding more simply, in a logical way, for example: Without a principle of universal *human* equality, there can be no derivation of racial equality from a more fundamental principle.

11. Cicero's circle model has contemporary influence. See Martha Nussbaum, "Kant and Stoic Cosmopolitanism," *The Journal of Political Philosophy* 5, no. 1 (1997): 27, 6n, citing Julia Annas, *The Morality of Happiness* (Oxford: Oxford University Press, 1993), 262–76, on Hierocles as a source.

12. Cicero, *On Obligations*, trans. and ed. Peter G. Walsh (Oxford: Oxford University Press, 2000), 19, Book 1, 51. For a wider discussion of the real life inequalities that Cicero benefited from, see Zack, *Ethics and Mores of Race*, 50–54.

13. See Moses I. Finley, *Ancient Slavery and Modern Ideology* (New York: Viking Press, 1980), 80, 112.

14. On the views of the Catholic Church regarding slavery, see John T. Noonan Jr., "Development in Moral Doctrine," *Theological Studies* 54, no. 4 (1993): 662–77.

15. See Milton Meltzer, *Slavery: From the Rise of Western Civilization to the Renaissance*, vol. 1 of *Slavery: A World History* (New York: Da Capo Press, 1993), 223–30; Milton Meltzer, *Slavery: From the Renaissance to Today*, vol. 2 of *Slavery: A World History* (New York: Da Capo Press, 1993), 8.

16. Gal. 3:26–29.

17. Seneca, *De Beneficiis*, III.20, cited in Aquinas, *Summa Theologiae* II–II.104.5; Thomas Aquinas , "Obedience and Rebellion," in *On Law, Morality, and Politics*, trans. Richard J. Regan, ed. William P. Baumgarth (Indianapolis: Hackett Publishing Company, 1988), 183.

18. For textual citations and analyses, see chapters 1 and 2 of Naomi Zack, *Philosophy of Science and Race* (New York: Routledge, 2002), 9–40.

19. Locke excluded Catholics from religious toleration because of their allegiance to "foreign princes," and also atheists, because they could not swear on "oaths." See John Locke, *A Letter Concerning Toleration*, ed. Mario Montuori (The Hague: Martinus Nijhoff, 1963), 91, 93.

20. Immanuel Kant, *Grounding for the Metaphysics of Morals*, in *Kant's Ethical Philosophy*, trans. and ed. James W. Ellington (Indianapolis: Hackett, 1994), 36.

21. Ibid., 14.

22. John Stuart Mill, *The Subjection of Women*, in *On Liberty and Other Writings*, ed. Stefan Collini (Cambridge: Cambridge University Press, 1989), 13–14; on these inegalitarian assumptions of Mill's, see Thomas McCarthy, *Race, Empire, and the Idea of Human Development* (Cambridge: Cambridge University Press, 2009), 168.

23. For an illuminating and comprehensive discussion of the inequality posited by utilitarians, see Marco Guidi, "'Everybody to Count for One, Nobody for More than One': The Principle of Equal Consideration of Interests from Bentham to Pigou," in "John Stuart Mill," special issue of *Revue d'études* 4, no. 1 (2008): 40–69.

24. John Rawls, *A Theory of Justice*, rev. ed. (Cambridge, MA: Harvard University Press, 1999), 442.

25. Ibid.

26. "Last of all, we should recall here the limits of a theory of justice. Not only are many aspects of morality left aside, but no account is given of right conduct in regard to animals and the rest of nature. A conception of justice is but one part of a moral view." Ibid., 441, see also 15 and 448.

27. Evolution could make us morally good or bad and there is some evidence, or at least argument, that it could provide the kind of extension of basic moral impulses that are important for a sense of justice or reaction to injustice. See Robert Folger and Daniel P. Skarlicki. "The Evolutionary Bases of Deontic Justice," *Justice, Morality, and Social Responsibility* (Charlotte, NC: Information Age Pub, 2008), 29–62. Also, Judith N. Shklar, *The Faces of Injustice* (New Haven, CT: Yale University Press, 1990), 87–88, where she claims anecdotally that infants and animals react to perceptions of injustice as unfairness.

28. See Naomi Zack, "Racial Inequality and a Theory of Applicative Justice," *Philosophy and the Black Experience*, The American Philosophical Association Newsletter 13, no. 1 (2013), 6–11.

29. About rulings employing this doctrine, see Adam Winkler, "Fatal in Theory and Strict in Fact: An Empirical Analysis of Strict Scrutiny in the Federal Courts," *Vanderbilt Law Review* 59, no. 3 (2006): 793–869.

30. Amarta Sen, "Equality of What"? The Tanner Lecture on Human Values, Stanford University, May 22, 1979, *Artikler*, http://www.akira.ruc.dk/.

31. Amartya Sen, "The Possibility of Social Choice," Nobel Lecture, published by Trinity College, Cambridge, CB2 1TQ, UK, December 8, 1998, 178–215. http://www.cse.iitb.ac.in/~damani/ctaraReading/AmartyaSenSocialChoice.pdf; Also published in *American Economic Review*, 89, 1999.

32. Amartya Sen, *The Idea of Justice* (Cambridge, MA: Harvard University Press, 2009).

33. G. A. Cohen, "Equality of What? On Welfare, Goods and Capabilities," *Recherches Économiques de Louvain/Louvain Economic Review* 56, no. 3/4, Alternatives to Welfarism (1990): 357–82, published by Department of Economics, Universite Catholique de Louvain Stable URL: http://www.jstor.org/; idem, "On the Currency of Egalitarian Justice,"*Ethics* 99, no. 4 (July 1989): 906–44. Stable URL: http://links.jstor.org/.

34. Sen, Nobel Lecture, 183, 193–94.

35. See Drew DeSilver, "U.S. Income Inequality, On Rise for Decades, Is Now Highest since 1928," *Pew Research Center*, http://www.pewresearch.org/fact-tank/2013/12/05/u-s-income-inequality-on-rise-for-decades-is-now-highest-since-1928/. The issue of increasing income inequality does not actually rise to a live political issue because there is nothing in the formal structure of law or its wider practice that would count it as illegal. Concern about such inequality is either part of moral discourse or in demonstrations, for example, "Occupy Wall Street," where a fundamental discontent with the economic system of capitalism is expressed.

36. Sen, Nobel Lecture, 182–84.

37. Ibid., 190ff. et passim.

38. Cohen, "Equality of What? On Welfare, Goods and Capabilities," quotes pages 368 and 370.

39. Amartya Sen, *Inequality Reexamined*, Russell Sage Foundation, 1992, 4.

40. Amartya Sen, *The Idea of Justice*, 291, 293, and 293–94.

41. See ibid., xi–xiii, xvi, 9, 15–18, 70, 96–105, 301–2.

42. Ibid., 297.

43. See "Why Judges and Prosecutors Engage in Plea Bargaining," *NOLO Law for All*, http://www.nolo.com/legal-encyclopedia/why-judges-prosecutors-engage-plea-bargaining.html.

4. THE DISTRIBUTION OF PROCEDURAL JUSTICE

1. John Rawls, *A Theory of Justice* (Chicago: University of Chicago Press, 1971), 54.

2. Ibid., 297.

3. See Amartya Sen, *Development as Freedom* (New York: Alfred A. Knopf, 1999), preface.

4. Samuel Fleischaker, *A Short History of Distributive Justice* (Cambridge, MA: Harvard University Press, 2004), 62–68. Fleischaker identifies Adam Smith's thought as the pivot between the Aristotelian and contemporary idea of distributive justice. Earlier, Judith Shklar gave up on the Aristotelean meanings of distributive justice, in favor of what she called "primary justice." Judith N. Shklar, *The Faces of Injustice* (New Haven, CT: Yale University Press, 1990), 18.

5. See Iris Young, *Inclusion and Democracy* (Oxford, UK: Oxford University Press, 2002), 31–32. See also Ben Eggleston, "Procedural Justice in Young's Inclusive Deliberative Democracy," *Journal of Social Philosophy* 35, no. 4 (Winter 2004): 544–49. In terms of Rawls, Eggleston interprets Young as beginning with a notion of perfect procedural justice but cashing it out in terms of an inclusion requirement that more resembles Rawlsian imperfect procedural justice.

6. Martin Gustafsson, "On Rawls's Distinction between Perfect and Imperfect Procedural Justice," *Philosophy of the Social Sciences* 34 (2004): 300–305.

7. Ibid., 204, quoted from Rawls, *A Theory of Justice*, 74.

8. In a different kind of response to the tautology or triviality problem, it may be feasible to supplement the standard of procedural justice with values other than justice, such as ethics or religion, for cases where procedural justice results in inegalitarian outcomes that appear to violate the spirit of principles

on which just procedures are based. Emanuela Ceva, distinguishing between pure procedural justice and "substantive concerns," argues for such an approach. However, Ceva doesn't take into account the Rawlsian notion of imperfect procedural justice, which would seem theoretically able to accommodate such substantive/distributional issues, because procedural justice is known to be imperfect. Her examples of conscientious objection and civil disobedience lead to a model of just procedure coexisting with an allowance for exemptions from it that are based on non-public values. See Emanuela Ceva, "Just Procedures with Controversial Outcomes: On the Grounds for Substantive Disputation within a Procedural Theory of Justice," August 26, 2009, *Phil Papers, Springer and Business Media*, http://philpapers.org/rec/CEVJPW-2.

9. It is not clear, however, that probable cause doctrine remains legally binding on police procedures. For discussion of these and related issues, see Naomi Zack, *White Privilege and Black Rights: The Injustice of US Police Racial Profiling and Homicide* (Lanham, MD: Rowman and Littlefield, 2015), chaps. 2 and 3.

10. Will Kymlicka interprets competing theories of justice with these foci as sharing an ideal of human equality in *Contemporary Political Philosophy: An Introduction* (Oxford, UK: Oxford University Press, 1990). I am merely pointing this out, here, in order to proceed with the reductive analysis of procedural to distributional justice in this chapter. As argued in chapter 3, it is difficult if not impossible to provide a factual foundation for equality as an ideal.

11. See Jonathan Kozol, *Savage Inequalities* (New York: Random House, 1991). For an update, see Michael Busch, "Keeping Faith with the Kids: An Interview with Jonathan Kozol," *Huffington Post*, http://www.huffingtonpost.com/michael-busch/poverty-education_b_2013593.html, October 25, 2012.

12. Eisenhower was reluctant to address racial segregation but did enforce the law of *Brown*. See Kenneth Janda, Jeffrey Berry, and Jerry Goldman, *The Challenge of Democracy: American Government in Global Politics* (Boston: Cengage, 2008), 234–35ff.

13. Thomas Frank, "TSA Proposes Screening Private Jet Passengers," *USA Today*, August 7, 2014, http://abcnews.go.com/Travel/story?id=5999405.

14. Rawls, *A Theory of Justice*, 65–73.

15. Robert Nozick held that new forms of inequality would occur after the equalizing revolution, as a result of voluntary action. See Andrew Lister on this objection as attributed to Will Kymlicka, as well as Nozick, in "Mirage of Social Justice: Hayek Against (and For) Rawls," University of Oxford, Department of Politics and International Relations, *CSSJ* Working Paper SJ017, June 2011. Lister writes in a footnote: "This critique of Nozick's argument about liberty and patterns is originally due to Cheyney Ryan and G. A. Cohen;" Cheyney

Ryan, "Yours, Mine, and Ours: Property Rights and Individual Liberty," *Ethics* 87, no. 2 (1977): 126–41; G. A. Cohen, *Self-Ownership, Freedom, and Equality* (Cambridge: Cambridge University Press, 1995). Cohen's Wilt Chamberlain paper was first published in 1977, http://social-justice.politics.ox.ac.uk/materials/SJ017_Lister_MirageofSocialJustice.pdf, pp. 19–20, note 43.

16. See my comparison of applicative justice with equity in Naomi Zack, "Racial Inequality and a Theory of Applicative Justice," *Philosophy and the Black Experience*, The American Philosophical Association Newsletter, Fall 2013, Vol. 13, no. 1, 6–11.

17. "Wilt Chamberlain," *New World Encyclopedia*, http://www.newworldencyclopedia.org/entry/Wilt_Chamberlain and "Forbes List of Highest Paid Athletes, *Wikipedia*, July 9, 2015, https://en.wikipedia.org/wiki/Forbes%27_list_of_world%27s_highest-paid_athletes.

18. G. A. Cohen, "Robert Nozick and Wilt Chamberlain: How Patterns Preserve Liberty," *Erkenntnis* 11, no. 1, Social Ethics, Part 1 (May 1977): 5–23, 6.

19. Ibid., 16.

20. Ibid.

21. John Locke, *Two Treatises of Government*, Second Treatise, Chapter II, Secs. 6 and 7. http://www.constitution.org/jl/2ndtr02.htm.

22. Rawls, *A Theory of Justice*, 24–25.

23. Ibid., 27.

24. Ibid., 54.

25. This is not Nozick's argument, because, as Will Kymlicka interprets him, Nozick derives almost absolute private property rights from a Lockean notion of self-ownership. However, self-ownership is compatible with varied forms of distribution, including socialism, so that free-market capitalism with limited government is not the only result. Although Nozick does not derive self-ownership from absolute liberty, Kymlicka suggests that Nozick derives its value as a form of freedom, from the more important value of self-determination. See Kymlicka, *Contemporary Political Philosophy*, 94–125.

26. Cheyney C. Ryan, "Yours, Mine, and Ours: Property Rights and Individual Liberty," *Ethics* 87, no. 2 (January 1977): 126–41.

27. Eva Brems and Laurens Lavrysen, "Procedural Justice in Human Rights Adjudication: The European Court of Human Rights," *Human Rights Quarterly* 35 (2013): 176–200. Brems and Lavyrsen's references are (in a remarkable example of one discipline inspired by others but believing they have invented the wheel) to social psychologists: John Thibaut and Laurens Walker, *Procedural Justice: A Psychological Analysis* (Hillsdale, NJ: Erlbaum, 1975); E. Allan Lind and Tom R. Tyler, *The Social Psychology of Procedural Justice* (New York: Plenum Press, 1988).

28. Tom R. Tyler, *Why People Obey the Law* (New Haven, CT: Yale University Press, 2006), 8.

29. Such timelines are common and often presented as rallying points and encouragement for members of oppressed groups, as well as they serve as an accounting of real legal progress toward justice. See for instance, Library of Congress, "Civil Rights Resource Guide," http://www.loc.gov/rr/program/bib/civilrights/external.html.

30. Social theory comes with its own abstractions and problematic reifications. Nonetheless, it has the salutary general effect of keeping written law and legal ideals in perspective, rather than assuming that their mere existence is a guarantee of just practice. See, for instance, Wolfgang Schlachter, "The Sociology of Law as an Empirical Theory of Validity," *European Sociological Review* 19, no. 5 (2002): 537–49, European Academy of Sociology, Second Annual Lecture, Paris, November 16, 2002; Michael Freeman, ed., *Law and Sociology: Current Legal Issues 2005*, vol. 8 (New York: Oxford University Press, 2006), especially Freeman's preface, 1–15.

31. The full text of these amendments reads as follows.

AMENDMENT XIII
Passed by Congress January 31, 1865. Ratified December 6, 1865.
Note: A portion of Article IV, section 2, of the Constitution was superseded by the 13th amendment.
Section 1.
Neither slavery nor involuntary servitude, except as a punishment for crime whereof the party shall have been duly convicted, shall exist within the United States, or any place subject to their jurisdiction.
Section 2.
Congress shall have power to enforce this article by appropriate legislation.

AMENDMENT XIV
Passed by Congress June 13, 1866. Ratified July 9, 1868.
Note: Article I, section 2, of the Constitution was modified by section 2 of the 14th amendment.
Section 1.
All persons born or naturalized in the United States, and subject to the jurisdiction thereof, are citizens of the United States and of the State wherein they reside. No State shall make or enforce any law which shall abridge the privileges or immunities of citizens of the United States; nor shall any State deprive any person of life, liberty, or property, without due process of law; nor deny to any person within its jurisdiction the equal protection of the laws.
Section 2.

Representatives shall be apportioned among the several States according to their respective numbers, counting the whole number of persons in each State, excluding Indians not taxed. But when the right to vote at any election for the choice of electors for President and Vice-President of the United States, Representatives in Congress, the Executive and Judicial officers of a State, or the members of the Legislature thereof, is denied to any of the male inhabitants of such State, being twenty-one years of age,* and citizens of the United States, or in any way abridged, except for participation in rebellion, or other crime, the basis of representation therein shall be reduced in the proportion which the number of such male citizens shall bear to the whole number of male citizens twenty-one years of age in such State.

Section 3.

No person shall be a Senator or Representative in Congress, or elector of President and Vice-President, or hold any office, civil or military, under the United States, or under any State, who, having previously taken an oath, as a member of Congress, or as an officer of the United States, or as a member of any State legislature, or as an executive or judicial officer of any State, to support the Constitution of the United States, shall have engaged in insurrection or rebellion against the same, or given aid or comfort to the enemies thereof. But Congress may by a vote of two-thirds of each House, remove such disability.

Section 4.

The validity of the public debt of the United States, authorized by law, including debts incurred for payment of pensions and bounties for services in suppressing insurrection or rebellion, shall not be questioned. But neither the United States nor any State shall assume or pay any debt or obligation incurred in aid of insurrection or rebellion against the United States, or any claim for the loss or emancipation of any slave; but all such debts, obligations and claims shall be held illegal and void.

Section 5.

The Congress shall have the power to enforce, by appropriate legislation, the provisions of this article.

**Changed by section 1 of the 26th amendment.*

AMENDMENT XV

Passed by Congress February 26, 1869. Ratified February 3, 1870.

Section 1.

The right of citizens of the United States to vote shall not be denied or abridged by the United States or by any State on account of race, color, or previous condition of servitude—

Section 2.

The Congress shall have the power to enforce this article by appropriate legislation.
http://www.archives.gov/exhibits/charters/constitution_amendments_11-27.html

32. Robert J. Cottrol, Raymond T. Diamond, and Leland B. Ware, *Brown v. Board of Education: Caste, Culture, and the Constitution* (Lawrence: University Press of Kansas, 2003), 27.

33. Ibid., 26–27.

34. For the development of the one-drop rule in the late nineteenth century, see James Kinney, *Amalgamation!* (Westport, CT: Greenwood, 1985); Joel Williamson, *New People* (New York: Free Press, 1980). For an analysis of the failure of American society to recognize mixed black and white racial identities, see Naomi Zack, *Race and Mixed Race* (Philadelphia: Temple University Press, 1993).

35. Ibid., 31–33. See also *Plessy v. Ferguson* (No. 210), Argued: April 18, 1896, Decided: May 18, 1896, 163 U.S. 537; Keith Weldon Medley, *We as Freeman: Plessy v. Ferguson*, Greta, Louisiana: Pelican, 2003.

36. See Zack, *Race and Mixed Race*.

37. Cottrol et al. *Brown*, 40–46.

38. Cottrol et al. *Brown*, 34–40.

39. Summaries of the facts and reasoning in these cases are in Cottrol et al. *Brown*, 40–46.

40. *Brown v. Board of Education of Topeka* (No. 1.) 347 U.S. 483, Argued: December 9, 1952, Decided: May 17, 1954, Legal Information Institute, Cornell University, http://www.law.cornell.edu/supremecourt/text/347/483.

41. Mary L. Dudziak, "Desegregation as a Cold War Imperative," *Stanford Law Review* 41, no. 1 (November 1988): 61–120, Stable URL: http://www.jstor.org/stable/1228836, quotes pages 76–77.

42. Cottrol et al. *Brown*, 183–207.

43. Jonathan Kozol has extensively documented and analyzed this racially based unequal situation in U.S. K–12 education. See Jonathan Kozol, "An Unequal Education," *ERIC* (Institute of Education Services) 46, no. 5 (2000): 46–49; *Savage Inequalities: Children in America's Schools* (New York: Crown, 1991); and *The Shame of the Nation: The Restoration of Apartheid Schooling in America* (New York: Crown, 2005). Kozol has also addressed the pressures on black children during the period of forced school integration after *Brown*, in *Amazing Grace: The Lives of Children and the Conscience of a Nation* (New York: Crown, 1995).

44. John Iceland and Daniel H. Weinberg "Racial and Ethnic Residential Segregation in the United States 1980–2000," United States Bureau of the Census, 3–4.

45. Erica Frankenberg, Chungmei Lee, and Gary Orfield, *The Civil Rights Project Harvard University*, January 2003, 1–82, quote from page 4, http://www.civilrightsproject.harvard.edu.

46. See Edward J. Littlejohn and Leonard S. Rubinowitz, "Black Enrollment in Law Schools: Forward to the Past?" *T. Marshall Law Review* 12, no. 415 (1986): 415–55; American Bar Association, "American Lawyer Demographics," lawyer_demographics_2013.authcheckdam.

47. Derrick Bell, "*Brown v. Board of Education* and the Interest-Convergence Dilemma," *Harvard Law Review* 93, no. 518 (1980), reprinted in D. Bell, *Shades of Brown: New Perspectives on School Desegregation* (New York: Teachers College Press, 1980), cited by Dudziak, "Desegregation as a Cold War Imperative," 64, n. 8.

48. See Richard M. Dalfiume, "The 'Forgotten Years' of the Negro Revolution," *The Journal of American History* 55, no. 1 (June 1968): 90–106, http://www.jstor.org/stable/1894253.

49. "Executive Order 9981, Harry S. Truman Museum and Library," http://www.trumanlibrary.org/9981.htm. At the turn of the twenty-first century, the presence of African Americans in the US Navy was in the low single digits. On background cultural reasons for this, see John W. Bodnar, "How Long Does It Take to Change a Culture? Integration at the U.S. Naval Academy," *Armed Forces and Society* 25, no. 2 (Winter 1999): 289–306; ProQuest Social Sciences Premium Collection, 289; Sherie Mershon and Steven Schlosmann, *Foxholes and Color Lines: Desegregating the U.S. Armed Forces* (Baltimore: Johns Hopkins University Press, 1998).

50. Dudziak, "Desegregation as a Cold War Imperative," 93–98.

51. Dudziak, "Desegregation as a Cold War Imperative," quoted on page 102 from *President's Committee on Civil Rights To Secure These Rights*, 57.

52. Dudziak, "Desegregation as a Cold War Imperative," 64–65, quoted from "Brief for the United States as Amicus Curiae at 6," *Brown v. Board of Education*," 347 U.S. 483 (1954).

53. Louis Menard, "The Sex Amendment: How Women Got in on the Civil Rights Act," *The New Yorker*, July 21, 2014, 74–81, Kennedy quote page 77. Menard here offers an insightful essay review of two books, published in commemoration of the fifty-year anniversary of the 1964 Civil Rights Act: Clay Risen, *The Bill of the Century* (Bloomsbury) and Todd Purdum, *An Idea Whose Time Has Come* (Holt). While Menard's focus is on the part played by Alice Paul and her colleagues in getting Title VII into the bill, he is also mindful of the white male political control of the Civil Rights Act, claiming that both books make it clear "how deliberately the 1964 Civil Rights Act was conceived of as the accomplishment of white men" (page 76).

54. Ibid.

55. Ibid.

56. Menard, "The Sex Amendment," quotes from pages 79 and 80. It's interesting to note this use of "intersectionality" implying that black women would be protected as blacks after the Civil Rights Act was passed, black women's employment rights often came behind those of black men and white women. See Kimberle Crenshaw's now classic, "Mapping the Margins: Intersectionality, Identity Politics, and Violence against Women of Color," *Stanford Law Review* 43, no. 6 (July 1991): 1241–99, http://www.jstor.org/stable/1229039.

57. Menard's summary of these oppositions is interwoven throughout "The Sex Amendment." For a detailed account of the politics in terms of Johnson's actions, see Sylvia Ellis, *Freedom's Pragmatist: Lyndon Johnson and Civil Rights* (Gainesville: University Press of Florida, 2013); Zachary Karabell and Jonathan Rosenberg, *Kennedy, Johnson, and the Quest for Justice: The Civil Rights Tapes* (Charlottesville, VA: Miller Center of Public Affairs, 2003).

58. Menard, "The Sex Amendment," Johnson quote page 77.

59. Martin Luther King Jr. Nobel Peace Prize Acceptance Speech, 1964, http://www.nobelprize.org/nobel_prizes/peace/laureates/1964/king-acceptance_en.html.

60. Ibid.

5. DISCOURSE, PROPHECY, AND ATMOSPHERE

1. Lydia Saad, "U.S. Mood on Economy Up, Race Relations Sharply Down" Gallup, January 19, 2015, http://www.gallup.com/poll/181187/mood-economy-race-relations-sharply-down.aspx.

2. "Address by Franklin D. Roosevelt," 1941, The Joint Congressional Committee on Inaugural Ceremonies, http://www.inaugural.senate.gov/swearing-in/address/address-by-franklin-d-roosevelt-1941.

3. Debra Cassens Weiss, "Justice Department Finds 'Unconstitutional Policing' in Ferguson; Racial Bias, Revenue Focus Cited." *ABA Journal*, March 4, 2015, http://www.abajournal.com/news/. Concerning the nationwide aspects of this problem, see Gene Johnson, "Federal Bias Report Resonates across U.S.," *Register Guard* from *Associated Press*, March 9, 2015, http://registerguard.com/. The Department of Justice report can be found at, United States Department of Justice, Civil Rights Division, "Investigation of the Ferguson Police Department," March 4, 2015, http://www.justice.gov/.

4. See Matt Taibbi with Molly Crabapple, *The Divide: American Injustice in the Age of the Wealth Gap* (New York: Random House, 2014).

5. For discussion of Broken Windows Theory, see Naomi Zack, *White Privilege and Black Rights: The Injustice of US Police Racial Profiling and Homicide* (Lanham, MD: Rowman and Littlefield, 2015), 52, 98.

6. See Michelle Alexander, *The New Jim Crow: Mass Incarceration in the Age of Colorblindness* (New York: New Press, 2011). In chapter 6, I will take up the gap between written discourse, as represented by this book, and real life changes.

7. See "NYPD officers say they had stop-and-frisk quotas," Marina Carver, *CNN* , March 26, 2013, http://www.cnn.com/2013/03/22/justice/new-york-stop-and-frisk-trial/.

8. For a more comprehensive criticism of white privilege discourse, see Zack, *White Privilege and Black Rights*, chap. 1.

9. For instance, when death results from a failure of police to protect or rescue, constitutional arguments have run aground on judicial insistence that negative rights mean the subject is what government officials may not do, and not what they should have done and failed to do. See, for example, David P. Currie, "Positive and Negative Constitutional Rights," University of Chicago Law Review 53, no. 3 (Summer 1986): 864–90, http://www.jstor.org/stable/1599586.

10. See n. 8, supra.

11. In *The Color of Our Shame*, Christopher Lebron discusses the phenomenon identified by Vesla Weaver as "frontlash." After the legislation of the civil rights era was passed, new policies holding racial inequality in place came into being, including: President Johnson's LEAA (Law Enforcement Assistance Administration, known since 1984 as the Office of Justice Programs) that provided aid to local enforcement toward arrests and stipulated mandatory minimum sentences, with a disproportionate effect on minorities; Reagan's War on Drugs that famously has higher sentences for forms of cocaine more likely to be used in minority neighborhoods (*The Color of Our Shame: Race and Justice in Our Time* [New York: Oxford University Press, 2013], 80–86). See chapter 6 for discussion of frontlash.

12. On the tension between social movement rhetoric and litigation and the judicial interpretation of the US Constitution, see Tomiko Brown-Nagin, "Elites, Social Movements and the Law: The Case of Affirmative Action," *Columbia Law Review* (2005): 1436–528, https://www.law.virginia.edu/pdf/workshops/0405/brownnagin.pdf.

13. Hannah Arendt, "Thoughts on Politics and Revolution: A Commentary," interview by Adelbert Reif, in *Crises of the Republic*, Summer 1970, Denver Lindley, trans. in Hannah Arendt, *The Last Interview and Other Conversations* (Brooklyn: Melville House, 2013), 67–106, views referred to in text pages 68–78.

14. Ibid.

15. For description of this trend, see Michael Rizzo and Ronald G. Ehrenberg, "Resident and Nonresident Tuition and Enrollment at Flagship State Universities," in *College Choices: The Economics of Where to Go, When to Go, and How to Pay for It* (Chicago: University of Chicago Press, 2004), 303–54; John J. Cheslock and Matt Gianneschi, "Replacing State Appropriations with Alternative Revenue Sources: The Case of Voluntary Support," *Journal of Higher Education* (2008): 208–29.

16. That academic ideas or utopian visions do not immediately lead to social change is perhaps a good thing if one considers the disastrous consequences when trained philosophers have been influential in government; for example, Plato's adventures in Syracuse, members of the Khmer Rouge in Cambodia, Slobodan Milošević in Yugoslavia, not to mention varied totalitarian contributions from those such as Machiavelli, the Third Reich's Carl Schmitt, or Martin Heidegger during his rectorate at the University of Freiburg (see chapter 6).

17. John Rawls, *A Theory of Justice* (Cambridge, MA: Harvard University Press, 1999), 117–18.

18. Deborah Dinner, "A Firebrand Flickers," *Legal Affairs*, March/April 2006, http://www.legalaffairs.org/issues/March-April-2006/review_Dinner_marapr06.msp.

19. Redzo Mujcic and Paul Frijters, "Still Not Allowed on the Bus: It Matters If You're Black or White!" *IZA Discussion Paper No. 7300*, April 6, 2003; Britni Danielle, " White Privilege Is Real, and Now There's Research to Prove it," Takepart.com, Yahoo news , February 28, 2015, http://news.yahoo.com/white-privilege-real-now-research-prove-184105763.html.

20. See Alessandra Stanley, "Oscars 2015: Passionate Speeches, but Few Surprises," *New York Times*, February 23, 2015, http://mobile.nytimes.com/; Patrick T. Fallon, "The Show," *New York Times*, February 24, 2015, http://www.nytimes.com/.

21. For Oscar ratings and audience numbers, see http://deadline.com/.

22. Thanks to Janine Jones for pointing this out after reading an earlier draft of this chapter section.

23. See Vesla M. Weaver, "Frontlash: Race and the Development of Punitive Crime Policy," *Studies in American Political Development* 21, no. 2 (2007): 230–65. See also n. 11, supra.

24. Tara J. Yosso et al., "Critical Race Theory, Racial Microaggressions, and Campus Racial Climate or Latina/o Undergraduates," *Harvard Educational Review* 79, no. 4 (Winter 2009): 659–90.

25. See, for instance, this discussion of white student ignorance about black history and current racism: Jamicia Lackey, "Exposing Duke's Racial Atmosphere," *The Chronicle*, February 2, 2002, http://www.dukechronicle.com/arti-

cles/2002/02/21/exposing-dukes-racial-atmosphere#.VQdLGLl0zcs. Concerning discrimination in career advancement, see the use of "atmosphere" in Richard Prince, "CNN's Racial 'Atmosphere' Worries NABJ," Richard Prince's Journal-isms, *Maynard Institute*, October 8, 2014, http://mije.org/richard-prince/cnn-atmosphere-worries-nabj.

26. Darryl Pinckney, *Blackballed: The Black Vote and US Democracy* (New York: New York Review of Books, 2014), 56–74.

27. Aphorism/epigraph appearing on "Dr. Cornel West: Official Website," as "Lover of Music: I'm a blues man in the life of the mind. I'm a jazz man in the world of ideas," accessed March 29, 2015, http://www.cornelwest.com/index.html#.VRjkU7l0zcs.

28. The Cornel West Site: Youtube.Com had 87,300 entries on March 29, 2015. https://www.google.com/.

29. For intellectual biographic information on Cornel West, see George Yancy, ed. *Cornel West: A Critical Reader* (Malden, MA: Blackwell Publishers, 2001), 1–6; "Cornel West—Biography," The European Graduate School, http://www.egs.edu/faculty/cornel-west/biography/; Cornel West with Christa Buschendorf, *Black Prophetic Fire* (Boston: Beacon Press, 2014), 1–9.

30. Cornel West, "Afterward: Philosophy and the Funk of Life," in Yancy, *Cornel West*, 246–62.

31. Cornel West, *Prophesy Deliverance!: An Afro-American Revolutionary Christianity* (Philadelphia: Westminster Press, 1982), 15.

32. Cornel West, "Afterward: Philosophy and the Funk of Life," in Yancy, *Cornel West*, 349–50. West makes these comparative claims in his response to Lewis Gordon's article in the same volume. See Lewis R. Gordon, "The Unacknowledged Fourth Tradition: An Essay on Nihilism, Decadence, and the Black Intellectual Tradition in the Existential Pragmatic Thought of Cornel West," in Yancy, *Cornel West: A Critical Reader*, 38–58.

33. Ibid., 361.

34. See excerpt from 2015 film, *Religion and Revolution: A Dialogue between Cornel West and Bob Avakian*, https://www.youtube.com/watch?v=72EfAuUFDoE.

35. Cornel West with Christa Buschendorf, *Black Prophetic Fire* (Boston: Beacon Press, 2014), 100ff. (I will say more about Raymond Williams in chapter 6.)

36. Cornel West, "Afterward: Philosophy and the Funk of Life," in Yancy, *Cornel West*, 351.

37. Amy Goodman and Juan González, "Attica Is All of Us: Cornel West on 40th Anniversary of Attica Prison Rebellion," *Democracy Now!*: A Daily Independent Global News Hour, http://www.democracynow.org/2011/9/12/attica_is_all_of_us_cornel.

38. Cornel West with Christa Buschendorf, *Black Prophetic Fire* (Boston: Beacon Press, 2014), 139 and 141.

39. Goodman and González, "Attica Is All of Us."

40. Ibid.

41. West with Buschendorf, *Black Prophetic Fire*, 165.

42. Overlooked in Obama's status is the mixed race identity with which he began his campaign in 2007. For discussion of issues related to that transformation, which would only confuse matters to bring into the current text, see Naomi Zack, "The Fluid Symbol of Mixed Race," *Hypatia*, 25th Anniversary Issue, 25, no. 4 (Fall 2010): 875–90.

43. Amy Goodman and Juan González, "Cornel West on the Election of Obama," *Democracy Now!*: A Daily Independent Global News Hour, November 19, 2008, http://www.democracynow.org/2008/11/19/cornel_west_on_the_election_of.

44. West has been involved in an ongoing controversy within the African American intelligentsia concerning federal programs that he believes harm the poor and fail to support black people. "Ferguson Signifies the End of the Age of Obama," *CNN News International*, November 27, 2014, https://www.youtube.com/watch?v=0PD_ixQlrvc.

45. Ibid.

46. West, "Afterward: Philosophy and the Funk of Life," in Yancy, *Cornel West*, 347.

47. See notes 27 and 28, supra.

48. See Ian Ayres and Daniel Markovits, "Ending Excessive Police Force Starts with New Rules of Engagement," *Washington Post*, December 25, 2014, http://www.washingtonpost.com/.

49. David A. Snow, "Extending and Broadening Blumer's Conceptualization of Symbolic Interactionism," *Symbolic Interaction* 24, no. 3 (2001): 367–77.

50. On the tension between honoring King and the result that most streets named after him have been in poor black neighborhoods, see Derek Alderman, "A Street Fit for a King?," Department of Geography, University of Tennessee, Knoxville Tennessee, http://mlkstreet.com/. In Illinois alone, eighty-nine schools are named Lincoln. Although eighty-nine Illinois public schools carry Lincoln's name, there is less historical irony here because President Lincoln is a national hero, claimed by whites as well as blacks. *Chicago Tribune*, February 11, 2009, http://articles.chicagotribune.com/.

51. Carla Bernardo, "Tears as UCT Debates Rhodes Statue," *IOL News*, March 26 2015, http://www.iol.co.za/.

52. West constantly refers to music throughout his speech and writing, for example, in his discussion of Malcolm X: "Malcolm was music in motion; he

was Black music in motion; he was jazz in motion, and, of course, jazz has improvisation, swing, and the blues, as brother Wynton Marsalis says, these three fundamental elements." West with Buschendorf, *Black Prophetic Fire*, 118. For a critique of the Eurocentrism in West's references to music, see Gordon, "The Unacknowledged Fourth Tradition."

53. See excerpt from "Religion and Revolution: A Dialogue between Cornel West and Bob Avakian," https://www.youtube.com/watch?v=72EfAuUFDoE.

6. THE DISCOURSE OF POLITICAL ACTIVISM

1. Theodore Parker, *The Collected Works of Theodore Parker: Sermons, Prayers*, Frances Power Cobbe, ed., vol. 2 (London: Trubner and Co., 1879), 48, https://books.google.com/; rephrased in: "GRAND INSPECTOR INQUISITOR COMMANDER, Section XXXI, [Inspector Inquisitor]" in *Morals and Dogma of the Ancient and Accepted Scottish Rite of Freemasonry: Prepared for the Supreme Council of the Thirty-Third Degree, for the Southern Jurisdiction of the United States*, Albert Pike, ed., Charleston, A.M. 5641, 1905 [Copyright 1871], 825–841, quote page 838, http://books.google.com/.

2. Frederick Douglass, "If There Is No Struggle, There Is No Progress," West Indian Emancipation Speech, Canandaigua, New York, August 3, 1857, available at Black Past.org, http://www.blackpast.org/1857-frederick-douglass-if-there-no-struggle-there-no-progress.

3. Caroline Sotello Viernes Turner, Samuel L. Myers Jr., and John W. Creswell, "Exploring Underrepresentation: The Case of Faculty of Color in the Midwest," *Journal of Higher Education* 70, no. 1 (January/February, 1999), 27–59, see esp. page 30ff.

4. Antonio Gramsci, *Selections from the Prison Books* (London: Lawrence and Wishart, 1982), 9ff.

5. Cornel West with Christa Buschendorf, *Black Prophetic Fire* (Boston: Beacon Press, 2014), 104–5.

6. See excerpt from the 2015 film, *Religion and Revolution: A Dialogue between Cornel West and Bob Avakian*, https://www.youtube.com/watch?v=72EfAuUFDoE.

7. See, for instance, this well-constructed Kantian argument that says nothing about how real, live people can help the real, live beggars they encounter in the time between such an encounter and the beggar's next meal: Lucy Allais, "What Properly Belongs to Me: Kant on Giving to Beggars," *Journal of Moral Philosophy* (2014): 1–18.

8. "Two steps forward, one step back" connotes some progress, whereas Lenin, in critiquing early twentieth-century communist party discourse re-

ferred to "one step forward, two steps back." See Vladimir Illyich Lenin, "One Step Forward, Two Steps Back (The Crisis in Our Party), Lenin's Collected Works," translated by Abraham Fineberg and Naomi Jochel, Progress Publishers (Written in February–May, 1904), 1964, Moscow, vol. 7, 203–425. Transcription\Markup: D. Walters & K. Goins (2008). https://www.marxists.org/archive/lenin/works/1904/onestep/.

9. Thirteenth Amendment to the US Constitution, Primary Documents, Library of Congress, http://www.loc.gov/rr/program/bib/ourdocs/13thamendment.html.

10. Michelle Alexander, *The New Jim Crow: Mass Incarceration in the Age of Colorblindness* (New York: New Press, 2011), 30–45.

11. Alexander, *The New Jim Crow*, 42ff, 80–84.

12. Vesla M. Weaver, "Frontlash: Race and the Development of Punitive Crime Policy," *Studies in American Political Development* 21, no. 2 (2007): 230–65.

13. See Naomi Zack, *White Privilege and Black Rights: The Injustice of US Police Racial Profiling and Homicide* (Lanham, MD: Rowman and Littlefield, 2015), 52, 98.

14. Alexander, *The New Jim Crow*, 22. Alexander here refers to Loïc Wacquant, "The New Peculiar Institution: On the Prison as Surrogate Ghetto," *Theoretical Criminology* 4, no. 3 (August 2000): 377–89.

15. Ibid.

16. Jamie Peck and Nikolas Theodore, "Commentary. 'Work First': Workfare and the Regulation of Contingent Labour Markets," *Cambridge Journal of Economics* 24, no. 1 (2000): 119–38.

17. See Loïc Wacquant, "Deadly Symbiosis: When Ghetto and Prison Meet and Mesh," *Punishment & Society* 3, no. 1 (2001): 95–133. Wacquant notes that compared to 800,000 black men in custody, there were in 2000, 68,000 black women (see Wacquant's note 1 for his call for further research on black women in prison), http://loicwacquant.net/.

18. Alexander, *The New Jim Crow*, 6–8, 11ff.

19. Steven R. Donziger, *The Real War on Crime: The Report of the National Criminal Justice Commission* (New York: HarperPerennial, 1996). For further sources, see also, Avery F. Gordon, "Prison Industrial Complex: An Interview with Angela Davis," 1999, http://carbonfarm.us/amap/davis_globalism.pdf.

20. See "War Comes Home: The Excessive Militarization of American Policing," ACLU, https://www.aclu.org/war-comes-home-excessive-militarization-american-policing.

21. See Y. Bazin, "Bilderberg People," *Society and Business Review* 7, no. 1 (2012): 102–4; Yovan Byford, *Conspiracy Theories: A Critical Introduction*

(New York: Palgrave Macmillan, 2011); Harry Paul Jeffers, *The Bilderberg Conspiracy* (New York: Kensington Publishing, 2009).

22. Riva Siegel, "Why Equal Protection No Longer Protects: The Evolving Forms of Status-Enforcing State Action," *Stan. L. Rev.* 49 (1997): 1111–48, http://digitalcommons.law.yale.edu/cgi/viewcontent.cgi?article=2093&context=fss_papers.

23. Alexander, *The New Jim Crow*, 11.

24. On the lack of independent scientific foundation for social racial categories, see Albert Atkin, *The Philosophy of Race* (Oxford, UK: Acumen, 2012); Nina G. Jablonski, *Living Color: The Biological and Social Meaning of Skin Color* (Oakland: University of California Press, 2012); John Relethford, *The Human Species: An Introduction to Biological Anthropology* (New York: McGraw-Hill, 2009–2012); Naomi Zack, *Philosophy of Science and Race* (New York: Routledge, 2002).

25. Alexander is aware of the social construction of race but does not seem to draw the conclusion that it wasn't constructed once and for all before the twentieth century, but continues to be constructed on an ongoing basis. For discussion of contemporary post-9/11 constructions of race, see Falguni Sheth, *Toward a Political Philosophy of Race* (Albany: State University of New York Press, 2009). For accounts of earlier history, see Michael Omi and Howard Winant, *Racial Formation in the United States*, 3rd ed. (New York: Routledge, 2014). On the vagaries of how race and mixed race have been dealt with in the US Census, see Naomi Zack, "American Mixed Race: Theoretical and Legal Issues," *Harvard BlackLetter Law Journal* 17 (Spring 2001): 33–46; "Philosophy and Racial Paradigms," *Journal of Value Inquiry* 33, no. 3 (September 1999); 299–317. (Reprinted in *A Companion to African American Philosophy*, Tommy Lott and John Pittman, eds. [New York: Blackwell Publishers, 2002], 239–54).

26. Alexander, *The New Jim Crow*, 33–34.

27. David C. Anderson, *Crime and the Politics of Hysteria: How the Willie Horton Story Changed American Justice* (New York: Crown, 1995).

28. For discussion of this "trope" in writing by George Yancy, and later, in a speech by President Obama, see Naomi Zack, *White Privilege and Black Rights: The Injustice of U.S. Police Racial Profiling and Homicide* (Lanham, MD: Rowman and Littlefield, 2015), 22, for the purse clutching and door lock clicking context and chapters 2 and 3 for the legality of police killings of unarmed black men.

29. Ibid. See George Yancy, *Black Bodies/White Gazes: The Continuing Significance of Race* (Lanham, MD: Rowman and Littlefield, 2008), esp. chap. 1.

30. Alexander, *The New Jim Crow*, 107, 162, 199.

31. Ibid., 199–200.

32. See, for instance, Ryan S. King, Marc Mauer, and Tracy Huling, "Big Prisons, Small Towns: Prison Economics in Rural America." *Sentencing Project*, 2003, http://prison.ppjr.org.

33. For a comprehensive account of what poor people incarcerated under current drug laws face after their release, see Alexander, *The New Jim Crow*, chaps. 4 and 5, 140–220.

34. Alexander, *The New Jim Crow*, 57.

35. Talk Poverty.Org, "Basic Statistics," 2009–2015, Center for American Statistics, http://talkpoverty.org/basics/, consulted April 6, 2015.

36. Alexandra Kalev and Frank Dobbin, "Enforcement of Civil Rights Law in Private Workplaces: The Effects of Compliance Reviews and Lawsuits over Time," *Law and Social Inquiry* 31, no. 4 (2006): 855–903.

37. Raymond Williams, *The Long Revolution* (Cardigan, UK: Parthian, 2011).

38. Raymond Williams, "The Romantic Artist," in *Romanticism*, Robert F. Gleckner and Gerald E. Enscoe, eds. (Detroit, MI: Wayne State University Press, 1974), 261–86, quote page 270.

39. Raymond Williams, *Modern Tragedy*, Pamela McClellum, ed. (Peterborough, Ontario: Broadview, 2006), 102.

40. Williams, *The Long Revolution*, 387.

41. Ibid. See also the foreword by Anthony Barnett, page xvii.

42. I first introduced this idea of a history of the future in my *Inclusive Feminism: A Third Wave Theory of Women's Commonality* (Lanham, MD: Rowman and Littlefield, 2005), 121–22, 133–34.

43. Raymond Williams, *Towards 2000* (Harmondsworth, UK: Penguin, 1985), 268–69.

44. Jens Manuel Krogstad, "Hispanics Only Group to See Its Poverty Rate Decline and Incomes Rise," FactTank, Pew Research Center, http://www.pewresearch.org/.

45. Lucius Outlaw, "Toward a Critical Theory of 'Race,'" in *Race and Racism*, Bernard Boxill, ed. (Oxford, UK: Oxford University Press, 2000), 58–82.

46. Peter Kihss, "Dr. W. E. B. Du Bois Joins Communist Party at 93," November 23, 1961, Books, *The New York Times on the Web*, https://www.nytimes.com/books/00/11/05/specials/dubois-communist.html.

47. See "About Dr. King," The King Center: Since 1968, http://www.thekingcenter.org/about-dr-king.

48. Jeff Horwitch, Interview with Cornel West, Market Place, http://www.marketplace.org/topics/wealth-poverty/cornel-west-poverty-issues-us, September 12, 2012. See also Tavis Smiley, "The Poverty Tour: A Call for Conscience, Preview," October 6, 2011, Black/Culture/Connection, *PBS*, http:/

/www.pbs.org/black-culture/home/. Smiley here interviews white middle-class homeless people at a campsite outside of Ann Arbor, Michigan. Including the plight of homeless white people among the poor might be problematic in terms of thinking about public policy toward the poor, because the US homeless population has special problems of criminalization that are distinct from issues faced by poor African Americans who live in ghettos. Both groups are poor, of course, but so are most of those who are incarcerated. Statistics on contemporary homeless Americans vary widely and systematic theoretical or philosophical work on the taxonomies of homelessness and poverty remain to be done for the twenty-first century. In a way, the intersection of race with poverty is comparable to the intersection of homelessness with poverty because contemporary homeless people are abused, criminalized, and shunned in distinctive ways, because they are homeless. For current resources, see the Community Philosophy Institute University of Oregon Department of Philosophy's website, Homelessness and Home: http://homelessness.philosophy.uoregon.edu/.

49. See Henry J. Richardson III, "Dr. Martin Luther King, Jr. As an International Human Rights Leader," *Legal Studies Research Paper Series*, Temple University Beasley School of Law, Research Paper No. 2007-19 (September 27, 2007), 471–85, esp. 473–74. http://papers.ssrn.com/sol3/papers.cfm?abstract_id=1017143.

50. David J. Garrow, "Martin Luther King, Jr., and the Spirit of Leadership,"*Journal of American History* 74, no. 2 (September 1987), 438–47, http://links.jstor.org/.

51. For a tortured and petty account of the "court politics" aspect of West's relationship to Obama, see Michael Eric Dyson, "The Ghost of Cornel West," *New Republic*, April 19, 2015, http://www.newrepublic.com/.

52. For full discussion of Trayvon Martin and related cases, see Zack, *White Privilege and Black Rights*.

53. Michael S. Schmidt and Matt Apuzzo, "South Carolina Officer Is Charged with Murder of Walter Scott," *New York Times*, April 7, 2015, http://www.nytimes.com/.

54. Philip Gourevitch, "Should You Watch the Video?" *The New Yorker*, April 8, 2015, http://www.newyorker.com/.

55. West with Buschendorf, *Black Prophetic Fire*, "The Heat of Democratic Existentialism: Ella Baker," 89–108, quote page 90.

56. See, for instance, Major Garrett, "Think Globally, Act Locally," *NationalJournal*, http://www.nationaljournal.com/; Jeffrey Ball, "The Politics of Climate Change Stink, That's Why 'Think Globally, Act Locally' Is Back," *New Republic*, http://www.newrepublic.com/.

57. On the challenges faced by police and the uncurtailed executive functions of their work, since the 1960s, see Jerome H. Skolnick, *Justice without*

Trial: Law Enforcement in Democratic Society (New Orleans, LA: Quid Pro Books, 2011). On the nature of place and its history in influencing law enforcement practices, see Mona Lynch et al., "Policing the 'Progressive' City: The Racialized Geography of Drug Law Enforcement," *Theoretical Criminology* (2013): doi 1362480613476986. The authors write in their abstract: "Our goal is to begin sketching out a robust framework of 'place' as an orientation for examining discretionary local policing practices, especially as they impact marginalized groups and communities of color." Available at https://webfiles.uci.edu/. However, analyses of the disproportionate race-based application of enforcement sometimes overlook the obvious fact that poor people of color live in urban clusters that can be targeted as areas for law enforcement practices that would not be acceptable in white or racially integrated neighborhoods. cf. "The words of a former prosecutor, 'It's a lot easier to go out to the 'hood, so to speak, and pick somebody than to put your resources in an undercover [operation in a] community where there are potentially politically powerful people,'" in Alexander, *The New Jim Crow*, 124, from Lynn Lu, "Prosecutorial Discretion and Racial Disparities in Sentencing: Some Views of Former U.S. Attorneys," *Federal Sentencing Reporter* 19 (February 2007): 192.

58. See Jonathan Kozol, *Savage Inequalities* (New York: Random House, 1991). For an update, see Michael Busch, "Keeping Faith with the Kids: An Interview with Jonathan Kozol," *Huffington Post*, October 25, 2012, http://www.huffingtonpost.com/michael-busch/poverty-education_b_2013593.html.

59. Office of Policy Planning and Research United States Department of Labor, "The Negro Family: The Case for National Action," March 1965, http://www.dol.gov/dol/aboutdol/history/webid-meynihan.htm, accessed April 2015. Patrick Moynihan oversaw the production of this report while he was Assistant Secretary of Labor and continued to discuss it throughout his career. See "Interviews with Daniel Patrick Moynihan over His Career, with a Focus on the Moynihan Report," in New York's Moynihan, *Local Projects for the Museum of the City of New York*, http://www.youtube.com/watch?v=hPxkJZsz4Kc.

60. This is to think within an acceptance of a total market economy. Of course, there is another social theory tradition that valorizes a welfare state along the lines of the "decommodification of human rights." See Gosta Esping-Andersen, *The Three Worlds of Welfare Capitalism* (New York: Wiley, 2013), chaps. 2, 3, and 4, especially.

61. Ann Morrison, "March Jobs Report: Weak Job Growth, Black Women's Unemployment Continues to Rise," National Women's Law Center, April 4, 2015, http://www.nwlc.org/.

62. Ibid., "What You Can Do," http://www.nwlc.org/what-you-can-do/act-online.

63. Ryan J. Reilly and Jennifer Bendery, "Ferguson Activists, Encouraged by White House Meeting, Still Predict Uphill Battle," *Huffington Post*, December 4, 2014, http://www.huffingtonpost.com/.

64. John Swaine, "Ferguson Alternative Spring Break Offers College Students Chance to Take Action," *The Guardian*, February 8, 2015, http://www.theguardian.com/. There were reports that some students from historically black colleges did accept the offer. Jesse Bogan, "College Students Make Ferguson Their Spring Break Destination," *St. Louis Post Dispatch*, March 9, 2015, http://www.stltoday.com/.

65. John Locke, *An Essay Concerning Human Understanding*, abridgement by John W. Yolton (Rutland, VT: Charles E. Tuttle; London: J. M. Dent, 1995), book II, chap. 21, "Of Power," 105–24.

66. I. Berlin, "Two Concepts of Liberty," 1958 Inaugural lecture as Chichele Professor of Social and Political Theory at Oxford University, in Isaiah Berlin, *Four Essays on Liberty* (Oxford: Oxford University Press, 1969). Accessed from https://www.wiso.uni-hamburg.de/fileadmin/wiso_vwl/johannes/Ankuendigungen/Berlin_twoconceptsofliberty.pdf. Berlin says that he is using "liberty" and "freedom" interchangeably on page 2.

67. Ibid., 11 and 13.

68. Ibid., 13.

69. Ibid., 22–26.

70. This is not merely a situation resulting from the distant past but an ongoing disparity. See Rakesh Kochhar and Richard Fry, "Wealth Inequality Has Widened along Racial, Ethnic Lines since End of Great Recession," Pew Research Center, December 12, 2014, http://www.pewresearch.org/fact-tank/2014/12/12/racial-wealth-gaps-great-recession/.

71. The feminist phenomenon of consciousness-raising has been compared to other processes, such as psychotherapy. Annette M. Brodsky, "The Consciousness-Raising Group as a Model for Therapy with Women," *Psychotherapy: Theory, Research & Practice* 10, no. 1 (1973): 24–29, http://dx.doi.org/10.1037/h0087537. I have simplified Sartre's views here, because he requires authenticity in recognizing a preexisting metaphysical freedom, before such imagination is even possible. See James Miller, *History and Human Existence—From Marx to Merleau-Ponty* (Berkeley: University of California Press, 1979), chap. 9, "Sartre: Fear of Freedom," 156–97, http://ark.cdlib.org/ark:/13030/ft2489n82k/. If one adds to these approaches, consideration of traditional and conventional social ideologies and the liberatory ideological approach of dissolving "false consciousness" or "decolonizing minds," it should be clear that what is at issue is so "constructed" and normative on both sides that the true "facts" of any situation may become a hypothetical construct, which supports the importance of what might be viewed as "only subjective."

72. See Paolo Friere, *Pedagogy of the Oppressed* (New York: Herder and Herder, 1970); film *Fundi: The Story of Ella Baker*, Icarus Films, 1981, http://www.icarusfilms.com/cat97/f-j/ell2.html ("fundi" is a Swahili word for a person who passes on knowledge of skills to the next generation).

73. Shklar explains that a focus on cruelty or deliberate harm to another is a primary concern in a secular sense because the first religious sin is disrespect to God, in Judith N. Shklar, "Putting Cruelty First," *Daedalus* 111, no. 3 (Summer 1982): 17–28. For discussion of how putting cruelty first relates to other aspects of Shklar's political philosophy, see Kamila Stullerova, "The Knowledge of Suffering: On Judith Shklar's 'Putting Cruelty First,'" *Contemporary Political Theory* (2014): 13, 23–45.

74. Judith N. Shklar, *The Faces of Injustice* (New Haven, CT: Yale University Press, 1990), 7.

75. Ibid., 36, 116, 123–24.

76. Ibid., 91–92.

77. Ibid., 112.

7. POSTSCRIPT: AN INVITATION TO THE READER

1. For a range of perspectives on white ignorance concerning race, see Shannon Sullivan and Nancy Tuana, eds., *Race and Epistemologies of Ignorance* (Albany: State University of New York Press, 2007).

2. *White Privilege and Black Rights: The Injustice of U.S. Police Racial Profiling and Homicide* (Lanham, MD: Rowman and Littlefield, 2015), xi, 1–2, 63, 80, 95.

3. Michael S. Schmidt and Matt Apuzzo, "South Carolina Officer Is Charged with Murder of Walter Scott," *New York Times*, April 7, 2015, http://www.nytimes.com/2015/04/08/us/south-carolina-officer-is-charged-with-murder-in-black-mans-death.html. Please see the discussion of this case in chapter 6.

4. The film is about the trial for murder of Samuel L. Jackson's character, who took lethal revenge on the white rapists of his ten-year-old daughter. See "Watch *A Time to Kill* Online," PutLocker, http://putlocker.is/watch-a-time-to-kill-online-free-putlocker.html.

5. On the issue of bypassing an address to injustice through rhetoric suggesting that oppressors as well the oppressed should move ahead, see Rodney Roberts, "Race, Rectification and Apology," Naomi Zack, ed. *Oxford Handbook of Philosophy and Race* (Cambridge, MA: Oxford University Press, forthcoming 2016–2017).

6. "Obama Delivers Eulogy in Charleston," *New York Times*, June 27, 2015, http://www.nytimes.com/.

7. Martin Heidegger, "Only a God Can Save Us," Der Spiegel Interview, 1966, *Heidegger Texts online*, http://religiousstudies.stanford.edu/.

8. Thanks to Jon La Rochelle for asking me what the relationship was between the common narrative and local activism.

9. This reference is just to the title. I am not subscribing to or endorsing avant-garde French primitivism! For images of this painting, see https://www.google.com/search?q=gauguin.

SELECT BIBLIOGRAPHY

NEWS, MAGAZINE ARTICLES, AND OTHER MEDIA

Alderman, Derek. "A Street Fit for a King?" Department of Geography, University of Tennessee, Knoxville, Tennessee, http://mlkstreet.com/.

Ayres, Ian, and Daniel Markovits. "Ending Excessive Police Force Starts with New Rules of Engagement." *Washington Post*, December 25, 2014, http://www.washingtonpost.com/opinions/ending-excessive-police-force-starts-with-new-rules-of-*engagement*/2014/12/25/7fa379c0-8a1e-11e4-a085-34e9b9f09a58_story.html.

Ball, Jeffrey. "The Politics of Climate Change Stink, That's Why 'Think Globally, Act Locally,' Is Back." *New Republic*, April 22, 2014, http://www.newrepublic.com/article/117459/earth-day-2014-think-globally-act-locally-back.

Bazin, Y. "Bilderberg People." *Society and Business Review* 7, no. 1 (2012): 102–4.

Becker, Jo, Sheryl Gay Stolberg, and Stephen Labaton. "Bush Drive for Home Ownership Fueled Housing Bubble." *New York Times*, December 21, 2008, http://www.nytimes.com/2008/12/21/business/worldbusiness/21iht-admin.4.18853088.html?pagewanted=all&_r=0.

Bernardo, Carla. "Tears as UCT Debates Rhodes Statue." *IOL News*, March 26, 2015, http://www.iol.co.za/news/south-africa/western-cape/tears-as-uct-debates-rhodes-statue-1.1837070#.VR8Asrl0zcs.

Bogan, Jesse. "College Students Make Ferguson Their Spring Break Destination." *St. Louis Post-Dispatch*, March 9, 2015, http://www.stltoday.com/news/local/crime-and-courts/college-students-make-ferguson-their-spring-break-destination/article_7d145d59-8139-558e-be78-8251191937bb.html.

Busch, Michael. "Keeping Faith with the Kids: An Interview with Jonathan Kozol." *Huffington Post*, October 25, 2012, http://www.huffingtonpost.com/michael-busch/poverty-education_b_2013593.html.

Bush, George W. "I'm the Decider and I Decide What Is Best . . ." http://www.crooksandliars.com/ and https://www.youtube.com/watch?v=irMeHmlxE9s.

"Cornel West—Biography." The European Graduate School, http://www.egs.edu/faculty/cornel-west/biography/.

Cornel West Site: Youtube.Com had 87,300 entries on March 29, 2015. https://www.google.com/search?sourceid=navclient&aq=&oq=youtube&ie=UTF-8&rlz=1T4ADRA_enUS481US481&q=youtube&gs_l=hp..0.0l5.0.0.0.9504...........0.xjQdne3A0cA#q=cornel%20west%20site%3ayoutube.com.

Cornel West, Dr. Cornel West. Official Website, http://www.cornelwest.com/index.html#.VRjkU7l0zcs.

CNN Marina. March 26, 2013, http://www.cnn.com/2013/03/22/justice/new-york-stop-and-frisk-trial/.

Daily Mail Reporter. " I've Never Escaped from That Moment: Girl in Napalm Photograph That Defined the Vietnam War 40 Years On." Daily Mail, UK News, June 1, 2012, http://www.dailymail.co.uk/news/article-2153091/Napalm-girl-photo-Vietnam-War-turns-40.html.

Danielle, Britni. " White Privilege Is Real, and Now There's Research to Prove It." Takepart.com, Yahoo news, February 28, 2015, http://news.yahoo.com/white-privilege-real-now-research-prove-184105763.html.

Dinner, Deborah. "A Firebrand Flickers." *Legal Affairs*, March/April 2006, http://www.legalaffairs.org/issues/March-April-2006/review_Dinner_marapr06.msp.

"Disability." *National Campaign to Restore Civil Rights* (1999–2014), http://www.rollbackcampaign.org/issues/item.disabilityrights2143.

Dyson, Michael Eric. "The Ghost of Cornel West." *The New Republic*, April 19, 2015, http://www.newrepublic.com/article/121550/cornel-wests-rise-fall-our-most-exciting-black-scholar-ghost.

Fallon, Patrick T. "The Show." *New York Times*, February 24, 2015, http://www.nytimes.com/interactive/projects/cp/oscars-2015/show?&from=promo.

Frank, Thomas. "TSA Proposes Screening Private Jet Passengers." *USA Today*, August 7, 2014, http://abcnews.go.com/Travel/story?id=5999405.

Fundi: The Story of Ella Baker. Icarus Films, 1981. http://www.icarusfilms.com/cat97/f-j/ell2.html.

Goodman, Amy, and Juan González. "Attica Is All of Us: Cornel West on 40th Anniversary of Attica Prison Rebellion." *Democracy Now!:* A Daily Independent Global News Hour http://www.democracynow.org/2011/9/12/attica_is_all_of_us_cornel.

———. "Cornel West on the Election of Obama." *Democracy Now!* A Daily Independent Global News Hour, http://www.democracynow.org/2008/11/19/cornel_west_on_the_election_of, Nov. 19, 2008.

Gordon, Avery F. "Prison Industrial Complex: An Interview with Angela Davis." (1999). http://carbonfarm.us/amap/davis_globalism.pdf.

Gourevitch, Philip. "Should You Watch the Video?" *The New Yorker*, April 8, 2015, http://www.newyorker.com/news/news-desk/should-you-watch-walter-scott-video.

Horwitch, Jeff. Interview with Cornel West, *Market Place*, http://www.marketplace.org/topics/wealth-poverty/cornel-west-poverty-issues-us.

Iceland, John, and Daniel H. Weinberg. "Racial and Ethnic Residential Segregation in the United States 1980–2000." Census 2000 Special Reports, United States Bureau of the Census. https://www.census.gov/prod/2002pubs/censr-3.pdf.

Kihss, Peter. "Dr. W. E. B. Du Bois Joins Communist Party at 93." November 23, 1961, *New York Times*, https://www.nytimes.com/books/00/11/05/specials/dubois-communist.html.

King, Ryan S., Marc Mauer, and Tracy Huling. "Big Prisons, Small Towns: Prison Economics in Rural America." *Sentencing Project*, 2003, http://prison.ppjr.org/files/tracy%20huling%20prisons%20economy%20study.pdf.

Lackey, Jamicia. "Exposing Duke's Racial Atmosphere." *The Chronicle*, February 2, 2002, http://www.dukechronicle.com/articles/2002/02/21/exposing-dukes-racial-atmosphere#.VQdLGLl0zcs.

Lemann, Nicholas. "Conflict of Interests." *The New Yorker*, August 11, 2008. http://www.newyorker.com/arts/critics/atlarge/2008/08/11/080811crat_atlarge_lemann?currentPage=all.

Mayerson, Arlene. "The History of the Americans with Disabilities Act." Disability Rights Education and Defense Fund, 1992. http://dredf.org/news/publications/the-history-of-the-ada/.

Menard, Louis. "The Sex Amendment: The Sex Amendment: How Women Got In on the Civil Rights Act." *New Yorker*, July 21, 2014, 74–81.

Miller, Michelle. "The Children Who Marched into Civil Rights History, *CBS News* , May 3, 2013, http://www.cbsnews.com/news/the-children-who-marched-into-civil-rights-history.

Morgenson, Gretchen, and Louise Story. "In Financial Crisis, No Prosecutions of Top Figures." *New York Times*, April 14, 2011, http://www.nytimes.com/2011/04/14/business/14prosecute.html?pagewanted=all&_r=0.

Morrison, Ann. "March Jobs Report: Weak Job Growth, Black Women's Unemployment Continues to Rise." National Women's Law Center, April 4, 2015, http://www.nwlc.org/our-blog/march-jobs-report-weak-job-growth-black-women%E2%80%99s-unemployment-continues-rise.

Moynihan, Patrick. "Interviews with Daniel Patrick Moynihan Over His Career, with a Focus on the Moynihan Report." In New York's Moynihan, *Local Projects for the Museum of the City of New York*, http://www.youtube.com/watch?v=hPxkJZsz4Kc.

Reilly, Ryan J., and Jennifer Bendery. "Ferguson Activists, Encouraged by White House Meeting, Still Predict Uphill Battle." *Huffington Post*, December 4, 2014, http://www.huffingtonpost.com/2014/12/02/ferguson-white-house_n_6257306.html.

"Religion and Revolution: A Dialogue between Cornel West and Bob Avakian." Film Excerpt, 2015, https://www.youtube.com/watch?v=72EfAuUFDoE.

Saad, Lydia. "U.S. Mood on Economy Up, Race Relations Sharply Down." Gallup, January 19, 2015, http://www.gallup.com/poll/181187/mood-economy-race-relations-sharply-down.aspx.

Schmidt, Michael S., and Matt Apuzzo. "South Carolina Officer Is Charged with Murder of Walter Scott." April 7, 2015, http://www.nytimes.com/2015/04/08/us/south-carolina-officer-is-charged-with-murder-in-black-mans-death.html.

Smiley, Tavis. "The Poverty Tour: A Call for Conscience, Preview." Black/Culture/Connection, *PBS*, October 6, 2011, http://www.pbs.org/black-culture/home/.

Stanley, Alessandra. "Oscars 2015: Passionate Speeches, but Few Surprises." *New York Times*, February 23, 2015, http://mobile.nytimes.com/2015/02/23/movies/awardsseason/oscars-2015-passionate-speeches-but-few-surprises.html?_r=0&referrer=.

Sullivan, Shannon, and Nancy Tuana, eds. *Race and Epistemologies of Ignorance*. Albany: State University of New York Press, 2007.

Swaine, John. "Ferguson Alternative Spring Break Offers College Students Chance to Take Action." *The Guardian*, February 8, 2015, http://www.theguardian.com/us-news/2015/feb/08/ferguson-alternative-spring-break-college-students-beyond-protest.

WEBSITES AND PUBLIC INFORMATION

ACLU. "War Comes Home: The Excessive Militarization of American Policing." https://www.aclu.org/war-comes-home-excessive-militarization-american-policing.

American Bar Association. "American Lawyer Demographics." lawyer_demographics_2013.authcheckdam.

British Parliament. "Birth of the English Parliament." *Living History*, http://www.parliament.uk/about/living-heritage/evolutionofparliament/originsofparliament/birthofparliament/overview/origins/.

Congress of the United States. "The Preamble to the Bill of Rights." http://www.archives.gov/exhibits/charters/bill_of_rights_transcript.html.

———. U.S. Constitution Amendments, http://www.archives.gov/exhibits/charters/constitution_amendments_11-27.html.

Desilver, Drew. "U.S. Income Inequality, on Rise for Decades, Is Now Highest since 1928." *Pew Research Center*, http://www.pewresearch.org/fact-tank/2013/12/05/u-s-income-inequality-on-rise-for-decades-is-now-highest-since-1928/.

Durose, Matthew R., and Patrick A. Langan. "Felony Sentences in State Courts." *Bureau of Justice Statistics Bulletin*, US Department of Justice, Office of Justice Programs 2002, http://www.bjs.gov/content/pub/pdf/fssc02.pdf, page 3. Accessed June 3, 2013.

Fair Vote. "Voter Turnout." *The Center for Voting and Democracy*, 2000–2014, http://www.fairvote.org/research-and-analysis/voter-turnout/.

Harry S. Truman Museum and Library. "Executive Order 9981." http://www.trumanlibrary.org/9981.htm.

Homelessness and Home. Community Philosophy Institute University of Oregon Department of Philosophy's website, http://homelessness.philosophy.uoregon.edu/.

King, Martin Luther. "About Dr. King." The King Center: Since 1968, http://www.thekingcenter.org/about-.

Kochhar, Rakesh, and Richard Fry. "Wealth Inequality Has Widened along Racial, Ethnic Lines since End of Great Recession." Pew Research Center, December 12, 2014. http://www.pewresearch.org/fact-tank/2014/12/12/racial-wealth-gaps-great-recession/.

King, Ryan S., Marc Mauer, and Tracy Huling. "Big Prisons, Small Towns: Prison Economics in Rural America." *Sentencing Project*, 2003, http://prison.ppjr.org/files/tracy%20huling%20prisons%20economy%20study.pdf.

Krogstad, Jens Manuel. "Hispanics Only Group to See Its Poverty Rate Decline and Incomes Rise." FactTank, Pew Research Center, http://www.pewresearch.org/fact-tank/2014/09/19/hispanics-only-group-to-see-its-poverty-rate-decline-and-incomes-rise/.

Library of Congress. "Civil Rights Resource Guide." http://www.loc.gov/rr/program/bib/civilrights/external.html.

Roosevelt, Franklin D. 1941 Address by "The Joint Congressional Committee on Inaugural Ceremonies." http://www.inaugural.senate.gov/swearing-in/address/address-by-franklin-d-roosevelt-1941.

Simon, George. "Understanding Denial as a Defense Mechanism." *Counseling Resource*, http://counsellingresource.com/features/2008/10/08/denial-as-defense-mechanism/.

Talk Poverty.Org. "Basic Statistics." 2009–2015, Center for American Statistics, http://talkpoverty.org/basics/. Accessed April 6, 2015.

United Nations. "Universal Declaration of Human Rights." http://www.un.org/en/documents/udhr/index.shtml#ap.

———. "The United Nations Universal Declaration of Human Rights: An Historical Record of the Drafting Process." http://www.un.org/depts/dhl/udhr/members_cduke.shtml.

U.S. Department of Justice, Civil Rights Division. "Investigation of the Ferguson Police Department." March 4, 2015, http://www.justice.gov/sites/default/files/opa/press-releases/attachments/2015/03/04/ferguson_police_department_report.pdf.

"Why Judges and Prosecutors Engage in Plea Bargaining." *NOLO Law for All*, http://www.nolo.com/legal-encyclopedia/why-judges-prosecutors-engage.

COURT CASES

Brown v. Board of Education of Topeka (No. 1.) 347 U.S. 483, Argued: Argued December 9, 1952, Decided: Decided May 17, 1954, Legal Information Institute, Cornell University, http://www.law.cornell.edu/supremecourt/text/347/483.

Plessy v. Ferguson (No. 210). Argued: April 18, 1896, Decided: May 18, 1896, 163 U.S. 537; Keith Weldon Medley, *We as Freeman: Plessy v. Ferguson*, Greta, Louisiana: Pelican, 2003.

BOOKS AND ARTICLES

Agamben, Giorgio. *The State of Exception*. Translated by Kevin Attell. Chicago: University of Chicago Press, 2005.

Alexander, Michelle. *The New Jim Crow: Mass Incarceration in the Age of Colorblindness*. New York: New Press, 2011.

Anderson, David C. *Crime and the Politics of Hysteria: How the Willie Horton Story Changed American Justice*. New York: Times Books, 1995.

Arendt, Hannah. *Eichmann in Jerusalem.* New York: Viking Press, 1963.

———. "Philosophy and Politics." *Social Research* 57, no. 1, Philosophy and Politics II (Spring 1990): 73–103.

———. "Thoughts on Politics and Revolution: A Commentary." Interview by Adelbert Reif, in *Crises of the Republic*, Summer 1970. Translated by Denver Lindley. In *Hannah Arendt: The Last Interview and Other Conversations*, 67–106. Brooklyn: Melville House, 2013.

Atkin, Albert. *The Philosophy of Race.* Oxford, UK: Acumen, 2012.

Aquinas, Thomas. "Obedience and Rebellion." In *On Law, Morality, and Politics*, Richard J. Regan, trans., William P. Baumgarth, ed., 173–83. Indianapolis: Hackett Publishing Company, 1988.

Baudrillard, Jean. *In the Shadow of the Silent Majorities or, the End of the Social and Other Essays*. Translated by Paul Foss, John Shonston, and Paul Patton. New York: Semiotext(e), 1978.

Bell, Derrick "*Brown v. Board of Education* and the Interest-Convergence Dilemma." *Harvard Law Review*. (93) 518 (1980), reprinted in D. Bell, *Shades of Brown: New Perspectives on School Desegregation.* New York: Teachers College Press, 1980.

Bennett, Jonathan. "Descartes's Theory of Modality." *The Philosophical Review* 103, 4 (1994). *Early Modern Texts*, http://www.earlymoderntexts.com/jfb/descmod.pdf.

Bentley, Arthur F. *The Process of Government*. Chicago: University of Chicago Press, 1908.

Berlin, I. "Two Concepts of Liberty." 1958 Inaugural lecture as Chichele Professor of Social and Political Theory at Oxford University, in Isaiah Berlin, *Four Essays on Liberty*. Oxford: Oxford University Press, 1969. Assessed from https://www.wiso.uni-hamburg.de/fileadmin/wiso_vwl/johannes/Ankuendigungen/Berlin_twoconceptsofliberty.pdf.

Bodnar, John W. "How Long Does It Take to Change a Culture? Integration at the U.S. Naval Academy." *Armed Forces and Society* 25, no. 2 (Winter 1999): 289–306.

Brems, Eva, and Laurens Lavrysen. "Procedural Justice in Human Rights Adjudication: The European Court of Human Rights." *Human Rights Quarterly* 35 (2013): 176–200.

Brodsky, Annette M. "The Consciousness-Raising Group as a Model for Therapy with Women." *Psychotherapy: Theory, Research & Practice* 10, no. 1 (1973): 24–29. http://dx.doi.org/10.1037/h0087537.

Brostrom, Kimberly D. " Teaching Inequality: Denial, Defensiveness, and the Diminishing of Oppression." *Faculty Focus*, June 17, 2013, http://www.facultyfocus.com/articles/teaching-and-learning/teaching-inequality-denial-defensiveness-and-the-diminishing-of-oppression/.

Brown-Nagin, Tomiko. "Elites, Social Movements and the Law: The Case of Affirmative Action." *Columbia Law Review* (2005): 1436–528, https://www.law.virginia.edu/pdf/workshops/0405/brownnagin.pdf.

Byford, Yovan. *Conspiracy Theories: A Critical Introduction*. New York: Palgrave Macmillan, 2011.

Ceva, Emanuela. "Just Procedures with Controversial Outcomes: On the Grounds for Substantive Disputation within a Procedural Theory of Justice." August 26, 2009, *Phil Papers, Springer and Business Media*. http://philpapers.org/rec/CEVJPW-2.

Cheslock, John J., and Matt Gianneschi. "Replacing State Appropriations with Alternative Revenue Sources: The Case of Voluntary Support." *Journal of Higher Education* (2008): 208–29.

Cicero. *On Obligations.* Translated and edited by Peter G. Walsh. Oxford: Oxford University Press, 2000.

Cohen, G. A. "Equality of What? On Welfare, Goods and Capabilities." Alternatives to Welfarism, *Recherches Économiques de Louvain / Louvain Economic Review* 56, no. 3/4 (1990): 357–82. Published by Department of Economics, Universite Catholique de Louvain Stable URL: http://www.jstor.org/stable/40723932, reprinted in M. Nussbaum and A. Sen, eds. *The Quality of Life*. Oxford: Oxford University Press (1993), 9–29.

———. "On the Currency of Egalitarian Justice." *Ethics* 99, no. 4 (July 1989): 906–44. http://links.jstor.org/sici?sici=0014-1704%28198907%2999%3A4%3C906%3AOTCOEJ%3E2.0.CO%3B2-4.
———. "Robert Nozick and Wilt Chamberlain: How Patterns Preserve Liberty." *Erkenntnis* 11, no. 1, Social Ethics, Part 1 (May 1977): 5–23.
———. *Self-Ownership, Freedom, and Equality*. Cambridge: Cambridge University Press, 1995.
Cottingham, John Robert Stoothuff, and Dugald Murdoch, trans. *The Philosophical Writings of Descartes*. Cambridge, UK: Cambridge University Press, 1991.
Cottrol, Robert J., Raymond T. Diamond, and Leland B. Ware. *Brown v. Board of Education: Caste, Culture, and the Constitution*. Lawrence: University Press of Kansas, 2003.
Crenshaw, Kimberle. "Mapping the Margins: Intersectionality, Identity Politics, and Violence against Women of Color." *Stanford Law Review* 43, no. 6 (July 1991): 1241–99, http://www.jstor.org/stable/1229039.
Currie, David P. "Positive and Negative Constitutional Rights." University of Chicago Law Review 53, no. 3 (Summer 1986): 864–90, http://www.jstor.org/stable/1599586.
Dalfiume, Richard M. "The 'Forgotten Years' of the Negro Revolution." *Journal of American History* 55, no. 1 (June 1968): 90–106. http://www.jstor.org/stable/1894253.
Donziger, Steven R. *The Real War on Crime: The Report of the National Criminal Justice Commission*. New York: HarperPerennial, 1996.
Douglass, Frederick. "If There Is No Struggle, There Is No Progress." West Indian Emancipation Speech, Canandaigua, New York, August 3, 1857, http://www.blackpast.org/1857-frederick-douglass-if-there-no-struggle-there-no-progress.
Du Bois, W. E. B. *Selections: The Correspondence of W. E. B. Du Bois, 1944–1963*. Vol. 3. Edited by Herbert Aptheker. Amherst: University of Massachusetts Press, 1978.
Dudziak, Mary L. "Desegregation as a Cold War Imperative." *Stanford Law Review* 41, no. 1 (November 1988): 61–120, http://www.jstor.org/stable/1228836.
Eggleston, Ben. "Procedural Justice in Young's Inclusive Deliberative Democracy." *Journal of Social Philosophy* 35, no. 4 (Winter 2004): 544–49.
Ellis, Sylvia. *Freedom's Pragmatist: Lyndon Johnson and Civil Rights*. Gainesville: University Press of Florida, 2013.
Esping-Andersen, Gøsta. *The Three Worlds of Welfare Capitalism*. New York: Wiley, 2013.
Friere, Paolo. *Pedagogy of the Oppressed*. New York: Herder and Herder, 1970.
Fleischaker, Samuel. *A Short History of Distributive Justice*. Cambridge, MA: Harvard University Press, 2004.
Folger, Robert, and Daniel P. Skarlicki. "The Evolutionary Bases of Deontic Justice." *Justice, Morality, and Social Responsibility*, 29–62. Charlotte, NC: Information Age Publishing, 2008.
Foucault, Michel. *The History of Sexuality*. Vol 1. An Introduction. Translated by Robert Hurley. Éditions Gallimard, 1976.
Freeman, Michael, ed. *Law and Sociology: Current Legal Issues 2005*. Vol. 8. New York: Oxford University Press, 2006.
Garrett, Major. "Think Globally, Act Locally. *National Journal*, May 6, 2014, http://www.nationaljournal.com/all-powers/think-globally-act-locally-20140506.
Garrow, David J. "Martin Luther King, Jr., and the Spirit of Leadership." *Journal of American History* 74, no. 2 (September 1987): 438–47, http://links.jstor.org/sici?sici=0021-8723%28198709%2974%3A2%3C438%3AMLKJAT%3E2.0.CO%3B2-.
Gramsci, Antonio. *Selections from the Prison Books*. London: Lawrence and Wishart, 1982.
Gross, Bertram M. "*The Process of Government; A Study of Social Pressures* by Arthur F. Bentley." *American Political Science Review* 44, no. 3 (September 1950): 742–48.
Gustafsson, Martin. "On Rawls's Distinction between Perfect and Imperfect Procedural Justice." *Philosophy of the Social Sciences* 34 (2004): 300–305.
Hall, Eric S., and Zorka Karanxha. "School Today, Jail Tomorrow: The Impact of Zero Tolerance on the Over-Representation of Minority Youth in the Juvenile System." *PowerPlay* 4, no. 1 (2012): 1–30.

Humphreys, Stephen. "Legalizing Lawlessness: On Giorgio Agamben's *State of Exception.*" *European Journal of International Law* 17, no. 3 (2006): 677–87, http://www.ejil.org/pdfs/17/3/208.pdf.

Ifill, Sherrilyn A. "Creating a Truth and Reconciliation Commission for Lynching." *Law & Inequalities* 21 (2003): 263–311. http://digitalcommons.law.umaryland.edu.

Jablonski, Nina G. *Living Color: The Biological and Social Meaning of Skin Color.* Oakland: University of California Press, 2012.

Jeffers, Harry Paul. *The Bilderberg Conspiracy.* New York: Kensington Publishing, 2009.

Kalev, Alexandra, and Frank Dobbin. "Enforcement of Civil Rights Law in Private Workplaces: The Effects of Compliance Reviews and Lawsuits over Time." *Law & Social Inquiry* 31, no. 4 (2006): 855–903.

Katz, Stanley N. "Thomas Jefferson and the Right to Property in Revolutionary America." *Journal of Law and Economics* 19, no. 3 (1976): 467–88.

King, Jr. Martin Luther Nobel Peace Prize Acceptance Speech, 1964. http://www.nobelprize.org/nobel_prizes/peace/laureates/1964/king-acceptance_en.html.

Kant, Immanuel. *Groundwork of the Metaphysics of Morals.* Translated and edited by Mary Gregor. Cambridge: Cambridge University Press, 1998.

Kinney, James. *Amalgamation!* Westport, CT: Greenwood, 1985.

Kimlicka, Will. *Contemporary Political Philosophy: An Introduction.* Oxford, UK: Oxford University Press, 1990.

Kohls, L. Robert, and John L. Knight. *Developing Intercultural Awareness: A Cross-Cultural Training Handbook.* Yarmouth, ME: Intercultural Press, 1982.

Kozol, Jonathan, *Amazing Grace: The Lives of Children and the Conscience of a Nation.* New York: Crown, 1995.

———. "An Unequal Education." *ERIC* 46, no. 5 (2000): 46–49.

———. *Savage Inequalities: Children in America's Schools.* New York: Random House, 1991. For an update, see Michael Busch, "Keeping Faith with the Kids: An Interview with Jonathan Kozol." *Huffington Post*, October 25, 2012, http://www.huffingtonpost.com/michael-busch/poverty-education_b_2013593.html.

———. *The Shame of the Nation: The Restoration of Apartheid Schooling in America.* New York: Crown, 2005.

Kress, Paul F. *Social Science and the Idea of Process: The Ambiguous Legacy of Arthur F. Bentley.* Urbana: University of Illinois Press, 1970.

Kropotkin, Peter. "Anarchism." *Encyclopedia Britannica*, 11th ed. Cambridge, UK: University Press, 1910.

———. *Selected Writings.* Edited by Hubert Read. London: Freedom Press, 1992.

Laslett, Peter. "*Two Treatises of Government* and the Revolution of 1688." Introduction, Part 3, in *Locke: Two Treatises of Government*, Peter Laslett, ed. Cambridge, UK: Cambridge University Press, 1967.

Lebron, Christopher. *The Color of Our Shame: Race and Justice in Our Time.* New York: Oxford University Press, 2013.

Lemann, Nicholas. "Conflict of Interests." *The New Yorker*, August 11, 2008. http://www.newyorker.com/arts/critics/atlarge/2008/08/11/080811crat_atlarge_lemann?currentPage=all.

Littlejohn, Edward J., and Leonard S. Rubinowitz. "Black Enrollment in Law Schools: Forward to the Past?" *T. Marshall Law Review* 12 (1986): 415–55.

Locke, John. *An Essay Concerning Human Understanding.* Abridgement by John W. Yolton, Rutland, VT and London: Charles E. Tuttle and J. M. Dent, 1991.

———. *A Letter Concerning Toleration.* Edited by Mario Montuori. The Hague: Martinus Nijhoff, 1963.

———. *Original Letters of John Locke, Algernon Sidney and Lord Shaftesbury: With an Analytical Sketch of the Writings and Opinions of Locke and Other Metaphysicians: 1847.* Edited by T. Forster, https://play.google.com/store/books/details?id=O7tCAAAAYAAJ&rdid=book-O7tCAAAAYAAJ&rdot=1.

———. *Locke: Two Treatises of Government.* Cambridge: Cambridge University Press, 1967.

Lu, Lynn. "Prosecutorial Discretion and Racial Disparities in Sentencing: Some Views of Former U.S. Attorneys." *Federal Sentencing Reporter* 19 (February 2007): 192.

Lynch, Mona et al. "Policing the 'Progressive' City: The Racialized Geography of Drug Law Enforcement." *Theoretical Criminology* 17, no. 3 (2013): 333–57.

Macpherson, C. B. *The Political Theory of Possessive Individualism.* Oxford, UK: Oxford University Press, 1962.

Maritain, Jacques. "The Grounds for an International Declaration of Human Rights." In *The Human Rights Reader: Major Political Essays Speeches, and Documents from Ancient Times to the Present*, Micheline R. Ishay, ed., pp. 2–6. New York: Routledge, 2007.

Mathiowetz, Dean. "'Interest' Is a Verb: Arthur Bentley and the Language of Interest." *Political Research Quarterly* 61, no. 4 (December 2008): 622–35.

Mershon, Sherie, and Steven Schlosmann. *Foxholes and Color Lines: Desegregating the U.S. Armed Forces.* Baltimore: Johns Hopkins University Press, 1998.

Mill, John Stuart. *On Liberty*. Kitchener, Ontario: Batoche Books, 2001, http://socserv.mcmaster.ca/econ/ugcm/3ll3/mill/liberty.pdf.

———. *The Subjection of Women*. In *On Liberty and Other Writings*. Edited by Stefan Collini. Cambridge: Cambridge University Press, 1989.

Miller, James. History and Human Existence—From Marx to Merleau-Ponty. Berkeley: University of California Press, 1979. http://ark.cdlib.org/ark:/13030/ft2489n82k/.

Mills, Charles. "Contract of Breach: Repairing the Racial Contract." In *Contract and Domination*, Carole Pateman and Charles W. Mills, eds., 106–33. Malden, MA: Polity Press, 2007.

———. "Rawls on Race/Race in Rawls." *Southern Journal of Philosophy* 47 (2009): 160–85.

Moskop, John C, and Kenneth V. Iserson. "Triage in Medicine, part II: Underlying Values and Principles." *Annals of Emergency Medicine* 49, no. 3 (2007): 282–87.

Moynihan, Patrick, Office of Policy Planning and Research United States Department of Labor. "The Negro Family: The Case for National Action." March 1965, http://www.dol.gov/dol/aboutdol/history/webid-meynihan.htm, accessed April 2015.

Mujcic, Redzo, and Paul Frijters. "Still Not Allowed on the Bus: It Matters If You're Black or White! *IZA Discussion Paper No. 7300.* April 6, 2003.

Noonan Jr., John T. "Development in Moral Doctrine." *Theological Studies* 54, no. 4 (1993): 662–77.

Outlaw, Lucius. "Toward a Critical Theory of 'Race.'" In *Race and Racism*, Bernard Boxill, ed., 58–82. Oxford: Oxford University Press, 2000.

Peck, Jamie, and Nikolas Theodore. "Commentary. 'Work First': Workfare and the Regulation of Contingent Labour Markets." *Cambridge Journal of Economics* 24, no. 1 (2000): 119–38.

Perry, Barbara. "'No Biggie': The Denial of Oppression on Campus." *Education, Citizenship and Social Justice* 5 no. 3 (November 2010): 265–79 , doi: 10.1177/1746197910387543.

Pinckney, Darryl. *Blackballed: The Black Vote and US Democracy*. New York: New York Review of Books, 2014.

Ratner, Sidney. "Arthur Bentley: 1870-1957." *Journal of Philosophy* 55, no. 14 (July 3, 1958): 573–78.

Rawls, John. *The Law of Peoples.* Cambridge, MA: Harvard University Press, 1999; Chicago: University of Chicago Press, 1971.

———. *A Theory of Justice.* Cambridge, MA: Harvard University Press, 1971.

Relethford, John. *The Human Species: An Introduction to Biological Anthropology.* McGraw-Hill, 2009–2012.

Rizzo, Michael, and Ronald G. Ehrenberg. "Resident and Nonresident Tuition and Enrollment at Flagship State Universities." In *College Choices: The Economics of Where to Go, When to Go, and How to Pay for It*, 303–54. Chicago: University of Chicago Press, 2004.

Richardson III, Henry J. "Dr. Martin Luther King, Jr. As an International Human Rights Leader." *Legal Studies Research Paper Series*, Temple University Beasley School of Law, Research Paper No. 2007-19 (September 27, 2007): 471–85. http://papers.ssrn.com/sol3/papers.cfm?abstract_id=1017143.

Rosenberg, Jonathan, and Zachary Karabell. *Kennedy, Johnson, and the Quest for Justice: The Civil Rights Tapes*, Miller Center of Public Affairs. New York: W. W. Norton, 2003.
Ryan, Cheyney C. "Yours, Mine, and Ours: Property Rights and Individual Liberty." *Ethics* 87, no. 2 (January 1977): 126–41.
Schlachter, Wolfgang. "The Sociology of Law as an Empirical Theory of Validity." European Academy of Sociology, Second Annual Lecture, Paris. *European Sociological Review* 19, no. 5 (November 16, 2002): 537–49.
Sen, Amartya, *Development as Freedom*. New York: Alfred A. Knopf, 1999.
———. "Equality of What?" The Tanner Lecture on Human Values, Stanford University, May 22, 1979, *Artikler*, http://www.akira.ruc.dk/~fkt/filosofi/Artikler%20m.m/Egalitarianism/Sen%20-%20Equality%20of%20What.pdf.
———. *The Idea of Justice*. Cambridge, MA: Harvard University Press, 2009.
———. *Inequality Reexamined*. New York: Russell Sage Foundation, 1992.
———. "The Possibility of Social Choice." Nobel Lecture, published by Trinity College, Cambridge, CB2 1TQ, Great Britain (December 8, 1998), 178–215. http://www.cse.iitb.ac.in/~damani/ctaraReading/AmartyaSenSocialChoice.pdf; also published in *American Economic Review* 89, 1999.
Sheth, Falguni. *Toward a Political Philosophy of Race*. Albany: State University of New York Press, 2009.
Shklar, Judith N. *The Faces of Injustice*. New Haven, CT: Yale University Press, 1990.
———. "Putting Cruelty First." *Daedalus* 111, no. 3 (Summer 1982): 17–28.
Siegel, Riva. "Why Equal Protection No Longer Protects: The Evolving Forms of Status-Enforcing State Action." *Stan. L. Rev.* 49 (1997): 1111–48, http://digitalcommons.law.yale.edu/cgi/viewcontent.cgi?article=2093&context=fss_papers.
Simmons, A. J. "Ideal and Nonideal Theory." *Philosophy & Public Affairs* 38 (January 13, 2010): 5–36.
Sklar, Judity. *The Faces of Injustice*. New Haven, CT: Yale University Press, 1992.
Skolnick, Jerome H. *Justice without Trial: Law Enforcement in Democratic Society*. New Orleans, LA: Quid Pro books, 2011.
Snow, David A. "Extending and Broadening Blumer's Conceptualization of Symbolic Interactionism." *Symbolic interaction* 24, no. 3 (2001): 367–77.
Sotello, Caroline, Viernes Turner, Samuel L. Myers Jr., and John W. Creswell. "Exploring Underrepresentation: The Case of Faculty of Color in the Midwest." *Journal of Higher Education* 70, no. 1 (January/February 1999): 27–59.
Stullerova, Kamila. "The Knowledge of Suffering: On Judith Shklar's 'Putting Cruelty First.'" *Contemporary Political Theory* (2014): 13, 23–45.
Sullivan, Shannon, and Nancy Tuana, eds. *Race and Epistemologies of Ignorance*. Albany: State University of New York Press, 2007.
Swinburne, Richard. "The Existence of God," http://users.ox.ac.uk/~orie0087/pdf_files/General%20untechnical%20papers/The%20Existence%20of%20God.pdf (accessed November 2014).
Taibbi, Matt, with Molly Crabapple. *The Divide: American Injustice in the Age of the Wealth Gap*. New York: Random House, 2014.
Truman, Harry S. *Off the Record: The Private Papers of Harry Truman*. Edited by Robert H. Ferrell. Columbia: University of Missouri Press, 1980.
Tyler, Tom R., *Why People Obey the Law*. New Haven, CT: Yale University Press, 2006.
Wacquant, Loïc. "Deadly Symbiosis: When Ghetto and Prison Meet and Mesh." *Punishment and Society* 3, no. 1 (2001): 95–133.
———. "The New Peculiar Institution: On the Prison as Surrogate Ghetto." *Theoretical Criminology* 4, no. 3 (August 2000): 377–89.
Weaver, Vesla M. "Frontlash: Race and the Development of Punitive Crime Policy." *Studies in American Political Development* 21, no. 2 (2007): 230–65.
West, Cornel, with Christa Buschendorf. *Black Prophetic Fire*. Boston: Beacon Press, 2014.
West, Cornel. *Prophesy Deliverance!: An Afri-American Revolutionary Christianity*, Philadelphia: Westminster Press, 1982.
Williams, Raymond. *The Long Revolution*. Cardigan, UK: Parthian, 2011.

———. *Modern Tragedy*. Edited by Pamela McClellum. Peterborough, Ontario: Broadview, 2006.

———. "The Romantic Artist." In *Romanticism*, Robert F. Gleckner and Gerald E. Enscoe, eds. Detroit, MI: Wayne State University Press, 1974.

———. *Towards 2000*. Harmondsworth, UK: Penguin, 1985.

Williamson, Joel. *New People*. New York: Free Press, 1980.

Winant, Howard. *Racial Formation in the United States*. 3rd ed. New York: Routledge, 2014.

Winkler, Adam. "Fatal in Theory and Strict in Fact: An Empirical Analysis of Strict Scrutiny in the Federal Courts." *Vanderbilt Law Review* 59, no. 3 (2006): 793–869.

Winslow, Gerald R. *Triage and Justice*. Berkeley: University of California Press, 1982.

Wood, Ellen Meiksins. "The Agrarian Origins of Capitalism." *Monthly Review*, July 1, 1998, http://www.monthlyreview.org/798wood.htm.

Yancy, George. *Black Bodies/White Gazes: The Continuing Significance of Race*. Lanham, MD: Rowman and Littlefield, 2008.

———. *Cornel West: A Critical Reader*. Malden, MA: Blackwell Publishers, 2003.

Yosso, Tara J. et al. "Critical Race Theory, Racial Microaggressions, and Campus Racial Climate for Latina/o Undergraduates." *Harvard Educational Review* 79, no. 4 (Winter 2009): 659–90.

Zack, Naomi. "American Mixed Race: Theoretical and Legal Issues." *Harvard BlackLetter Law Journal* 17 (Spring 2001): 33–46

———. *Bachelors of Science: Seventeenth Century Identity, Then and Now*. Philadelphia: Temple University Press, 1996.

———. *The Ethics and Mores of Race: Equality after the History of Philosophy*. Lanham, MD: Rowman and Littlefield, 2011.

———. *Ethics for Disaster*. Lanham, MD: Rowman and Littlefield, 2009, 2011.

———. "The Fluid Symbol of Mixed Race." *Hypatia* 25, no. 4 (Fall 2010): 875–90. 25th Anniversary Issue.

———. *Inclusive Feminism: A Third Wave Theory of Women's Commonality*. Lanham, MD: Rowman and Littlefield, 2005.

———. "Philosophical Theories of Justice, Inequality, and Racial Inequality." *Graduate Faculty Philosophy Journal*, Special Issue on Race in the History of Philosophy, New School University, 2014, 353–68.

———."Philosophy and Racial Paradigms." *Journal of Value Inquiry* 33, no. 3 (September 1999): 299–317.

———. *Philosophy of Science and Race*. New York: Routledge, 2002.

———. *Race and Mixed Race*. Philadelphia: Temple University Press, 1993.

———. "Racial Inequality and a Theory of Applicative Justice." *Philosophy and the Black Experience*, American Philosophical Association Newsletter 13, no.1 (2013), 6–11.

———. *White Privilege and Black Rights: The Injustice of U.S. Police Racial Profiling and Homicide*. Lanham, MD: Rowman and Littlefield, 2015.

Žižek, Slavoj "Biopolitics: Between Terry Shiavo and Guantanamo." *ArtForum*, December 2005, http://www.lacan.com/zizartforum1205.htm.

INDEX

"A Time to Kill" (film), 178
"Attica is all of us" Riverside church address, 138
"Equality of What?", 84; midfare, 86, 87, 88
"I have a dream" speech, 106–114
"one step forward, two steps back", 149
"Think Globally, Act Locally", 167–168
"What to do?", xi, 154

a theory of justice, 14, 20, 100
A Theory of Justice, xii, 21, 70, 84, 100
abstract general idea, equality as, 84, 87
abstract reasoning, Kantian morality and, 77
academic criticism, 6, 141
academic speech, 60–62; naïve view of its power, 127
African American women, employment, unemployment, 168
Agamben, Giorgio, 1, 6, 43, 44, 45, 45–46, 50, 52, 53, 54, 57, 62
Aid to Families with Dependent Children (AFDC), 159
air travel, fairness of searches, 95, 96
Alexander, Michelle, 1, 149, 154
Americans with Disabilities Act, 1990,: as empirical, political theory 10, 184n3
analyses, methods, subjects, and types, 21, 35, 60, 65, 73, 121, 126, 161, 211n57
anarchy, 50
applicative justice
as distribution of procedural justice, 90
as empirical political theory, 34; compaired to fairness, 82–83; equity and, 197n16; history of, 4–5; model of, 116; strict scrutiny and, 83
Aquinas, Thomas, 74, 76
Arendt, Hannah, 6, 47, 51–52, 61, 126–127
Aristotle: departure from Athens, 61; distributional justice, 88, 91
Arquette, Patricia, ignorance of intersectionality, 130
Atkin, Albert, 209n24
atmosphere, of race, 2, 128, 129, 130, 131, 132, 133, 204n25
Attica Prison, 1971 riot: anniversary in 2011, 138

backlash, 58, 66, 160
Baker, Ella, steadiness of, 136, 167, 171
bare life (*homo sacer*), 44, 52, 73
Bastiat, Frédéric, 35
Baudrillard, Jean, 55, 56, 57, 59, 62
behaviorism, sociological, 36
Bell, Derrick, 110
benevolence: Obama on grace and, 179; unimportant for Kant, 77
Bentley, Arthur F., xi, 6, 24–34, 39–40, 41, 42–43, 45, 47, 52, 54, 57, 58, 61–62, 66, 90, 94, 116, 117, 125, 126,

160, 174, 175
Berea College v Commonwealth of Kentucky, 107
Berlin, Isiah, 169–170
Bilderberg group, 153
Bill of Rights, Preamble, 15
biopower, 47, 49
Black Bodies/White Gazes, 209n29
black identity, as criminal, 163
Black Lives Matter, xii, 165
black male crime, 157
black poverty, rate, 162, 163
Black Prophetic Fire , 136
Black Prophetic Tradition, descriptive and normative, 6, 135, 137, 138, 139, 139–141, 149, 165, 167
blackpoor, 163, 164
Blacks should not be treated as whites are not treated., 119
blueprint, model of society, 32–33, 39, 66
Bodnar, John W., on integration of U.S. Navy, 201n49
boundaries, in historical and political analysis, 160–162
broken window theory/policy, 122, 150
Brown v. Board of Education of Topeka, 107–109, 166; reported as blow to communism, 111
Brown, Justice Henry Billings, 106
Brown, Michael, 119
Buchanan v. Warley, 107
Buschendorf, Christa, 136, 137

California v. Bakke, 65
capabilities approach, 86, 96
Chamberlin, Wilt (example), 98–40
Christian philosophers, 75–76
Cicero, 73, 74–75
civil government (Locke), 47
Civil Rights Act of 1964, 112–113
civil rights, timeline of, 104, 108, 149, 198n29
Clinton administration, 159
Clyatt v. United States, 107
Code of Justinian, 185n12
Cohen, G.A., 84–86, 97–100
Cold War, *Brown* decision during, 165, 166
Color-blind/ness, 10, 11, 82, 83, 112, 162, 177–178
common narrative of race, 176, 177, 177–178, 180
common people, their aspirations, 49, 69, 153
communication: public philosophical skills for, 141; technological changes in, 61
communism, fear of and racial discrimination, 111
comparative approach, to justice/injustice, 1, 3, 6, 93, 114
comparative justice, 83
complicance, with law, 13, 14, 18–32, 77, 83, 96, 118–119, 171
consciousness raising, for freedom, 171
contexts of origin, of political theories, 9, 15–20
cosmopolitanism, Cicero's, 73, 74–75
Crenshaw, Kimberle, 202n56
criminalblackman, stigma of, 158
crisis, of race in early 21st c, 133
critical theory, of race, 164
cruelty, Shklar, 172, 214n73

debt, mortgage, 16
demonstrations, as form of discourse, 55, 112, 115
Descartes, divine voluntarism, 41–42
deontology versus consequentialism, 99
Development as Freedom, 195n3
Dewey, John, 24, 188n47
dignity, 68, 69, 70, 77, 95, 99, 114, 135, 137, 139, 186n16
discourse, subject and term, 117; academic liberatory, 98, 115, 175; oppositional/counter, 39, 43; political activist, 165, 168, 169; speech and action distinction, 147–148, 174
distributive justice: Aristotelian meaning, 88, 91; contemporary meaning, 91
divine voluntarism, 41–42
Douglass, Frederick, 137, 145
Dred Scott v. Sanford, 16
Du Bois, W. E. B., communism of, 164
Dudziak, Mary, 109
Dukakis, Michael, 156

Dyson, Michael Eric criticism of Cornel West, 211n51

economic inequality, 59
electorate, percent who vote, 55
empirical political theory, 9, 21–22, 23, 30, 184n1
empirical standard, for political progress, 23
end-in-itself (Kant), 77
Engels, Friedrich, 50, 52
entitlements, 68, 78, 79
epistemology, of social race, 156
Equal Protection Clause, 1875 law and, 105
equality: objective, normative, legal,: rhetorical or heuristic, 6, 74, 84; racial, human, 67
equity, courts of, 97, 197n16
ethics : as motive for law, 2; disaster, 30; journalistic, 166; Sancrit literature on jurisprudence and, 21
eugenics movement, 106
European Court of Human Rights, procedural justice in, 103
Executive Order 9981, 110, 201n49
exile, from society, 53
explanation and correction of injustice, 121–122

The Faces of Injustice, 173
fairness, 13, 18, 19, 21, 23, 67, 70, 78, 81, 82–83, 86, 91, 100; factual equality and, 82
fascination, spectacles and, 56, 131
Ferguson, Missouri, racial discourse and,, 92, 139, 168, 202n3, 206n44
First Amendment, protection of racist expressions by, 133
Folkways, 106
formal equality, xi, 31, 65, 66, 133
Foucault, Michel, 49
Fourth Amerndment, 121, 170
Fraser, E. Franklin, 168
freedom, as a negative right, 203n9
freedom to achieve, 88
free speech, 49, 69, 147; broader than freedom of action (J.S. Mill), 191n3
Fleishacker, Samuel, 91
Friere, Paolo, 171
frontlash, 132, 203n11

Galatians, 75
Gallup, 219
General Equality Principle (GEP), 68, 70, 71, 73
Giddings, Franklin, 29
Giles v Harris, 106
global capitalism, 158; global finance, 140
global system, 153, 154, 168, 169; global justice, 153
Golden Rule, 82
good will, Kant's principle of volition, 77
government, as apparatus of state, 6, 24, 42, 43, 71
governmental normality, 41, 43, 45, 57–58
government, protection of rights by, 70, 72, 115, 123
Gramsci, Antonio, 47, 146
Griffiths, Martha, early intersectionality and, 113
groups and interests, Bentley's view, 36, 37, 39, 58

Harvard Civil Rights Project, 2003, 110
Hegel, race, and racism, 76
Hispanic/Latino protests, 58
history of philosophy, human inequality in, 67, 73–78
history, accounts of progress,
holdings, institution of, 101
Holmes, Justice Oliver Wendall, 106, 188n47
homer sacer (bare life), 44, 52, 73
Horton, Willie, 156, 157
human equality, idea of, xii, 4, 6, 52, 66–68, 68, 71, 73–74, 75, 76, 77–78, 79–81, 82, 84, 91, 94, 192n10, 196n10
human family, membership in (UDHR), 69, 70, 73
humanism, humanist ideals and, 57, 60, 67, 71, 128, 135, 140, 153
Hume, on race, and racism of, 76
hyper-reality, 56

iconography, 157
idea of justice, as analytically prior to injustice, 19

The Idea of Justice, 86

ideal and nonideal theories, distinction, 13–15
ideal equality, 65–67
ideal theory, 9–20
ideas, power of, 29–30
ignorance, behind veil, 9–13
images, importance of, ln3
immigration, US minors from Central America to U.S., 59
immigration and Naturalization Act of 1965, 4
imperatives, Kantian categorical or hypothetical, 68–69
Iñárritu Alejandro G., 2015 Best Picture Award, 130
injustice discourse: academic injustice discourse, 125–126; legal system and, 118–120
injustice theory, 3, 34, 117
integration: higher education, 65; K-12, 109–110; legal profession, 110
intrinsic human worth, 68
Invitation to the Reader (of this book), 180

Jefferson, Thomas, 16
Johnson, President Lyndon Baines, xi, 112, 113, 150, 165, 203n11
journalism, new oppositional political, 58
jury service, racial restrictions, 105
just process, 87, 99
justice and injustice, asymmetry of, 121
justice, as ideal, 5, 70

Kennedy, President John F., civil rights and, 112
kindness and courtesy, compatible with inequality, 74–75
King, Jr. Martin Luther, 112, 114, 142, 146, 164, 167
kingdom of ends, 68
Kozol, Jonathan, 196n11, 200n43, 212n58
Kropotkin, Peter, 25, 50
Ku Klux Klan, 105
Kymlicka, Will, 97, 196n10, 197n25

Laslett, Peter, 189n23
law and government limits, 35, 40, 44, 193n26
Law Enforcement Assessment Administration (LEAA), 150, 208n11
law of nature, 47, 48
The Law of Peoples, 185n7
The New Jim Crow, 149, 155
lawyers, race of in U.S., 110
Left, recent defeat of, 147
Lenin, Vladimir Illyich, 149, 207n8
liberatory scholarship, 5
libertarians, 99
liberty, as distributed, 171–173
liberty, tension with equality, 3
life of the mind, 6, 47, 51–52, 58, 61, 126
Lister, Andrew, 97, 98, 196n15
Locke, John, 1, 16, 17, 47–49, 50, 61, 62, 76, 169, 185n10, 189n23
logos, 51, 61
The Long Revolution, 6, 161–162, 166–167, 174
Lynching: government complicity in,: Bentley's account,

MacPherson, C. B.,1n10 2n3
magic words : of academics, 125; prophecy and, 136, 141
Malcolm, Roger, 109
Manifest Destiny, 44
Martin, Trayvon, 165
masses, silent (Baudrillard), 55
Mathiowitz, Dean, 39
maxim, of action (Kant), 77
Mayweather, Floyd (income), 98
McCabe v Achison, Topeka, and Santa Fe Railroad, 107
McCarthy era, 61
McKinnon, Katherine, 128
media, social justice activism and, 58
Menard, Louis, 112, 202n56
Mill, John Stuart,
Mills, Charles, 19, 73
minimum sentencing, 150
moral equality, Rawls's idea of,
morality, Kant's restrictions on, 70, 76–77
Motion Picture Academy Awards, 2015,, 130–131
Moynihan Report (Patrick Moynihan), 168, 212n59

Mujcic, Redzo, and Paul Frijters, 129

National Association for the Advancement of Colored People (NAACP), 109, 110, 137, 167
National Women's Law Center, 168
National Women's Party (NWP), 112–113
natural law, ancient, 41, 74–75
negative liberty, 169, 170, 172
Nietzsche, Frederick, 73
niggerization, of America according to Cornel West, 138
Nobel Peace Prize, 114, 115, 164
nonideal theory, 5, 9, 14, 15, 20, 22, 30, 187n23
Nozick, Robert, 98–99, 101, 196n15, 197n25; Lockean private property from self-ownership,4n25
niti and *nyaya* (Sen), 18–19, 21, 32–34

Obama, President Barack: as criticized by Cornel West, 168; invocation of religion, 179–180; meeting with activists in Ferguson, Mo., 168
Occupy, movement, 58–59
On Liberty, 78, 191n3, 193n22
one-drop rule, of black identity, 106, 200n34
organic intellectual, 47, 145–147
original position, according to Rawls, 17, 18, 20, 127
Outlaw, Lucius, 164
Overton, Richard, 183n1

Pan-African Congress, 165
Parker, Theodore, 145
Paul, Alice, 112
Pearson, Karl, 27
Penn, Sean, racist remark at 2015 Academy Awards, 130
peonage, of blacks after Reconstruction, 106, 107
philosophers, in politics, 61, 141, 190n40, 204n16
Philosophy of Science and Race, 193n18, 209n24
Plato, 61, 73, 127, 189n15, 204n16
Plessy v Ferguson, 106
Plessy, Adolphus, 106
police racial profiling, xii, 5, 93, 140, 156, 172
political activism, xiii, 61, 145, 147, 148, 174
political content (Bentley), 30, 35, 40, 44, 66, 193n26
The Political Theory of Possessive Individualism, 185n10, 189n23
polls, interpretation of, 56, 128
Poor People's Campaign, 164
positive law, 20, 22, 71, 80, 81, 82, 147
Poverty Tours, 164
poverty, feminization of, 168
power, distribution of, 67
pragmatic theory of government (Bentley's), 9, 24
principles of justice, 10, 16, 18, 20, 79, 118
prison-ghetto system, 152
prison-poverty system, 159
private property rights, 100, 101, 185n10
private property, rights to and freedom/ liberty, 100–102
privilege, 10, 44, 49, 68, 82–83, 83–84, 121–124, 128, 130, 179
procedural justice, 6, 18, 87, 104–105, 108; distinct from distributive justice, 90–91; distribution of, 96–98, 113, 115, 171; flexibility of, for elites, 94; liberty and, 100; perfect and imperfect, 89, 106–107; psychological value of, 103, 197n27; supplemented by other values, 195n8
The Process of Government , 25, 28, 57, 62

progress and regress, 136, 149, 151, 152, 154, 160, 162
prophecy, not predictive (West), 137
Prophesy Deliverance!, 135
public housing funding, 159
public opinion (Bentley), 39
pure violence (Benjamin), 45

Race and Epistemologies of Ignorance, 184n5
race,: new constructions of social,, 156; lack of scientific foundation for biological,6n25

racial climate, ambiguity of, 129, 131, 132, 133
racial contract (Charles Mills), 73
racial equality principle (REP), 68
racism, without racists, discourse of, 124
Rawls, ethics of disaster, 30
Rawls, John, 100–101, 127; ideal theory, xii, 9–22; ideal and nonideal theory, 22; Rawlsians, 97–99
Rawlsian deliberation, xii, 12, 13, 30
Reagan, President Ronald,, 150, 158
real inequality, 66, 75, 128
real world politics, 72
realistic utopia, of ideal theory, 20
reason, in diagnosis of justice/injustice, 21
rebellion, as last resort, 74–71
recognition: and protection of human rights,, 51, 68, 69, 71, 72, 73, 78, 91, 111; race and, 124, 129, 130, 131, 161, 170, 173, 177, 178, 179
reduction, Bentleyan pragmatic: metaphysical reduction of things to processes, 32; reduction of government apparatus to process, 66; reduction of law to government, 39; reduction of law and government to group activities, 6; reduction of government to process, 94; sociological reduction, 34, 36; written law reducted to legal action, 33
reduction of procedural justice to distributional justice, 171
Reif, Adelbert, 1970 interview with Hannah Arendt, 126
Relethford, John, 209n24
Reconstruction Amendments XIII, XIV, XV of U.S. Constitution,4n36 @@: era of "Redemption" following, 150
revisionist history, 6, 148–149, 150, 154, 169
revolution, progress versus,, 2
rhetoric, egalitarian, 84, 87, 94, 101
Rice, Tamir, 177
Roe v. Wade, 65
Roosevelt, President Franklin D., 44, 117
rule of law, 70, 72
rules of engagement, for police officers, 206n48
Ryan, Cheyney C., xiii, 97
safety net services, clients of, 151
Sartre, Jean-Paul, 171, 213n71
Schmitt, Carl, 45
Scott, Walter, 165
segregation, residential and education, 95, 110, 154, 163, 167
Sen, Amartya, 1, 5, 20–10
In The Shadow of the Silent Majorities, 55–57, 59
shared humanity, 177–178, 179, 180
Sharpton, Rev. Al , criticized by Cornel West, 139
Sheth, Falguni, 209n25
Shklar, Judith,, 1, 172–174, 174, 175
Siegel, Riva, social stratification and legal system, 155
Simmons, A. J., 14
Small, Albion, 25
Smiley, Travis and Cornel West, 164, 210n48
social causes, of social events, 25–27
social choice theory, impossibility theorem in, 158–159
social Darwinists, 106
social identity, 11, 142
social science metrics, 57
social values, 89, 101, 130
social well-being, income and wealth as measures of, 85
social will, of state, 30
sociology of law, 104
soul stuff (Bentley's critique of), 27
Spencer, Herbert, 25
St. Paul, 73, 75–76
state of exception, 41–46; Agamben, 43, 44, 45, 45–46, 54, 62; Bentley's omission of, 46, 62; Benjamin, 45; divine voluntarism and, 41–42; War on Terror, 58
Standard Oil Company, Bentley's account, 37
The State of Exception, 54
state of nature, 35, 47–50
stoic tradition, 74
"The Stone" New York Times, 60
stops and Frisks, 121, 123, 129, 152, 157, 170
Strauder v West Virgina , 105
strict scrutiny, by U.S. Supreme Court, 83

structured feeling, of Long Revolution, 161
suffrage, of freed male slaves and women, 73, 78
Summer, William Graham, 106
Swinburne, Richard, 189n15
symbols, discourse and, 4, 86, 142
symbolic interactionism, 206n49; symbolic meaning, 131

Taibbi, Matt, 202n4
Ted Talks, 60
"The Decider", 41
Theory of Applicative Justice, 1, 3, 183n2, 197n16
Truman, Harry S., 9, 110–90

U.S. Criminal Justice System, 140, 165
U.S. foreign policy, and racial bias, 111, 166, 176
U.S. police methods, foreign combat and, 152
U.S. Supreme Court, view of racial discrimination, 83, 105
unfreedoms, removal of, 89
United Nations, 69, 71, 110, 115; Universal Declaration of Human Rights (UDHR), 69–73, 78, 115, 190n40, 192n6
United States v. Cruikshank, 1876, 105, 107
utilitarianism, 78, 84
utility, individual, 78, 84–86

veil of ignorance, xii, 11, 13, 17–18, 78, 82
Vietnam War, protest, 126, 165, 184n3
violence, against blacks after World War II, 109
Von Jhering, Rudolph, 25, 26

Wacquant, Loïc, 151, 167, 208n17
Wallace, Governor George, 112
War on Drugs, 148, 150, 151, 158, 163, 203n11
War on Terror, 58
Warren, Justice Earl, 108, 109
Weaver, Vesla M., 132
Wells, Ida B., Cornell West about, 137
West, Cornel, 134–141, 143, 149–154, 162, 167, 206n52, 210n48, 211n51
Western medicine, method compared to ideal theorizing, 12–13
White House, expulsion of Du Bois, King, and West, 165
white ignorance, about racism, 176
white privilege, 121, 124, 128–129; discourse, 123
White Privilege and Black Rights, xii
white race, U.S., European immigrant assimilation to, 156
white supremacist ideology, 65
Williams, Raymond, 1, 6, 162–167
women's equality, Civil Rights Act, and, 112–113
Wood, Frederic Alan, 27
workfare, 151, 168
world peace, as absence of rebellion, 71

Yahoo News, 129
Yancy, George, 205n29, 206n46, 209n28
Yates, Ashley, 168
Yick Wo v Hopkins, 1879, 105

Žižek, Slavoj, 44
Zweck, 26

ABOUT THE AUTHOR

Naomi Zack received her PhD in philosophy from Columbia University in 1970 and has been professor of philosophy at the University of Oregon since 2001. She has published broadly and given talks nationally and internationally on urgent contemporary issues. Her latest book, *White Privilege and Black Rights: The Injustice of US Police Racial Profiling and Homicide* (2015) addressed the social reality and law attending murderous treatment of unarmed young black men in the twenty-first-century United States. Zack's monograph, *The Ethics and Mores of Race: Equality after the History of Philosophy* (Rowman & Littlefield, 2011, 2015) provides historical background in philosophy, for that work, as well as this text and her book in progress, *Starting from (Racial) Injustice: Historical and Contemporary Anti-Oppression Political Theory*. Zack's other recent books are *Ethics for Disaster* (2009 and 2010), *Inclusive Feminism: A Third Wave Theory of Women's Commonality* and *The Handy Answer Philosophy Book* (2010. Zack's earlier books include *Race and Mixed Race* (Temple, 1993); *Bachelors of Science* (1996)*; Philosophy of Science and Race* (2002), and the short textbook, *Thinking About Race*, 2nd edition (2006). Zack's published work also includes numerous book chapters, articles, and book reviews. Recent interviews are archived on the *NY Times* Opinionator Stone (http://opinionator.blogs.nytimes.com/category/the-stone/ November 5, 2014) and Public Radio International "To the Best of Our Knowledge" (http://www.ttbook.org/book/lets-stop-talking-about-privilege October 17, 2015).

Professor Zack teaches a variety of subjects on all levels. In addition to courses and seminars on race and diversity, she teaches courses on disaster, feminism, and Locke, Berkeley, Hume, and twentieth-century analytic philosophy. With the help of philosophy graduate students, Zack designed and curated entries for "Philosophical Installations," a website of (now) 1588 philosophy videos of philosophers and other theorists and critics performing their craft(s) outside the classroom. http://philinstall.uoregon.edu/ Zack also organized the project on Homelessness for the UO Philosophy Department's Community Philosophy Institute, including a multimedia website, "Homelessness and Home," with posted art, videos, photographs, narratives and scholarly articles, as well as local events and services. http://homelessness.philosophy.uoregon.edu/ Ongoing contributions are welcome for both websites, which are accessible for classroom use and to the wider local, national, and global community. Contact: nzack@uoregon.edu

www.ingramcontent.com/pod-product-compliance
Ingram Content Group UK Ltd.
Pitfield, Milton Keynes, MK11 3LW, UK
UKHW041631031026
15587UKWH00001B/216